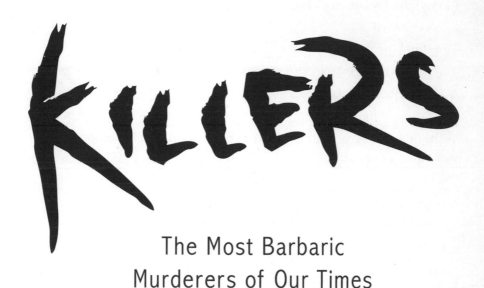

KILLERS

The Most Barbaric Murderers of Our Times

nigel cawthorne

summersdale

KILLERS

Summersdale Publishers Ltd
46 West Street
Chichester
West Sussex
PO19 1RP
UK

www.summersdale.com

Printed and bound in Great Britain

ISBN 1 84024 485 2

Contents

Introduction

Murder is close to the human heart. We have all said in anger or irritation 'I'll kill you' or 'I could have killed so-and-so'. No matter how little we meant it, everybody wonders at one time or another whether they could actually kill. How can we be sure that no murderer lurks within? Once that anger wells up inside, who can know how far things could go? Can you be sure that you could control that murderous rage? What would happen if you had too much to drink? Or if stress made you snap? And if you killed once and got away with it, would the temptation to murder again be too much?

Then again we are all potential victims. You are not even safe in your own home – most murders occur within families – or on the streets even in broad daylight – there could be a sniper on the roof intent on killing whoever steps into their sights. At night, things get worse. A sex killer could be lurking in the shadows. A murderer eager to kill for Satan or some other perverted cause might be climbing in through that unlocked window. Nowhere is safe. It is not just your own safety that you have to worry about. Your friends and family are also at risk. Ian Brady and Myra Hindley – the Moors Murderers – preyed on defenceless children, torturing and murdering them for their own perverted gratification. Myra Hindley is now dead and Ian Brady, unrepentant, still refuses to reveal where all the bodies are buried, despite the evident distress of the families of their victims. More recently two American high-school students went on a rampage, slaughtering their fellow pupils: even at school our young ones are at risk. The UK, America and Australia have all been terrorised by hideous killings: in England sullen loner Michael Ryan devastated the quiet village of Hungerford with inexplicable acts of murderous violence; America was horrified by the actions of a lone sniper who picked off innocent victims in Austin, Texas; and in Australia a gang of lesbian vampires killed their victim to drink his blood. There have also been those killers who were motivated by an overwhelming sexual desire. In the 1960s the Boston Strangler used his sexual charisma to talk his way into women's apartments and, often persuaded them to take their clothes off and have sex before he murdered them. The Yorkshire Ripper followed his nineteenth-century namesake by slaughtering prostitutes or those who he thought were prostitutes. He claimed he was doing God's work. Ted Bundy's insatiable libido sent him on a nation-wide killing spree and Dennis Nilsen killed men he had picked up so that they would not leave him. He then dissected their bodies, cooked them and flushed them down the toilet. Jeffery Dahmer came up with another solution. He ate his victims. Like Brady and Hindley, couples can become so deeply involved that they will kill anyone who gets in their way – even family members. Charles Starkweather and his girlfriend Caril Fugate killed her family, before going on a killing spree which has inspired several films. No one is sure how many people were murdered by Fred and Rosemary West as they usually picked on transients who no one would miss, and the case of Dr Harold Shipman, who killed at least 215 people proves that sometimes you cannot even trust your own family doctor. Emanuel Tanay, a professor of psychiatry at Wayne State University, pointed out that murder is not the crime of criminals, but that of ordinary citizens. The great majority of murders are family affairs, committed by outwardly ordinary people who never murder or commit any other crime – except on the one fateful occasion. And when the psychotic killer strikes, the result is often wholesale slaughter.

 Killers details these shocking cases and takes you inside the minds of the people who committed these horrendous crimes. Are they inhuman beasts who are beyond compassion or understanding? Or are they human beings just like us, but who have simply overstepped a line? You decide. In the meantime, be on your guard. Anyone around you could be a potential killer. There may even be one lurking inside.

– Chapter 1 –

Natural Born Killers

Charles Starkweather

ACCOMPLICE: CARIL FUGATE (THE YOUNGEST WOMAN EVER TO BE TRIED FOR FIRST-DEGREE MURDER IN THE US)

NATIONALITY: AMERICAN

NUMBER OF VICTIMS: 11 KILLED

FAVOURED METHOD OF KILLING: SHOOTING, STABBING

BORN: 1938

REIGN OF TERROR: DECEMBER 1957

STATED MOTIVE: 'GENERAL REVENGE UPON THE WORLD AND ITS HUMAN RACE'

EXECUTED: 25 JUNE 1959

Charles Starkweather was born on 24 November 1938 in a poor quarter of Lincoln, Nebraska. He was the third of eight children – seven boys and a girl. His father, Guy Starkweather, was a convivial man who liked a drink. A handyman and a carpenter, he suffered from a weak back and arthritis, and could not always work. His wife, Helen, a slight, stoical woman, worked as a waitress and, after 1946, became practically the sole provider for her large family.

Although the Starkweathers knew little of their roots, the first Starkweather had left the old world in the seventeenth century, sailing from the Isle of Man in 1640. The name was well known across the mid-West and there was even a small town called Starkweather in North Dakota. Somehow the name Starkweather seemed eerily redolent of the wind sweeping the Great Plains.

Charles Starkweather had happy memories of his first six years, which he spent playing with his two elder brothers, Rodney and Leonard, helping around the house with his mother and going fishing with his dad. But all that changed in 1944 on his first day at school. When they enrolled at Saratoga Elementary School, all the children were supposed to stand up and make a speech. When it came to Starkweather's turn, his classmates spotted his slight speech impediment and began to laugh. Starkweather broke down in confusion. He never forgot that humiliation.

Starkweather soon gained the impression that the teacher was picking on him, and he believed that the other children were ridiculing him because of his short bow-legs and distinctive red hair. Later, from his condemned cell, he wrote: 'It seems as though I could see my heart before my eyes, turning dark black with hate of rages.' On his second day at school he got into a fight, which he found relieved his aggression. He claimed to have been in a fight almost every day during his school life, though his teachers remembered little of this.

Despite his high IQ Starkweather was treated throughout his school career as a slow learner. It was only when his eyes were tested at the age of 15 that it was discovered he could barely see the blackboard from his place at the back of the class. He was practically blind beyond 20 feet.

Starkweather felt that life had short-changed him. He was short, short-tempered, short-sighted and short on education. He was forced, by poverty, to wear second-hand clothes. Classmates called him 'Little Red' and he remembered every perceived slight. It made him as hard as nails.

Starkweather's reputation as a fighter spread throughout Lincoln and toughs from all over the city came to take him on. He said later that it was the beginning of his rebellion against the whole world, his only response to being made fun of. At the age of 15, he was challenged by Bob von Busch. They fought each other to a standstill. Afterwards they became firm friends. Von Busch was one of the few people who saw the amusing and generous side to Starkweather's nature. The rest of the world saw barely repressed hostility.

Starkweather dropped out of Irving Junior High School in 1954, when he was just 16 years old, taking a menial job in a newspaper warehouse. His boss treated him as if he was mentally retarded and he hated it.

Although Starkweather continued to love and respect his mother, his relationship with his father sometimes degenerated into open hostility. In 1955 they had a fight and Starkweather went to stay with Bob von Busch and his father. The two teenagers were car fanatics. They spent a lot of their spare time at Capitol Beach, the local race-car track. Starkweather raced hot rods there and participated in demolition derbies. The two boys also took to joyriding in stolen cars, occasionally stripping them down for spare parts.

When von Busch started dating Barbara Fugate, Starkweather began to see less of him. Then, in the early summer of 1956, Bob took Starkweather to a drive-in cinema on a double date with Barbara and her younger sister Caril. Caril Fugate was just 13 years old, though she could easily have passed for 18. She and Barbara were the daughters of Velda and William Fugate, a drunkard and a convicted peeping Tom. The couple had divorced in 1951 and Barbara and Caril's mother married again. The family lived at 924 Belmont Avenue, an unpaved road in the poor quarter of Lincoln.

Caril Fugate seemed the perfect mate for the moody Charlie Starkweather. Although she was short – five foot one – she was self-confident and most people found her opinionated and rebellious. She often wore a man's shirt with the sleeves rolled up, blue jeans and boots. Like Starkweather, she did badly at school. Considered slow, she had little experience of life. She had left Lincoln only once, for a holiday in Nebraska's Sand Hill.

To the girls of Lincoln, Charles Starkweather did not seem like much of a catch. He had never had a proper girlfriend before. He was just five foot five, with bow-legs, a pug face and the reputation of a hoodlum. But Caril liked him. His tough, rebel image appealed to her. She did not care about his working-class origins or his dead-end job. Far more fascinating were the stories he told of his fantasies about being a cowboy or the fastest hot-rod driver in town. What's more, with his slicked-back hair and cigarette dangling from his lips, he looked the spitting image of the latest teenage idol, James Dean, on whom Starkweather consciously modelled himself.

Starkweather liked Caril too. He liked the way she wore make-up and swore. After their first date, Caril went out with another local boy. Starkweather tracked him down and threatened to kill him if he saw Caril again.

After that Caril Fugate and Charles Starkweather started going steady. It made Starkweather feel good to be wanted. They lived in a world of their own and with Caril, he forgot about his problems. He quit his job at the warehouse. He had been working part-time as a rubbish collector with his brother Rodney since he was 13. Now he worked the rubbish trucks full-time. He earned a pittance but he got off work early enough to meet Caril from school every day.

Their parents were against the match. Caril's mother and stepfather thought that 17-year-old Starkweather was too old for Caril and they thought that he was leading their daughter astray. Starkweather's father, who co-owned Starkweather's pale blue 1949 Ford sedan, banned Caril – whom Starkweather had taught to drive – from taking the wheel. In the late summer of 1957, however, Caril was involved in a minor accident with the car. Starkweather's father hit his son so hard that he knocked him through a window.

Starkweather left home for good. He moved in with Bob von Busch, who had just married Barbara. Soon he was persuaded to move out of their cramped apartment and he took a room of his own in the same apartment block, one of the very few in town at the time.

Starkweather and Caril went on dates to the cinema, sometimes alone, sometimes with Bob and Barbara. Or they would just drive around, listening to distant rock 'n' roll stations on the radio. Starkweather also liked to get out of the small city of Lincoln, which had a population of just 100,000 in 1958. He found Nebraska's capital city claustrophobic and felt contempt for the local people's law-abiding, Christian ways. Lincoln had just three murders a year before Starkweather went on his spree, and boasted more churches per head than any other city in the world. Out in the huge, flat countryside around Lincoln, Starkweather felt at home. He had craved the solitary life of a backwoodsman since he was a child.

'When the sun was setting in its tender glory,' he later wrote of an early experience of the wilderness, 'it was as though time itself was standing still. The flames still burn deep down inside of me for the love of that enchanted forest.'

Out in the woods he would experience that feeling again.

'I would sit down against a large tree,' he said. 'I gazed above and between the lagged limbs into the sky for miles and miles.'

Death, he said, had come to him in a vision

Caril shared that romantic view of the natural world. She would accompany him on hunting trips and, in the evening, they would lie back, holding hands, and stare up into the clear, starry, black Nebraskan sky. There he told her of the deal he had made with death. Death, he said, had come to him in a vision. Half-man, half-bear, it had taken him down to hell, but hell was not as he had always imagined, 'it was more like beautiful flames of gold'. The few other people he had trusted enough to tell his vision to had thought him crazy and had changed the subject. But Caril said she loved him and that she wanted to go there, to hell, with him. And in his love for her, Starkweather thought, at last he had found 'something worth killing for'. His one great aim in life now was for Caril to see him 'go down shooting, knowing it was for her'.

Starkweather liked to buy presents for Caril – soft toys, a record player and a radio, so she could enjoy music at home. He also bought her jewellery, including a locket with 'Caril' and 'Chuck', her nickname for him, engraved on it. But buying presents on the $42 a week he earned as a garbage collector did not come easy – especially when there was rent to pay and a car to keep on the road. Starkweather soon began looking around for an easier way of making money.

Nebraska was on the eastern edge of the old Wild West. Cattle ranchers had wrested it from the Sioux and it had been cowboy country until the cereal farmers fenced it in and forced the cattlemen to move on. Starkweather felt himself very much part of that old tradition. He loved guns and spent hours stripping them down and oiling them. And he loved to shoot. Although he was short-sighted, he was a good shot and practised shooting from the hip like an old time gunfighter. He also loved detective films and true crime comics, and he began to fantasise about being a criminal. But he was not interested in being a burglar or a sneak thief. To Starkweather, crime meant armed robbery.

Although he had had a few adolescent scrapes, he had never been in any real trouble with the law. Now, to keep Caril, he started planning a criminal career. Bank robbery was plainly the pinnacle of the profession, but he thought he had better start small – by knocking over a petrol station. He chose the Crest Service Station on Cornhusker Highway that ran out of Lincoln to the north. He used to hang out there tinkering with his car and knew the petrol station pretty well. A couple of times, when he had been locked out of his room for not paying the rent, he had slept there in his car, surviving on chocolate bars and Pepsi from the vending machines. The petrol station attendant would wake him at 4.15 a.m. so that he would be on time for work.

On 1 December 1957 a new attendant named Robert Colvert had just taken over. Colvert was 21 and just out of the Navy, where he had been known as 'Little Bob'. He was nine stone, and around five foot five. Earlier that year he had got married. His wife Charlotte was expecting and he had taken the night job at the petrol station to support his growing family. He was new to the job and barely knew Starkweather, though they had had a row the day before when he refused to give Starkweather credit on a toy dog he wanted to buy for Caril.

It was a freezing night and a bitter Nebraskan wind was blowing in from the plains, when Starkweather pulled into the service station around 3 a.m. Colvert was alone. Starkweather was nervous. He bought a pack of cigarettes and drove off. A few minutes later he came back. This time he bought some chewing gum and drove off again. The coast was clear. It was now or never.

Starkweather loaded the shotgun he had stolen from Bob von Busch's cousin, Sonny. He pulled a hunting cap down over his red hair and tied a bandanna around his face.

Back at the petrol station, Starkweather pointed the shotgun at Colvert and handed him a canvas money bag. Colvert filled the bag with the notes and loose change from the till. But then Starkweather's plan went badly wrong. Although he knew the station's routine and how much money was kept there overnight, the new man did not know the combination of the safe and could not open it. Starkweather forced him into the car at gunpoint. Colvert drove. Starkweather sat in the passenger seat, the shotgun trained on Colvert. They headed for Superior Street, a dirt road a little way north, used by teenagers as a lovers' lane.

The only witness to what happened next was Starkweather. He claimed that, as they got out of the car, Colvert made a grab for the gun.

'I got into a helluva fight and shooting gallery,' he said. 'He shot himself the first time. He had hold of the gun from the front, and I cocked it and he was messing around and he jerked it and the thing went off.' Colvert was hit and fell, but he was not dead. He tried to stand up.

The killing filled him with a feeling of serenity he had not experienced since childhood

Starkweather reloaded the shotgun. He pressed the barrel to Colvert's head and pulled the trigger. 'He didn't get up any more.'

Although Starkweather had been nervous before, the killing filled him with a feeling of serenity he had not experienced since childhood. He felt free, above the law. The robbery had earned him just $108. Five months later, on 24 April 1958, Robert Colvert's widow Charlotte gave birth to a daughter.

When Starkweather picked up Caril later that day, he told her about the robbery, but claimed that an unnamed accomplice had done the shooting. That evening he threw the shotgun in a creek. A few days later he fished it out, cleaned it and put the gun back in Sonny's garage. It had not even been missed.

During the police investigation, several of the other service station attendants mentioned Starkweather's name, but no one came to visit him. He paid off his back rent, had his car resprayed black and spent ten dollars on second-hand clothes, paying with the loose change he had got from the till in the petrol station. The owner of the store was suspicious and reported the matter to the police. But no effort was made to question him.

The fact that no one seemed even to suspect him of the robbery and murder gave Starkweather a great deal of satisfaction. It was his first taste of success. Until then he had always been the underdog. Now he had showed that he could outwit authority.

'I learned something, something I already knowed,' he said. 'A man could make money without hauling other people's rubbish.'

He stopped turning up for work and was fired. He spent his time going to the cinema, reading comics, playing records, working on his car and practising shooting and knife-throwing. The money from the robbery did not last long. He got behind with the rent again and ended up sleeping in his car in a garage he had rented. But it did not bother him. He knew he could get cash again as soon as he wanted. And the idea of killing again did not bother him one little bit.

On Sunday 19 January 1958 there was a terrible row. Caril was putting on weight and her family feared she was pregnant. When Starkweather turned up, Caril told him that she was sick of his wild ways and that she never wanted to see him again. He did not take her seriously. He had already arranged to go hunting jackrabbits with Caril's stepfather, Marion Bartlett, two days later, and he figured that he would see her then.

On the morning of 21 January 1958 Starkweather helped his brother Rodney out on the rubbish round, then went to check that his room was still padlocked. It was. His hunting rifle was inside and he had to borrow Rodney's, a cheap, single-shot, .22 bolt action rifle. He took some rugs he had scavenged from his rubbish round with him to Belmont Avenue and gave them to Caril's mother, Velda, as a peace offering. Velda was not appeased. As Starkweather sat cleaning his brother's rifle in the living-room, she told him that her husband Marion was not going hunting with him and that he should leave and never come back. When he did not respond, according to Starkweather: 'She didn't say nothing. She just got up and slammed the shit out of me... in the face.' As Starkweather ran from the house, he left the rifle. A few minutes later, he returned to collect it. Caril's father was waiting. 'The old man started chewing me out. I said to hell with him and was going to walk out through the front room, and he helped me out. Kicked me right in the ass. My tail hurt for three days.'

But that was not the end of it. Starkweather walked down to the local grocery store and phoned the transport company where Marion Bartlett worked. He told them that Mr Bartlett was sick and would not be in for a few days. Then he drove his car over to a friend's house nearby, left it there and walked back to Belmont Avenue. Caril and her mother were still yelling their heads off when Starkweather turned up. Velda accused him of making her daughter pregnant and began slapping him around the face again. This time he hit back, knocking her back a couple of steps. She let out a strange cry – 'a war cry', Starkweather thought. Marion Bartlett came flying to the rescue. He picked Starkweather up by the neck and dragged him towards the front door. But Starkweather was younger and stronger. He kicked the old man in the groin and wrestled him to the ground. Bartlett managed to slip from Starkweather's grasp and went to look for a weapon. Starkweather thought he had better do the same.

As Starkweather hurriedly slipped a .22 cartridge into his brother's hunting rifle, Marion Bartlett ran at him with a claw hammer. Starkweather fired, shooting the old man in the head. Velda Bartlett grabbed a kitchen knife and threatened to cut Starkweather's head off. Starkweather reloaded the rifle, but Caril grabbed it from him. She threatened her mother, saying she would blow her to hell. The older woman did not take her daughter's threat seriously and knocked her down. Starkweather grabbed the rifle back and shot the old woman in the face. He hit her with the butt of the gun as she fell, then hit her twice more.

Caril's two-and-a-half-year-old sister Betty Jean was screaming. Starkweather hit her with the rifle butt too. She screamed all the louder, so Starkweather picked up the kitchen knife and threw it at her. He said he aimed for the chest, but the knife pierced her neck, killing her. Caril then pointed out that her stepfather was still alive in the bedroom.

Starkweather went through and finished Marion Bartlett off, stabbing him repeatedly in the throat.

The house fell quiet. Starkweather reloaded his gun and sat down to watch television. 'I don't even remember what was on,' he later told police. 'I just wanted some noise.' That evening he and Caril wrapped the bodies of her murdered family in rugs and bedclothes and dragged them out into the frozen backyard. They stuffed Velda's body into an outside toilet. Betty Jean's body was placed in a box on top of it. Marion Bartlett's corpse was hidden in a disused chicken coop.

Back in the house the two teenagers tidied up as best they could. They mopped up some of the blood and mess with rags and splashed perfume around to hide the smell. Then they went into the living-room to watch television together.

Caril later claimed that she had not been present during the slaughter of her family. She had come home to find Starkweather there with a gun and her family gone. She said that he had told her that he was planning a big bank robbery. Her parents had found out and the family had been taken hostage by the rest of the gang. He had only to make one phone call and they would be killed, unless she cooperated. Starkweather said that Caril had participated in the slaughter of her family, egging him on.

The young couple settled down together for what Starkweather would later describe as the best week of his life. They were alone together with no one to push them around. Certainly he had no conscience troubling him. Later he confessed: 'Shooting people was, I guess, a kind of thrill.'

In Starkweather's eyes they were now living like kings. With money taken from Marion Bartlett's pockets he made the occasional run to the local grocery store to stock up on chewing gum, ice cream, potato chips and Pepsi. Caril claimed that he tied her up when he went out. Starkweather denied it.

They lived, for the first time, as man and wife. The two of them played cards, watched television a lot and tended the family pets – two parakeets, a dog called Nig and a puppy called Kim which Starkweather had bought for Caril. Everything would have been idyllic except for the bodies in the backyard.

Visitors were warned off by a sign on the kitchen door saying: 'Stay away Every Body is sick with the Flue [sic].' Caril told those who knocked that the family was sick and they were in quarantine, while Starkweather hid in a room off the hall with his rifle cocked.

Then on Saturday, 25 January Caril's sister Barbara came to visit with Bob von Busch and their newborn baby. Caril spotted her sister before she was halfway up the pathway. She called out that the whole family had the flu and that the doctor had said no one should come near the house. But Barbara, who was concerned that her mother had not been in touch, kept on coming. Fearing the game was up, Caril screamed: 'Go away! If you know what's best you'll go away so Mother won't get hurt.'

Barbara stopped, turned around and went back to Bob's car. Something in her sister's voice scared her. Once the baby was safely home, Bob von Busch and Rodney Starkweather returned to the house to find out what was going on. Again, Caril sent them away. Her mother's life would be in danger if they did not go, she said.

They reported the matter to the police and a patrol car was sent out to Belmont Avenue that evening. Caril gave the officers the regular story about the family having the flu. She also mentioned that her family did not get on with Bob von Busch – that was why he had called the police. Noting that Caril was calm and controlled, the policemen left their inquiries at that.

After the police had left, Starkweather took his brother's rifle to the house of a mutual friend. He called Barbara von Busch to reassure her. He had bought some groceries for Caril's family, he said, and he left a message for Rodney, saying that he should go and pick up his gun at the friend's house. When Rodney went to collect his rifle, he noticed it was damaged. The butt plate had been knocked off.

The next day, Starkweather's sister Laveta arrived at Belmont Avenue. She was not put off by the story of the flu. She was one of Caril's few friends and, when she would not go away, Caril pulled her close. Her brother was inside planning a bank robbery, Caril confided, and that was why she could not come in. Laveta went home and told her father what had happened. He did not believe a word of it. But the next day he began to get concerned.

On Monday morning Velda's mother Pansy Street was also getting worried. She turned up at Belmont Avenue and shouted until Caril showed herself. When Mrs Street refused to believe the flu story, Caril reverted to the story about her mother being in danger. Mrs Street went straight to the police station. While she was there, Guy Starkweather phoned, relating the story Laveta had told him. The police sent a second squad car out to Belmont Avenue. When they knocked on the door, they got no answer. So they broke in.

But Charles Starkweather and Caril Fugate had already figured that the game was up. Caril had packed a bag with some clothes and a few family snapshots. Starkweather had wrapped his hunting knife in a blue blanket, along with Marion Bartlett's shotgun, the barrel of which he had sawn down, and a .32 pistol he had found in the house. And they slipped out of the house the back way. By the time the police turned up, everything was neat and tidy. With nothing to excite their suspicions, they took Pansy Street home and let the matter rest.

Bob von Busch and Rodney Starkweather were not so easily satisfied. At 4.30 p.m. they went over to Belmont Avenue to check the place out for themselves. Almost immediately they found the Bartletts' bodies. The hunt was now on, but the young fugitives had several hours' start.

After picking up two spare tyres from Starkweather's garage the couple stopped at the Crest Service Station to fill up with petrol and buy maps. Then they turned south, out of Lincoln, on to the open highway, heading across the frozen farmlands of the Great Plains. They stopped at the small town of Bennet, where Starkweather bought some ammunition at a service station and they ate a couple of hamburgers. Starkweather often came to Bennet to spend time in the surrounding countryside. An old family friend, 70-year-old August Meyer, had often let him hunt on his land in return for half the kill.

Meyer lived two miles east of Bennet, down a dirt track. Starkweather thought they might be safe there, for the night at least. But there had been a six-inch fall of snow and the track was muddy. Their car got stuck. Nearby was a derelict schoolhouse with a cyclone cellar, where the children would have taken shelter from the tornadoes that tore across the Great Plains every spring. Starkweather and Caril went down into the cellar to warm up before traipsing up to Meyer's farm on foot, ostensibly to ask the old man's assistance in shifting the car. However, at the farmhouse Starkweather shot Meyer and his dog. He later claimed that he had shot Meyer in self-defence when, after a heated argument the old man had gone into the house to get a coat, but came out on the porch firing a rifle.

'I felt a bullet go by my head,' Starkweather said. But Meyer's gun had jammed after the first shot. 'Meyer started running back in the house, and I shot him at almost point-blank range with the sawn-off.'

He also blamed the incident on Caril: 'Caril got pissed off because we got stuck,' he said. 'She said that we ought to go up and blast the shit out of him because he did not shovel the lane.'

Caril said that Starkweather had simply asked Meyer if he could borrow some horses to drag the car out of the mud, then shot the old man as he went into the barn.

Starkweather dragged Meyer's body into the wash-house and covered it with a blanket. The two of them ransacked his house for money, food and guns. Their total haul was less than a hundred dollars. It included a pump-action, .22 calibre repeating rifle, some socks, gloves, a shirt, a straw hat and some jam and biscuits. They took a brief nap before trudging back to the car. After an hour or two of digging they managed to shift it. But it slid off the track into a ditch and Starkweather damaged the reverse gear trying to back it out. Eventually they were rescued by a farmer, a neighbour of Meyer's, who towed the car out with his truck. Starkweather insisted on giving the farmer two dollars for his trouble.

They drove up towards Meyer's farmhouse, where Starkweather planned to stay the night. But Caril insisted they turn back. When they did, the car got stuck in the mud again. It was already dark so they abandoned the car and headed back to the derelict school, intending to spend the night in the cyclone cellar. On the way they were offered a lift by 17-year-old Robert Jensen, the son of a local store-owner, and his fiancée, 16-year-old Carol King. When Starkweather explained his car trouble, Jensen offered to take them to the nearest service station where they could telephone for help. As they got in the back seat, Jensen asked why they were carrying guns – Starkweather had the .22 and Caril the sawn-off shotgun. Starkweather insisted they were not loaded.

Starkweather later claimed that, at this point, he toyed with the idea of ringing the police and turning himself in. But when they reached the service station, it was closed. On their brief acquaintanceship, Starkweather had already decided that these two high-school kids were exactly the sort of people he hated – clever, popular at school, conservative, middle class. Jensen was a football player. King was a cheerleader, drum majorette and a member of the school choir. They planned to get married once they graduated. It struck Starkweather that if he turned himself in, Jensen would get the credit. He could not bear the thought of this chubby, all-American boy being fêted as a hero.

He put his gun to the back of Jensen's head and told him to hand over his wallet to Caril, who emptied it and handed the money to Starkweather. He then ordered Jensen to drive them back to Lincoln but after a couple of miles, he changed his mind and told him to drive back to the derelict school where they had been stuck earlier that day. He said he was going to leave Jensen and King there and take their car – a dark blue, souped-up 1950 Ford with whitewall tyres.

When they got there, Starkweather left Caril in the car, listening to the radio, while he marched his prisoners off at gunpoint As they walked down the steps into the cellar, Starkweather shot Jensen from behind. Later he claimed that Jensen had tried to grab the gun but, when the body was found, there were six shots in the left ear. Starkweather made several conflicting statements about how King died. He was alone with her for 15 minutes and claimed to have shot her when she started screaming. Later he claimed that Caril had killed her.

Carol King was killed with a single shot from behind. When their bodies were found the next day, Jensen was found lying on his stomach in a pool of blood at the bottom of the stairs. King was partly nude and lying on top of him. Her coat had been pulled over her head, her jeans and panties were round her ankles. And her back was scratched and streaked with mud as if she had been dragged across the floor. She had been stabbed viciously, several times, in the groin, The autopsy found internal damage to the vagina, cervix and rectum. It had been caused by a rigid, double-edged blade that could not have been Starkweather's hunting knife. But doctors found no semen and no indication of sexual assault. Starkweather at first said that he had raped King, but later admitted only to having been tempted to rape her and pulling down her jeans. Caril, he insisted, had then murdered and mutilated King in a fit of jealousy.

Starkweather closed the heavy storm doors on the cellar and went back to Jensen's car. But it, too, was stuck in the mud. He and Caril managed to dig it out by about 10.30 p.m. Starkweather claimed that he was now determined to abandon his killing spree and give himself up to the police, but Caril talked him out of it. They headed back to Lincoln to see if the Bartletts' bodies had been discovered yet.

Squad cars lined Belmont Avenue and Number 924 was crawling with policemen. Starkweather slowly drove by. Then he headed west out of Lincoln with the vague idea of finding refuge with his brother Leonard who lived in Washington State, over a thousand miles away. But after about three hours' driving, before they had even crossed the state line out of Nebraska, they turned back and headed for Lincoln once more. Starkweather was tired, had a streaming cold and the car was not running too well. The idea was to rest up in one of the wealthy mansions in the country club area of town, steal a new car and make a run for it again the following night. Starkweather knew the area well. He had collected rubbish there and deeply resented its affluent residents. It was 3.30 a.m. when they arrived back in Lincoln. They parked up in the secluded street and took a nap. When they awoke in the early morning they began cruising the streets, hunting for a suitable property. Starkweather pointed out several possibilities before they settled on the five-bedroomed mansion belonging to millionaire industrialist C. Lauer Ward. It was just down the street from the garage Starkweather rented.

Mr Ward was the 47-year-old president of Lincoln's Capital Bridge Company and Capital Steel Company, and had gone to work before Starkweather rang the doorbell. The 51-year-old maid, Lillian Fencl, answered the door. She had been with the Wards for 26 years and may have known Starkweather from this time as a rubbish man in the area. Starkweather and Caril brandished their guns and forced their way into the house.

Mrs Ward, a 46-year-old graduate of the University of Nebraska who was active in community affairs, was the only other person at home; the Wards' 14-year-old son, Michael was at boarding school in Connecticut. By then the Bartlett murders were front-page news so when Starkweather ordered Mrs Ward and Lillian Fencl to carry on with their household chores, they readily agreed to cooperate. Meanwhile Starkweather went wandering about the mansion's elegant rooms, amazed by their opulence. Before noon, he ordered Mrs Ward – not the maid – to serve him pancakes in the library, then petulantly changed his order to waffles.

While Starkweather was enjoying his late breakfast, 25 armed policemen were surrounding August Meyer's farm. Starkweather's abandoned car had been found nearby and the police were convinced the two fugitives were holed up there. A bulletin on the radio news said that they would be taken just as soon as the tear gas arrived. But when the gas cleared and the state troopers went in all they found was August Meyer's dead body. The bodies of Robert Jensen and Carol King were found soon after. Within the hour a hundred policemen were combing the frozen countryside.

Around 1 p.m. Starkweather allowed Mrs Ward to go upstairs to change. When he went to check on her, he claimed she came out of her son's room with a .22 calibre pistol and took a shot at him. She missed and turned to run. Starkweather threw his hunting knife at her. It stuck in her back. He dragged the groaning woman into her bedroom and put her on the bed. The Wards' dog then began to worry him. He broke its neck with a blow from his rifle butt. Later, suspecting that Mrs Ward might try and make a phone call, he bound and gagged her and covered her with a sheet.

Later in the afternoon Starkweather called his father and asked him to tell Bob von Busch that he was going to kill him for coming between him and Caril. He also wrote a note, addressed to 'the law only', saying that he and Caril had intended to commit suicide after he had killed the Bartletts but Bob von Busch and others prevented them by coming round to the house.

Around 6 p.m. Mr Ward arrived home. When he came in through the kitchen door he was confronted by Starkweather brandishing a rifle. Ward made a grab for the gun and in the ensuing fight, the rifle fell down the stairs into the basement. Ward tumbled down after it, and Starkweather followed. Starkweather got to the gun first, and shot Ward in the back as he turned and ran back up the stairs. Despite his wounds, Ward kept going. He ran through the kitchen and the living-room and was opening the front door when Starkweather caught up with him. He shot Ward again, this time in the side of the head.

'I asked him if he was all right,' Starkweather said later, 'but he did not answer.'

Starkweather took the maid upstairs, took ten dollars from her purse and tied her up. He left Caril to watch her, while he took seven dollars from Mrs Ward and tried to dye his hair black with shoe polish. Caril packed some clothes while Starkweather loaded up Mrs Ward's blue Packard with tins of food he found in the kitchen. As evening fell they drove down Belmont Avenue one last time, then headed west out of Lincoln on Highway 34.

Next morning a relative of Lauer Ward's went to his house to find out why he had not shown up at work. He found Ward dead just inside the front door. The two women were dead too. Both had been stabbed repeatedly, with the same double-edged blade that had been used to mutilate Carol King. The knife was never found. Starkweather maintained that the two women had been alive when he left them. But Caril said later that Starkweather had admitted to her that he had killed

Mrs Ward with a kitchen knife and that, after he had tied Lillian Fencl up and stabbed her, she screamed. So he put a pillow over her face and kept on stabbing her every time she hollered.

News of the killings spread quickly. A picture of Starkweather and Caril grinning was on the front page of the evening paper. Now nine were dead and Starkweather was still in the area. People in Bennet and Lincoln barricaded themselves in their houses. Gun stores were packed. People were buying anything that would shoot. One shop reported selling over forty guns in two hours as parents armed themselves to escort their children to school. Lincoln's mayor posted a $1,000 reward for Starkweather's capture. Soon a hundred-strong posse gathered outside the sheriff's department – though some of its members were not entirely sober. The governor called out the National Guard. Soldiers cruised in jeeps with machine guns mounted on them. The city was sealed off and searched block by block. And an aircraft circled the city, looking for the blue Packard Starkweather had stolen. But the fugitives were long gone. They pressed on westwards throughout the night. They claimed that, as they went, they wrote notes, boasting of what they had done, and tossed them out of the window. None were ever found.

In the small hours of morning Starkweather fell asleep at the wheel and only just managed to keep the car out of a drainage ditch at the side of the road. He persuaded Caril that having sex was the only thing that would wake him up enough to keep driving. It did not work. Ten minutes later he pulled off the road again to sleep.

At first light they set off again. At around 9 a.m. they crossed the state line into Wyoming and found themselves in the Badlands – an area scarred by ravines that provided a safe haven for the outlaws of the Wild West. At midday they stopped in the small town of Douglas where they filled the car with petrol and bought Pepsi and chocolate bars to keep themselves going. It was there that they heard on the radio that the Wards' bodies had been found and police were looking for Mrs Ward's Packard. Starkweather decided to look for another car.

About twelve miles beyond Douglas, Starkweather saw a Buick parked off the highway. In it, Merle Collison, a 37-year-old shoe salesman, was asleep. Married with two children, he was on his way home from a sales trip to Grand Falls, Montana. Starkweather woke Collison and told him they were going to swap cars. Collison left the door locked and ignored him. Starkweather got the .22 pump-action rifle from the Packard and shot at Collison twice through the window of the car. Collison agreed to the trade and opened the door. But Starkweather cold-bloodedly blasted him seven times – in the nose, cheek, neck, chest, left arm, right wrist and left leg. The fugitives transferred their belongings – and their booty – into Collison's Buick. With Collison still jammed in the front seat and Caril in the back, Starkweather tried to drive off. But the handbrake was stuck fast. Caril said Starkweather turned to Collison's corpse for help. 'Man, are you dead?' Starkweather asked when there was no reply.

While Starkweather struggled with the handbrake, Joe Sprinkle, a 29-year-old geologist, drove by. Seeing Collison slumped in the front seat of the Buick, he thought there had been some sort of accident. He stopped and walked back to the Buick.

'Can I help?' he asked. Starkweather stuck the rifle in his face and explained that he could.

'Raise your hands. Help me release the emergency brake or I'll kill you,' Starkweather snarled.

It was then that Sprinkle noticed the bullet wounds in Collison's dead body. Instinctively he grabbed for the gun. Sprinkle knew that if he did not get the gun away from Starkweather he was a dead man. As the two men grappled in a life-or-death struggle in the middle of the highway, Wyoming Deputy Sheriff William Romer drove by. He pulled up about 25 yards down the road. Caril got out of the Buick and ran down to the patrol car.

'Take me to the police,' she said, pointing at Starkweather. 'He just killed a man.'

Sensing the danger, Starkweather spun round, letting go of the gun. Sprinkle lost his balance and fell back into a shallow ditch. Abandoning the Buick, Starkweather ran back to the Packard and roared off back towards Douglas. The deputy put out an all-points bulletin and, with Caril on board, gave chase. A few miles down the road he was joined by another police car. In it were County Sheriff Earl Heflin and Douglas Chief of Police Robert Ainslie. With the two police cars in hot pursuit Starkweather pushed his speed up to 100 mph. When he hit Douglas, the traffic slowed him and Heflin got off a couple of pot shots at his tyres with his handgun. For a moment, Ainslie got close enough to lock bumpers, but the bumper tore loose as Starkweather jumped a red light and overtook a lorry on the inside. As he cleared the town, Starkweather put his foot down on the accelerator again and his speed climbed towards 120 mph. Heflin got out his rifle and started shooting at the Packard. One shot smashed the back window. Starkweather screeched to a halt. Bleeding copiously, he thought he had been shot. In fact, a piece of flying glass had nicked his ear.

The police pulled up behind him. Starkweather got out of the car and started to walk towards them. The police shouted for him to put his hands up. As the police shot at the road in front of him, Starkweather put his hands behind him and coolly tucked in his flapping shirt tail. Then he lay face down on the road and surrendered.

The police blustered about his arrest.

'He thought he was bleeding to death. That's why he stopped. That's the kind of yellow son of a bitch he is,' the arresting officer told reporters.

However, in the public's mind, Starkweather was already a new kind of brooding anti-hero. When the prisoners were taken to the state penitentiary they were met by a crowd of newsmen, photographers and news cameramen. Caril, with her head covered by a scarf, played up to the cameras. But it was Starkweather, ignoring the media, who got all the attention. Wearing tight jeans, a black motorcycle jacket, cowboy boots with a butterfly design on the toe, handcuffed and with a cigarette dangling from his lips, he was the perfect young rebel killer. America had already been rocked by the image of the wayward teenager. They had seen a brooding James Dean in *Rebel Without a Cause* and a cocky and threatening Marlon Brando as the motorcycle gang leader in *The Wild One*. Elvis Presley had just burst on the scene with wild pelvic gyrations that scared the pants off conservative middle-America. But here, in the person of Charles Starkweather, was the embodiment of their fears. Here was the ultimate juvenile delinquent. Local Nebraskan newspaper the *Omaha World Herald* captured the mood. In a vitriolic leader it declared: 'The Starkweather story brought back to mind a thousand others. The sideburns, the tight blue jeans, the black leather jacket have become almost the uniform for juvenile hoodlums. And the snarling contempt for discipline, the blazing hate for restraint, have become a familiar refrain in police stations and juvenile courts.' FBI chief J. Edgar Hoover promised a nation-wide crackdown on juvenile crime.

At first Caril told police that she had been Starkweather's captive and had had no part in the murders. She had only gone along with him because her family were held hostage. But later she undermined her story by saying that she had witnessed their murders. She then became incoherent and had to be sedated.

Starkweather remained unrepentant. In a note to his parents, ostensibly apologising for the trouble he had caused them, he wrote: 'I'm not real sorry for what I did 'cos for the first time me and Caril had more fun, she helped me a lot, but if she comes back don't hate her she had not a thing to do with the killing all we wanted to do was get out of town.' He later compared himself to a soldier, killing only when he had to, to achieve an objective.

He quickly confessed to all the murders – except those of Clara Ward and her maid Lillian Fencl. As far as he knew, he maintained, they were alive when he left the house. Despite being charged with the murder of Merle Collison in Wyoming, Starkweather was quickly extradited back to Nebraska. He was ridiculed for being afraid of flying when he refused to go back to Lincoln by plane. In fact he thought that travelling by car he would stand a better chance of escaping.

Caril Fugate and Charles Starkweather were both charged with first-degree murder, making Caril the youngest woman to be tried on this charge in the US. They both pleaded not guilty and were tried separately. Starkweather's lawyer tried to get him to enter an insanity plea. Starkweather refused.

'Nobody remembers a crazy man,' he said, insisting that all the killings had been in self-defence.

★★★

Starkweather's trial for the murder of 17-year-old high-school student Robert Jensen began on 5 May 1958. The prosecution quickly established that the six bullets in Jensen's head had all been shot from behind, demolishing Starkweather's self-defence argument. Throughout the prosecution case, Starkweather acted cool, chewing gum and rocking back on his chair. The only time he showed any emotion was when an ex-employer said that Starkweather was the dumbest man who ever worked for him. Starkweather went crazy and had to be restrained.

The ex-employer's testimony was part of the defence lawyer's strategy to show his client was mentally incompetent. In fact, Starkweather had an above-average IQ. The defence attorney also read out some of Starkweather's confessions, hoping to show that his state of mind was abnormal and confused.

When Starkweather took the stand, he was asked why he was mad at Caril when they were at the derelict school. He replied that it was because of what she had done.

'What did she do?' he was asked.

'Shot Carol King,' said Starkweather.

This was not the first time that Starkweather accused Caril of killing Carol King. During his time on remand he had begun to fall out of love with her. He had also accused her of finishing off Merle Collison when his gun jammed.

Three psychiatrists appeared for the defence. They claimed that Starkweather had a diseased mind. But, under cross-examination, they admitted that this did not amount to a recognised mental illness and none of them were prepared to have Starkweather certified insane. Prosecution psychiatrists agreed that Starkweather had an anti-social personality disorder, but was legally sane. The jury also agreed. They returned a guilty verdict and recommended the electric chair.

During his court appearance, Starkweather become a TV celebrity, appearing on the news each night. Many teenagers identified with the cool and unrepentant Starkweather. Fan mail flooded in, though some urged him to turn to God. Admirers overlooked the fact that one of his first victims was Caril's stepsister, a two-and-a-half-year-old child.

Five months later Caril Fugate became the youngest woman ever to be tried for first-degree murder in the US. She was tried for being an accomplice in Jensen's murder. Although there was no suggestion that she had actually pulled the trigger, her admission that she had taken Jensen's wallet meant that this case would be easier to prove than one where it was simply her word against Starkweather's.

If I fry in the electric chair, then Caril should be sitting on my lap

Starkweather himself was the prosecution's star witness. Taking the stand, he told the jury that he no longer loved Caril and did not care if she lived or died. At one time he was even reported as having said: 'If I fry in the electric chair, then Caril should be sitting on my lap.'

He said that she had known he was involved in the murder of the filling-station attendant Robert Colvert and that she had been present when he had killed her family. She had gone with him willingly and had even expressed a desire to be shot down with him when the denouement came.

Caril's attorney believed that she was innocent, but could not shake Starkweather's story, which was partially corroborated by witnesses to their spree and early statements to the police. She was found guilty and sentenced to life imprisonment.

She continued to protest her innocence, but settled in to become a model prisoner at the state women's reformatory at York, Nebraska. In 1972 she was the subject of a documentary called *Growing up in Prison* and in 1976 was released on parole. In 1983 she appeared on TV to protest her innocence once more and took a lie detector test on camera. It indicated that she was telling the truth. However, a public opinion poll in Nebraska showed that most people did not believe her.

On death row Starkweather spent his time writing. He also talked for more than eighty hours to James Melvin Reinhardt, a professor of criminology at the University of Nebraska, explaining why he had taken to crime. His main motive was to take 'general revenge upon the world and its human race'.

'The people I murdered had murdered me,' he said. 'They murdered me slow, like. I was better to them. I killed them in a hurry.'

Poverty was another reason. 'They had me numbered for the bottom,' he said. He blamed the world and was sure that other people hated him 'because I was poor and had to live in a goddamned shack'. But there was a way out of this class trap – 'all dead people are on the same level,' he said.

He saw his murderous spree as the only way out of a life of drudgery. 'Better to be left to rot on some high hill, and be remembered,' he wrote, 'than to be buried alive in some stinking place.'

Now Starkweather had everything he wanted. He was going to die – but he was famous. Nothing gave him more pleasure than to see his name in the papers.

Professor Reinhardt published *The Murderous Trail of Charles Starkweather*, which alleged that Starkweather was paranoid and that this problem was self-inflicted. Starkweather's own account was published in *Parade* magazine under the title 'Rebellion'. The piece was heavily cut and ended up as a homily to wayward youth, advising commitment to God, regular church-going, and respect for authority. 'If I had followed these simple rules, as I was advised to many times, I would not be where I am today,' it concluded.

In fact, Starkweather did have something of a change of heart in prison. His murderous rampage seemed to have quenched his hatred. A gentler side took over. One of his prison guards said: 'If somebody had just paid attention to Charlie, bragged on his drawing and writing, all of this might not have happened.'

At the parole board Starkweather spoke of his remorse and his new-found Christian faith. It did no good. The execution was scheduled for 22 May 1959. He wrote to his father, talking of repentance and his hopes of staying alive. The execution was delayed by a federal judge, then rescheduled for 25 June.

When the prison guards came for him, he asked: 'What's your hurry?' Then, in a new shirt and jeans, he swaggered ahead of them to the electric chair with his hands in his pockets. Outside, gangs of teenagers cruised the streets, playing rock 'n' roll on their car radios. Fifteen years later the Starkweather story was retold in the 1974 cult film *Badlands*, starring Martin Sheen and Cissy Spacek. The story then formed the basis of Oliver Stone's controversial 1994 film *Natural Born Killers*, starring Woody Harrelson and Juliette Lewis.

– Chapter 2 –

The Boston Strangler

Albert DeSalvo

NATIONALITY: AMERICAN

NUMBER OF VICTIMS: 13 KILLED

FAVOURED METHOD OF KILLING: STRANGULATION
– HE ALWAYS TIED THE LIGATURE IN A BOW ON THE
VICTIM'S BODY

BORN: 1931

REIGN OF TERROR: 1962–64

APPREHENDED: HE WAS NEVER CAUGHT OR FORMALLY IDENTIFIED

No one was ever prosecuted for the murders committed by the Boston Strangler, who terrorised the women of New England between 1962 and 1964. However, the Boston Police Department named the main suspect who they believed had brutally murdered 13 young women. His name was Albert DeSalvo.

DeSalvo was the son of a vicious drunk. When he was 11, DeSalvo watched his father knock his mother's teeth out then bend her fingers back until they snapped. But this was nothing unusual in the DeSalvo household.

When they were just children, Albert and his two sisters were sold to a farmer in Maine for nine dollars, but later escaped. After he got back home, his father taught him how to shoplift, taking him to the store and showing him what to take. His father would also bring prostitutes back to the apartment and make the children watch while he had sex with them.

Soon the young DeSalvo developed a lively interest in sex, making many early conquests among the neighbourhood girls, as well as earning a healthy living from the local gay community who would pay him for his services. In the army, DeSalvo continued his sexual adventuring, until he met Irmgaard, the daughter of a respectable Catholic family in Frankfurt. They married and returned to the US in 1954, where DeSalvo was dishonourably discharged from the army for sexually molesting a nine-year-old girl. Criminal charges were not brought because the girl's mother feared the publicity.

DeSalvo pursued a career in breaking and entering, but at home he was the perfect family man. However, his sexual appetite was more than his wife could cope with. He demanded sex five or six times a day. This annoyed Irmgaard and finally repelled her. So DeSalvo found an outlet as the 'Measuring Man'.

He began hanging around the student areas of Boston, looking for apartments shared by young women. He would knock on the door with a clipboard, saying that he was the representative of a modelling agency, and ask whether he could take their measurements. Sometimes his charm succeeded in seducing the women – sometimes they would seduce him. Other times he would just take their measurements, clothed or naked, and promise that a female representative would call later. He never assaulted any of the girls. The only complaints were that no one came on a follow-up visit.

About that time, DeSalvo was caught housebreaking and sent to jail for two years. The experience left him frustrated. When he was released he started a new career, breaking into houses throughout New England and tying up and raping women. At that time, he was known as the 'Green Man' because he wore a green shirt and trousers. The police in Connecticut and Massachusetts put the number of his assault in the hundreds. DeSalvo himself claimed more than a thousand – bragging that he had tied up and raped six women in one morning.

DeSalvo confined his activities to Boston and added murder to his repertoire, killing 55-year-old Anna Slesers in her apartment on 14 June 1962. DeSalvo had left her body in an obscene pose, with the cord he had used to strangle her tied in a bow around her neck. This was to become his trademark.

Over the next month he raped and strangled five women, including 85-year-old Mary Mullen, (even though, he said, she reminded him of his grandmother) and 65-year-old nurse Helen Blake. Within two days he killed 75-year-old Ida Irga and 67-year-old Jane Sullivan. By this time, the Boston police force had realised that they had a serious maniac on their hands and had begun questioning all known sexual deviants. But DeSalvo was overlooked because he only had a record for burglary and housebreaking. The only official record of his sexual deviancy was in his army file.

DeSalvo cooled off for a bit and took a long autumn break. But by his eighth wedding anniversary on 5 December, his mind was so overheated with violent sexual images that he thought it was going to explode. He saw an attractive girl going into an apartment block. He followed her and knocked on her door. Using his usual ploy, he pretended to be a maintenance man sent by the landlord to check the pipes. She did not let him in so he tried the next apartment. The door was opened by a tall, attractive, 25-year-old black woman named Sophie Clark. DeSalvo reverted to his Measuring Man routine. He remarked on her stunningly curvaceous body and, when she turned her back, he attacked her. Once he had subdued her, he stripped her and raped her. Then he strangled her. He left her naked body, like the others, propped up with the legs spread and the ligature he had used to strangle her tied in a bow under her chin.

Three days later, DeSalvo went back to one of the women he had previously visited as the Measuring Man – 23-year-old secretary Patricia Bissette. She invited him in for a cup of coffee and when she turned her back he grabbed her round the throat and raped her, then strangled her with her own stockings.

DeSalvo's next victim escaped. She fought back so violently, biting, scratching and screaming that he fled. This seems to have been something of a turning-point in DeSalvo's career. But she was so distraught after the attack that the description she gave was next to useless.

From then on the Boston Strangler's attacks became even more violent. On 9 March 1963, he gained access to 69-year-old Mary Brown's apartment by saying he had come to fix the stove. He carried with him a piece of lead pipe which he used to beat her head in. He raped her after he had killed her, then stabbed her in the breasts with a fork which he left sticking in her flesh. He maintained his *modus operandi* by strangling her, but this time the victim was already dead.

Two months later, DeSalvo took a day off work. He drove out to Cambridge, Massachusetts, where he spotted a pretty girl, 23-year-old student Beverley Samans, on University Road. He followed her to her apartment. Once inside he tied her to the bedposts, stripped, blindfolded, gagged and raped her repeatedly before strangling

There were 22 savage wounds on her body

her with her own stockings. But this time, it was not enough. Before he left the apartment, he pulled his penknife from his pocket and started stabbing her naked body. Once he started he could not stop. He stabbed and stabbed her. Blood flew everywhere. There were 22 savage wounds on her body. Once the frenzy subsided, he calmly wiped his fingerprints from the knife, dropped it in the sink and went home.

DeSalvo killed again on 8 September, raping and strangling 58-year-old Evelyn Corbin with her own nylons, which he then left tied in a bow around her ankle. The city was in panic. The killer seemed to come and go at will. With no description of the man and no clues, the police were powerless. In desperation they brought in Dutch psychic Peter Hurkos, but he failed to identify the Strangler.

While America – and Kennedy's home state of Massachusetts particularly – was in mourning following the assassination of the president, he struck again. He raped and strangled 23-year-old dress designer Joan Gaff in her own apartment, leaving her black leotard tied in a bow around her neck

DeSalvo admitted later that he did not know why he had killed Joan. 'I wasn't even excited,' he said. After he left her apartment, he went home, played with his kids and watched the report of her murder on TV. Then he sat down and had dinner, without thinking of it again.

On 4 January 1964, the Boston Strangler struck for the last time. He gained access to the flat of 19-year-old Mary Sullivan, tied her up at knifepoint and raped her. This time he strangled her with his hands. Her body was found propped up on her bed, her buttocks on the pillow and her back against the headboard. Her head rested on her right shoulder, her eyes closed and viscose liquid was dripping from her mouth. Her breasts and her sexual organs were exposed and there was a broom handle protruding from her vagina. More semen stains were found on her blanket. Between her toes he placed a card he found in the apartment which read 'Happy New Year'.

Later that year, a woman reported being sexually assaulted by a man using the Measuring Man routine, but otherwise all the activity of the Boston Strangler stopped. This coincided with the arrest of DeSalvo for housebreaking. Held on bail, DeSalvo's behaviour became disturbed and he was transferred to the mental hospital at Bridgewater, where he was diagnosed as schizophrenic.

Although they had him in custody, the police still had no idea that DeSalvo was the Boston Strangler. But in Bridgewater, another inmate, jailed for killing a petrol pump attendant and also a suspect in the Boston Strangler case himself, listened to DeSalvo's manic ramblings and began to put two and two together. He got his lawyer to interview DeSalvo.

In these taped interviews, DeSalvo revealed facts about the murders – the position of the bodies, the nature of the ligature and the wounds inflicted – that the police had not revealed. He also admitted to two murders that had not already been attributed to the Boston Strangler.

DeSalvo was a mental patient, so he was not prosecuted for the rapes and murders he confessed to. But there was no doubt that he was, indeed, the Boston Strangler. DeSalvo was transferred to Walpole State Prison. He was found dead in his cell in 1973, stabbed through the heart.

– Chapter 3 –

Australian Spree Killers

Eric Edgar Cooke

NATIONALITY: AUSTRALIAN

NUMBER OF VICTIMS: 2 INJURED, 7 KILLED

FAVOURED METHOD OF KILLING: SHOOTING

EXECUTED: 26 OCTOBER 1964

In **1963,** on a summer Saturday night in a comfortable Perth suburb, a gunman started picking off people, seemingly at random. Nicholas August, a poultry dealer and a married man, was out with Ocean beach barmaid Rowena Reeves. They were sharing a drink in the car around 2 a.m. on 27 January when Rowena saw a man. Thinking he was a peeping Tom, August told him to 'bugger off'. The silent figure did not move, so August threw an empty bottle at him. 'Look out,' screamed Rowena to her companion. 'He's got a gun.' The man raised a rifle and took careful aim at August's head. At the last moment, Rowena pushed August's head down and the bullet nicked his neck and then lodged in her forearm. It bled profusely. Rowena yelled at him to start the car and run the gunman down. August sped off, with bullets singing past them. By the time he reached the hospital, Rowena was unconscious. Both survived the incident. Just over an hour later and a couple of miles away, 54-year-old George Walmsley was shot when he opened his front door after hearing the doorbell. The bullet hit him in the forehead and he was dead by the time his wife and daughter, woken by the shot, got downstairs. Around the corner at Mrs Allen's boarding house, John Sturkey, a 19-year-old agricultural student from the University of Western Australia, was sleeping on the verandah. At around 4 a.m. fellow student Scott McWilliam was awoken by Mrs Allen's niece Pauline. 'There's something wrong with John,' she said. McWilliam went out on to the veranda. A strange noise was coming from Sturkey's throat. McWilliam raised his head. There was a bullet hole between his eyes. Next morning Brian Weir, who lived nearby in Broome Street, did not show up for training at the Surf Life Saving Club. One of the crew went round to get him out of bed. Brian was found with a bullet wound in his forehead and serious brain damage. He would die from his wounds three years later. The police had little to go on and the press offered a £1,000 reward for the capture of the 'Maniac Slayer' (Australia didn't their currency to the Australian dollar until 1966). Local homeowners slept with loaded guns next to their beds. Nothing happened for three weeks. Then the killer struck again. Joy Noble was up early making breakfast one Saturday morning when she glanced out of the kitchen window of her West Perth home. Outside she saw the naked body of a young woman spread-eagled on the back lawn. At first she thought it was her daughter and she ran through the house shouting: 'Carline.' In fact, it was the body of Constance Lucy Madrill, a 24-year-old social worker who lived in nearby Thomas Street. She had been raped, strangled and dumped on the Nobles' lawn. The attack had taken place in the girl's own apartment, while her flatmate, Jennifer Hurse, slept. No one could explain why the attacker had dragged her all the way to the Nobles' lawn, then abandoned her. An Aborigine had probably done it, the police concluded – even though there were no records of Aborigines in Western Australia attacking white girls. And it certainly had nothing to do with the shootings three weeks before, the police said. Six months passed uneventfully. Then on the thundery night of 10 August, Shirley McLeod, an 18-year-old science student at the University of Western Australia, was babysitting Carl and Wendy Dowds' eight-month-old son, Mitchell. When the Dowdses returned from their party they found Shirley slumped on the sofa with a peaceful look on her face like she had just fallen asleep but in fact, she had been shot by a .22 rifle and was quite dead. Baby Mitchell was unharmed. There could be no doubt that this killing was linked with the murders in January. Perth experienced mass panic. The *West Australian* advised people to lock their doors at night – unheard of in Perth before that time. Babysitters were warned not to sit near windows, and there were proposals to close the old alleyways that ran down the back of people's houses. The police began to fingerprint every male over the age of 12 in the city, at a rate of 8,000 a week. Then, on Saturday 17 August an elderly couple were out picking flowers in Mount Pleasant when they spotted a rifle hidden in some bushes. It was a Winchester .22. The police believed that it had not been discarded but hidden there so it could be used again. They staked out the area for two weeks before a truck driver named Eric Edgar Cooke turned up, looking for the gun.

Cooke had been born in Perth in 1931 with a harelip and a cleft palate. Early operations improved his condition, but his speech remained blurred and indistinct and his appearance was mocked by others. From an early age he suffered severe headaches and blackouts. These were aggravated by a fall from a bicycle and a dive into shallow water at 14. Doctors suspected brain damage, but X-rays and an exploratory operation revealed nothing. At home as a teenager, his father had beaten him regularly. At 16 he spent three weeks in hospital after trying to protect his mother from one of his father's onslaughts. He told the doctors he had been fighting with other boys. Expelled from several schools, Cooke had quit completely by the age of 14. He had taken a series of manual jobs, none of which lasted long, before being called up for National Service. In the army, he was taught how to handle a rifle.

In November 1953 he married an 18-year-old immigrant from England called Sally. The couple had seven children – four boys and three girls. Their first child was born mentally handicapped and their eldest daughter, one of twins, was born without a right arm. Nevertheless it was a happy household. Cooke was a faithful husband and a loving father. Other childrenfromalloverthe neighbourhood cametoplayin the Cookes'house. However, behind it all was what Sally Cooke described as her husband's 'restlessness'. She could not keep him at home. He constantly went out on sprees of petty thieving. He had burgled some 250 houses and spent three short terms in prison before the police picked him up as a murder suspect. At the police station Cooke claimed to have been at home on the night Shirley McLeod was killed. His wife said he was not. Then Cooke confessed. On the way home from bowling that day, he had started looking for somewhere to burgle. He found a house in Pearse Street with its back door open and went in. There was a couple sitting in the lounge, so Cooke crept into the bedroom to look for money. Instead he found a Winchester .22. He took it, and some cartridges, thinking he could probably sell it later. He said he remembered parking his car again on the way home, then – later – finding the rifle in his hand with a spent cartridge in the breach. It was only the next day, when he saw a report about the babysitter's murder on the television, that he realised what he had done.

The next day he was taken to the scene of Lucy Madrill's murder and confessed to that killing as well. He said he had been robbing the girls' flat when he had knocked over a framed photograph. Lucy had woken up and he had hit her. She tried to scream but he throttled her. He dragged her through into the next bedroom, strangled her with a lamp flex, then raped her. He had intended to hide the body. He dragged it outside and left it on the Nobles' lawn while he looked for a car to steal. But he could not find one, so he stole a bicycle instead and rode home.

Later he confessed to the spree on 27 January. He had shot five people that night because he 'wanted to hurt somebody', he said. Out on his usual Saturday night prowl, he had stolen a Lithgow single-shot .22 and a tan-coloured Holden sedan. He had been driving aimlessly when he saw a man and a woman in a parked car. The interior light went out, so Cooke thought he would stop and spy on the couple. He took the rifle with him. And when they spotted him and threw a bottle at him, he shot back. In Broome Street he stopped again, intent on doing a bit more burglary. He clambered over some railings and climbed up on to a balcony. Inside some French windows a man lay sleeping. The bed barred Cooke's way into the room, so he shot from the hip at the sleeping body. The result was Brian Weir's irreversible brain damage. Prowling around the block, Cooke saw a man sleeping on the verandah. Another shot from the hip ended John Sturkey's young life. The next killing was even more deliberate. He leant the rifle against the garage of a house he had picked randomly in Louise Street and went to ring the front doorbell. Then he ran back to the gun and aimed at the doorway. When a man answered the door, Cooke shot him. Then he threw the rifle off the Narrows Bridge into the Swan River and

I'm just a cold-blooded killer

returned the Holden to the house where he had stolen it. In the morning the owner noticed that the bulb of the interior light had been removed, but the matter was too petty to report to the police. Only the death of John Sturkey upset Cooke. 'He was so young,' he told the police. 'He never had a chance. I will never meet him because he is up there and I'll be down there. I'm just a cold-blooded killer.' With that last sentence, Cooke ruled out the possibility of being found not guilty by reason of insanity. Cooke also confessed to the murder of 33-year-old divorcée Patricia Vinico Berkman in 1959. Her lover, local radio personality Fotis Hountas, had found her body in bed in her flat in South Perth. She had been stabbed repeatedly in the head and chest. She left a nine-year-old son. And Cooke said that he had killed wealthy society beauty Jillian Brewer later that year. Aged 22, she too had been viciously murdered in her own flat. The killer had used a hatchet and a pair of scissors. There were no fingerprints. The doors were locked from the inside and there was no sign of any windows being forced. The police were mystified. Four months after the killing, 20-year-old deaf-mute Darryl Beamish, arrested for molesting four little girls, had confessed to the Brewer murder through a sign-language interpreter. At his trial, Beamish claimed the confession had been forced out of him. The prosecutor produced no other evidence.

Nevertheless, Beamish was found guilty and sentenced to death. Cooke's confession, on the other hand, was extraordinarily detailed. His description of the flat on the night of the murder fitted exactly with the photographs taken by the scene-of-crime photographer. He even explained the locked doors – he had stolen the key to the flat on a previous raid. On 17 March 1964, Beamish appeared before the appeal court with Cooke's statement. However, the three appeal court judges – one was the original trial judge, the other two had dismissed Beamish's appeals on two previous occasions – did not believe Cooke's confession. But they did commute Beamish's sentence from death to life imprisonment. Cooke was hanged in Fremantle Prison on 26 October 1964.

Julian Knight

NATIONALITY: AUSTRALIAN

NUMBER OF VICTIMS: 7

FAVOURED METHOD OF KILLING: SHOOTING

STATED MOTIVE: HE CLAIMED HIS KILLING SPREE WAS A RESULT OF HIS DESIRE TO MAKE AN HEROIC LAST STAND AND GO DOWN FIGHTING

Cooke's January night rampage is peculiar, but he otherwise exhibited the profile of a serial, rather than a spree, killer. In 1987 a lone gunman loosed off a hail of bullets in a more typical, random, mindless spree killing. At 9.30 p.m. on Sunday 9 August, young Alan Jury was driving along Hoddle Street near the suburb of Clifton Hill, Melbourne, when he heard a noise like a firecracker. His windscreen shattered. Quickly realising that someone was shooting at him, he stamped down on the accelerator and roared away from the danger. At the next service station he reported that a gunman was firing at passing cars. In the car behind him, Rita Vitcos also heard a bang and saw sparks fly off the surface of the road. She too accelerated away. Later, when she got out of the car, she found two bullet-holes in the driver's door and realised how lucky she had been. Twenty-three-year-old Vesna Markonsky's windscreen exploded as she drove down the Street. She jammed on the brakes. When the car came to a halt she discovered that a bullet had hit her in the left arm. She got out and a second bullet hit her, then a third. Her boyfriend

Zoran, who was with her in the car, jumped out to help her. More bullets filled the air as he and a young doctor, who had stopped his car behind Vesna's, ran towards the wounded girl. The doctor collapsed, hit. Another car pulled up behind Zoran's. A bullet hit the driver in the right temple. He died instantly. A girl student stopped to help. She too was gunned down. When Zoran reached Vesna, he cradled her in his arms. She spoke a few words, then lost consciousness. Constable Belinda Bourchier arrived in a police car shortly afterwards. Zoran ran to her and tried to pull her revolver out of its holster. Covered in blood and in a state of shock, he yelled at her that he wanted to kill the bastard who had just murdered his girlfriend. More shots screamed past them. 'Let's get out of here,' said Constable Bourchier, and they ran for cover behind some trees at the edge of the road. The gunman continued firing with deadly accuracy. More windscreens shattered and cars careered across the road. A motorcyclist swerved and crashed. He lay in the road trapped under his bike and two more bullets slammed into his body. After ten minutes of shooting, the police turned up in force. The shots were coming from the 'nature strip', a grass verge alongside Clifton Hill railway station. The police set up roadblocks and closed off the area. A police helicopter was called in. It flew in low over the nature strip. Its searchlight swept the ground. But the gunman had vanished. A few minutes later a police car, turning into Hoddle Street from the north, came under fire. A policeman on a roadblock there was also winged by a bullet. Another shot struck the helicopter flying overhead, but bounced off its armoured underside. Spotting the gunman near the track, a signalman managed to stop an oncoming train. He ran up the line, expecting to be shot in the back. But the gunman now seemed to be firing into the ground. The signalman reached the train and told the driver to reverse. When he looked back, the gunman had disappeared. In a street close by, two constables in a police car spotted a man with a rifle running along the road. They pursued him. The gunman turned in to a lane and they stopped the car, closing off the end. Out of the darkness of the lane came a hail of bullets. One shot hit Constable John Delahunty in the head. He flung himself to the ground and managed to crawl towards the gunman. His partner, Constable Lockman, crawled after him. They got within a few yards of where they believed the gunman to be when the wounded Delahunty saw his head rise above some bushes. Delahunty leapt to his feet and fired his revolver. The gunman ducked back down behind the bushes. A moment later a voice called out, 'Don't shoot me, don't shoot me.' 'Put your gun down and come out with your arms up,' Delahunty shouted back. A dark silhouette rose from behind the bushes. 'Don't shoot me,' said the gunman again as he walked forward with his arms high above his head. He had a small moustache, a military haircut and identified himself as 19-year-old Julian Knight.

Knight was an illegitimate child who had been adopted when he was a baby. His adoptive father was a career army officer, whom he greatly admired, and it was an emotional shock when his parents divorced when he was 12. Although he was generally regarded as bright, his schoolwork soon began to deteriorate. His reports said he was lazy, too easily distracted and too complacent about his abilities. He always had difficulty accepting authority. Unlike other spree killers, Knight was not shy. He had girlfriends and something of a reputation as the 'class clown' at Fitzroy High School. But from an early age he was preoccupied with Charles Whitman and other lone snipers. Eventually he was expelled from school for his violent outbursts. Then he was accepted by the Royal Military College at Duntroon. He was almost 19 when he went to the Military College in January 1987. An army assessor described him as immature, overconfident and stubborn. He could not knuckle down to army discipline. In May he was charged with eight offences, including four counts of being absent without leave. Then, on 31 May, after a weekend confined to barracks, he slipped out and got drunk in a nightclub near Duntroon. A sergeant encountered him and ordered him out. Knight stabbed him twice in the face with a penknife. He was charged with assault and discharged from Duntroon in July 1987, after only seven months.

Back at the police station, Knight seemed calm and subdued. He described how he had started the evening by drinking a dozen glasses of beer in a local pub to alleviate a terrible feeling of depression. Since his discharge, his whole life had been turned upside down. His mother had changed his bedroom into a sitting room, so he was forced to camp in his own home (just a few yards from Hoddle Street, on the other side of the railway tracks). His girlfriend had left him. He owed the bank thousands of dollars. A car he had hoped to sell had broken

He decided to go down fighting

down that afternoon, and something had snapped. He had decided it was time to die – but to commit suicide offended his sense of military honour. Since his schooldays, he had fantasised about wars, particularly heroic 'last stands'. He decided to go down fighting. He left home that evening at 9.25 p.m., carrying a shotgun and two rifles. He crossed the railway line to the nature strip. He knelt down, took careful aim and started to shoot at the cars coming down Hoddle Street. He kept on shooting until he had used up all his ammunition. He claimed to have hoped that a 'battle' might develop, but no one shot at him until Constable Delahunty fired his revolver. He groped in his pocket for the last bullet he said he had saved for himself. It had gone. So he surrendered, like a soldier who was surrounded and had run out of ammunition. In the space of 45 minutes Knight had fired at more than 50 cars, hitting 26 people. Seven of his victims were dead, or dying in the nearest hospital. Two days later, when what he had done had sunk in, Knight had a nervous breakdown and had to be confined to a padded cell. In November 1988 he was sentenced to life imprisonment. Julian Knight will not be eligible for parole until the year 2013.

Frank Vitkovic

NATIONALITY: AUSTRALIAN

NUMBER OF VICTIMS: 8

FAVOURED METHOD OF KILLING: SHOOTING

Melbourne **had scarcely recovered** from the shock of the Hoddle Street rampage when four months later another mad gunman claimed a further eight victims. On 8 December 1987, 22-year-old Frank Vitkovic went to the Australia Post office, initially intending to kill an old schoolfriend against whom he harboured a grudge. He was suffering from depression and severe headaches. But the gun misfired and his friend escaped. Vitkovic then began to shoot at random.

Twenty-year-old Judy Morris photographed the last sunset of her life on Monday from the roof of her father's funeral parlour. 'It's beautiful,' said Judy, a Telecom Credit Union teller, as she pointed her camera at the horizon. 'I want it on film so I can always remember.' She was speaking to her fiancé, 19-year-old Jason Miles, an apprentice chef she had met just a year before. According to Judy's father, Ken Morris, it was Jason who had coaxed his shy daughter out of her shell. Shortly before sunset that night Judy told her fiancé that something was worrying her. Her workmates at the Credit Union on the fifth floor of the Australia Post building, at 191 Queen Street, had met about security that morning. The tellers had complained that the bullet-proof screens they had asked for a year before had still not been installed. 'She was horrified at not having any security at work,' Jason said. 'Not for herself, but for everyone else.'

As Jason moved to go that night, Judy said: 'Don't go.' They lay in each other's arms for a long time. It was as if she knew her time was up, he said.

Next morning Judy Morris waved to her mother, Nola, as she walked to the train station and called out that she would see her that night. Six-and-a-half hours later Frank Vitkovic caught another train to Queen Street and entered the blue-tiled foyer of the Australia Post building. As Judy and Jason had contemplated the happy course of their own lives the previous evening it is likely that Vitkovic had already decided the course of his. Vitkovic came from the West Preston area of North Melbourne, home to many European immigrants of the late 1950s and 1960s. Yugoslav house painter Drago Vitkovic and his wife lived in a small white-painted weatherboard house on May Street, the very picture of respectability. The front lawn had been covered with concrete to give more off-street space for Mr Vitkovic's brown Valiant station wagon and the family's two other small vehicles.

In these affluent surroundings, their son Frank grew into a good-looking, big framed youth who was over six feet tall. At high school he was placed in the top five per cent of students. Vitkovic also had a passion for playing tennis, becoming something of a legend on the twin clay courts of St Raphael's tennis club. A strong backhand drive floored many opponents and scared others. Margaret O'Leary, a former club secretary, recalled that Vitkovic sometimes aimed his returns at an opponent's body. It was enough to help him win the club championship in 1983.

The young sons of immigrant families in the club quickly identified with Vitkovic. They became known in the clubhouse as 'the ethnics'. Mrs O'Leary recalled that some of the young men idolised Vitkovic and his confidence blossomed. 'The topic of conversation was always Frank Vitkovic,' she said. 'He found it very hard to lose.'

Everyone agreed that Vitkovic was destined for bigger things. Nobody was surprised when, in 1984, he won a place at Melbourne University's Law School. To start with everything went fine. Vitkovic told tennis-club friends he was 'breezing through'. But in early 1986 things began to go wrong. Midway through his last year, Vitkovic abandoned his studies and helped his father paint houses. Those who knew him still detected no hint that Vitkovic was having problems. His family were good people. Nobody ever expected anything bad to happen to Frank. Vitkovic returned to Law School at the beginning of 1987, but it was a brief and unhappy experience. He left his studies again soon after because of 'unsatisfactory progress'. He also sought help from Melbourne

I've got to get rid of my violent impulses

University's Counselling Service during this period. He did not work after leaving university. Vitkovic kept a file of Melbourne newspaper clippings of Julian Knight's massacre on Hoddle Street, underlining sections of the clippings in red. He also kept *Rambo* videos in his bedroom. In mid-September he had obtained a gun permit from the Central Firearms Registry in Melbourne after failing just one of the 14 questions. It was: 'Should firearms be unloaded before you enter a house or building?' He had answered: 'No.' Around the same time, a salesman from Precision Guns and Ammo in Victoria Street, West Melbourne, sold Vitkovic an M-1 semi-automatic rifle for £275. Vitkovic sawed the stock and barrel off the 75-centimetre weapon to make it easy to conceal. The night before he went into the Australia Post building, he wrote in his diary: 'The anger in my head has got too much for me. I've got to get rid of my violent impulses. The time has come to die. There is no other way out.'

Judy Morris returned to her office from her 1 p.m. lunch-break on top of the world. Not only had she had the spectacular picture of the sunset developed, but she had bought a new outfit – white slacks with braces and a matching pink blouse. She showed them to her closest friend, a young supervisor who also worked behind the Credit Union counter. Judy also passed the pictures of the sunset around her friends in the Credit Union. Twenty-two-year-old Con Margellis, one of the regular staff, may have seen them. Margellis is the only apparent link between Vitkovic and the 1,000 people working that day in the Queen Street offices. He lived just a few streets from the Vitkovics in West Preston. He and Vitkovic had been at school together and had been friends for a number of years.

At 4.10 p.m. that Tuesday Vitkovic emerged from the lift and greeted Mr Margellis inside the fifth-floor Credit Union office with the word 'G'day.' He then brought out the carbine from under his green top and began firing shots in the direction of his friend. Police ruled out any homosexual relationship between them. Nor was there any dispute over a woman. Nevertheless Vitkovic was now shooting with murderous intent at his former classmate. The Telecom Credit Union staff scattered in fear. Someone pressed the alarm button. Judy Morris and her best friend ran towards the glass exit doors. A shot rang out. Both women fell. They lay on the ground until Vitkovic finished shooting and disappeared out of the exit to the lift wells. Margellis was safe. He had hidden in the women's toilets. But Judy Morris was dead. The security doors shut tight behind Vitkovic, trapping him outside. He kicked the doors, trying to get back in. He went to the lifts and waited until one of the pink arrows flashed up. Then he rode to the twelfth floor. The Philatelic Bureau was quiet when Vitkovic burst in. In the customer sales section he let rip with automatic rifle-fire. The bureau's 29-year-old supervisor Warren Spencer was killed while trying to take cover behind the office photocopier. His 24-year-old wife, Susan, mother of their two children, who also worked at the bureau, watched in horror as her husband died. Twenty-year-old Julie McBean and 18-year-old Nancy Avigone were shot dead at their desks.

Below, Melbourne became aware of the shootings. As crowds began to gather in the street, Vitkovic took a sniper's perch from a broken twelfth-floor window. He fired several bullets at the first motorcycle police officers who arrived at 4.15 p.m. Vitkovic ran down the stairs to the eleventh floor, which housed the Australia Post accounts department. In the stairwell Vitkovic fired one volley that blew a fist-sized hole in the office window to his right. Turning left he confronted Michael McGuire in the data-processing room, where McGuire trained staff and fixed machines. Vitkovic fired at point-blank range into the young father of three. One bullet passed through the partition McGuire sheltered against and punched a crater in the corridor wall. McGuire had been hoping to be home early that night. His youngest daughter was celebrating her fifth birthday. The staff in the accounts department now found their escape path blocked by the killer. The shots rang out as Vitkovic entered the room, his fire concentrated to the far corners of the room. Thirty-two-year-old Rodney Brown was shot beside the desk he had worked at for seven years. He died later in the arms of an ambulanceman. Thirty-eight-year-old Marianne van Ewyk and Catherine Dowling, 28, died as they cowered under their desks. Van Ewyk, who had emigrated from Holland as a child, had worked with Australia Post since she was a teenager. Next to her desk was a school-term calendar to keep track of holidays she could spend with her only son. At the same time Frank Vitkovic was downstairs, waiting for the lift, Marianne's husband, Bernie Sharp, had rung her to warn her of a rail strike.

The accounts department assistant manager Tony Gloria then put an end to the massacre. A quiet man who was never known to lose his temper, he tackled the gunman. A head shorter than Vitkovic, he grabbed the killer around the waist. Another of the office workers, who had been shot in the shoulder, helped to drag Vitkovic down. A third man grabbed the rifle and hid it in the fridge. Vitkovic, who was now bent on taking his own life, struggled to make his way through to a broken window. Gloria fought to save him. Office workers in nearby buildings saw the struggle and the shower of glass that preceded the killer as he fell to the pavement 60 metres below, where he died.

– Chapter 4 –

Sniper in the Tower

Charles Whitman Jr

NATIONALITY: AMERICAN

NUMBER OF VICTIMS: 16 KILLED, 30 INJURED

FAVOURED METHOD OF KILLING: SHOOTING, STABBING

BORN: 1941

PROFESSION: EX-US MARINE

MARRIED: YES

REIGN OF TERROR: 1 AUGUST 1966

FINAL NOTE: 'THE INTENSE HATRED I FEEL FOR MY FATHER IS BEYOND ALL DESCRIPTION'

It was a perfect summer day in Austin, Texas. By mid-morning on 1 August 1966, the temperature had already soared to 36 degrees in the shade and the hot air hung heavy over the downtown campus of the University of Texas. The students had taken the opportunity to linger in the sunshine when classes changed at 11.30. But by 11.45, all was quiet again under the university's 28-storey limestone tower.

At 11.48, 17-year-old Alec Hernandez was cycling across the campus, delivering newspapers, when a .35 rifle bullet ripped through his leg. It slammed into his saddle and catapulted him from his bike. Then, out of the clear, blue sky, more bullets came raining down. Three students, late for class, fell in quick succession.

At first, no one could figure out what was happening. There was a distant report, then someone would crumple to the ground. On the fourth floor of the tower building 23-year-old postgraduate student Norma Barger heard what she took to be dynamite exploding. In fact, it was the sound of a deer-hunting rifle echoing from the low buildings that nestled around the tower. When she looked out of her classroom window, she saw six bodies sprawled grotesquely on the mall beneath her. At first she thought it was a tasteless joke. She expected them to get up and walk away laughing. Then she saw the pavement stones splashed with blood – and more people falling beneath the sniper's deadly rain of fire.

Eighteen-year-old Mrs Claire Wilson, who was eight months pregnant, was heading across the mall to her anthropology class when a bullet ripped into her belly. She survived, but her unborn child's skull was crushed and the baby was later born dead. Nineteen-year-old freshman Thomas Eckman, a classmate and aspiring poet, was kneeling beside the injured mother-to-be when another bullet shot him dead.

Thirty-three-year-old post-graduate mathematician Robert Boyer was looking forward to his trip to England. He had already secured a teaching post in Liverpool, where his pregnant wife and two children were waiting for him. But when he stepped out on to the mall, heading for an early lunch, he was shot, fatally, in the back. Secretary Charlotte Darehshori ran to help him and found herself under fire. She spent the next hour and a half crouched behind the concrete base of a flagpole, one of the few people to venture on to the mall and survive uninjured.

The sniper took a shot at a small boy. People began to take cover. A woman on the eighteenth floor of the administration block rang a friend in a nearby university building and said: 'Somebody's up there shooting from the tower. There's blood all over the place.' Soon hundreds were pinned down on the campus.

At 11.52, four minutes after the shooting started, the local police received a hysterical phone call. At first, all they knew was that there had been 'some shooting at the university tower'. In seconds, a 'ten-fifty' went out. All units in the vicinity were ordered to head for the university.

Soon the quiet of the Texas high noon was torn by the sound of sirens as more than a hundred city policemen, reinforced by some thirty highway patrolmen, state troopers, Texas Rangers and Secret Service men from President Lyndon Johnson's Austin office, converged on the campus – along with a number of ordinary gun-toting Texans.

One of the first policemen on the scene was rookie patrolman Billy Speed. He quickly figured out what was happening. He spotted the killer on the observation deck of the tower. The young patrolman took cover behind the base of a statue of Jefferson Davis and took careful aim. But before he could take a shot, the sniper shot him dead. Speed was just 23 and left a wife and baby daughter. The shot alerted the other lawmen. Volleys of small-arms fire cracked around the top of the tower. A few rounds smashed into the huge clock-face above the killer. Most pinged ineffectually off the four-foot-high wall around the observation deck, kicking up puffs of white dust.

Ducking down behind the low wall, the sniper was safe. Narrow drainage slits around the bottom of the wall made perfect gun ports. There the unknown gunman proved impossible to hit. And he kept finding new targets.

A hundred yards beyond Patrolman Speed, 29-year-old electrical repairman Roy Dell Schmidt was getting out of his truck on a call. He looked up at the tower and saw puffs of smoke coming from the observation gallery. The police told him to get back but, nonchalantly, Schmidt told a man standing next to him that they were out of range. They weren't. Seconds later, a bullet smashed into Schmidt's chest, killing him instantly.

To the west of the campus ran a main thoroughfare called Guadeloupe Street, known to the students as 'The Drag'. Among the window-shoppers on Guadeloupe Street that sunny lunchtime was 18-year-old Paul Sonntag. He was a lifeguard at Austin swimming pool and had just picked up his week's pay cheque. With him was 18-year-old ballet dancer Claudia Rutt who was on her way to the doctor's for the polio shot she needed before entering Texas Christian University. Suddenly Claudia sank to the ground, clutching her breast. 'Help me! Somebody, help me!'

she cried. Bewildered, Sonntag bent over her. The next shot took him out. Both were dead before help could get to them.

Further up Guadeloupe Street, visiting professor of government 39-year-old Harry Walchuk was browsing in the doorway of a news-stand. A father of six and a teacher at Michigan's Alpena Community College, he was hit in the throat and collapsed, dead, among the magazines. In the next block, 24-year-old Thomas Karr, who had ambitions to be a diplomat, was returning to his apartment after staying up all night, revising for a Spanish exam which he had taken at ten o'clock that morning. Before he reached his own front door, he dropped to the sidewalk, dying. In the third block, basketball coach Billy Snowden of the Texas School for the Deaf stepped into the doorway of the barbershop where he was having his haircut and was wounded in the shoulder.

Outside the Rae Ann dress shop on Guadeloupe Street, 26-year-old Iraqi chemistry student Abdul Khashab, his fiancée 20-year-old Janet Paulos – they were to have married the next week – and 21-year-old trainee sales assistant Lana Phillips fell wounded within seconds of each other. Homer Kelly, manager of Sheftall's jewellery store, saw them fall and ran to help. He was trying to haul them into the cover of his store when the shop window shattered. A bullet gashed the carpeting on the sidewalk outside his shop and two bullet fragments smashed into his leg. The three youths had to wait over an hour, bleeding on Sheftall's orange carpet, before an ambulance could get to them. In all, along picturesque, shoplined Guadeloupe Street, there were four dead and 11 wounded.

To the north, two students were wounded on their way to the biology building. Beyond that, far to the north of the campus, 36-year-old Associate Press reporter Robert Heard was running full tilt from cover to cover when he was hit in the shoulder. 'What a shot,' he marvelled as he winced with pain.

To the east, 22-year-old Peace Corps trainee Thomas Ashton was sunning himself on the roof of the Computation Center. A single round ended his life. A girl sitting at the window of the Business Economics Building was nicked by a bullet. But to the south was the worst killing field. The university's main mall had been turned into a no-man's land.

The university's main mall had been turned into a no-man's land

It was strewn with bodies that could not be recovered safely.

One man was responsible – one man 30 storeys up in the university tower had turned the peaceful campus into a free-fire zone. The Austin Police Department had never had anything like this to deal with before.

The bullet-scarred clock of the Austin tower was booming out its chimes at 12.30 when a local Texan turned up in camouflage fatigues and began chipping large chunks of limestone off the wall of the observation deck with a tripod-mounted, high-calibre M-14. Meanwhile a Cessna light aircraft circled the tower with police marksman Lieutenant Marion Lee on board. He tried to get a clear shot at the gunman but the turbulent air currents around the tower made aiming impossible. The plane was eventually driven away when the sniper put a bullet through the fuselage.

Down below an armoured truck laid down smoke cover and a fleet of ambulances, sirens wailing, began loading up the dead and wounded. Students braved the sniper's fire to haul other victims to shelter.

Austin Police Chief Robert Miles decided that he could not risk using helicopters against the sniper. His accurate fire could easily bring one down. So Police Chief Miles ordered his men to storm the tower. His directive was curt – 'Shoot to kill'.

Patrolmen Houston McCoy and Jerry Day found their way through the underground passageways that connected the university buildings into the foyer of the tower. There they met Patrolman Ramiro Martinez who had been at home cooking steaks when he heard news of the shootings on the radio. A handsome 29-year-old and veteran of six years with the Austin Police Department, he had driven to within a couple of blocks of the tower, then ran to the passageways, zigzagging across the open plaza with the sniper's bullets kicking up dust around him. None of the patrolmen had ever been in a gun fight before.

With them was 40-year-old retired Air Force tailgunner Allen Crum, who was a civilian employee of the university. Although he, too, had never fired a shot in combat, Crum insisted on accompanying the officers. He was given a rifle and deputised on the spot. That day, he was to see more action than during his entire 22 years in the Air Force. One of the four men punched the lift button. They were about to make the same 27-floor lift ride that the crazed gunman had taken less than two hours before.

Dressed in tennis sneakers, blue jeans and a white sports shirt under a pair of workman's overall, the gunman had pulled into a parking space reserved for university officials between the administration building and the library, at the base of the tower, at around 11 a.m. He unloaded a trolley and placed a heavy footlocker on it. Then he wheeled the trolley into the foyer of the building. The ground-floor receptionist thought he was a maintenance man.

When the lift door opened he wheeled the trolley into the lift and pushed the button for the top floor. During the 30-second ride, he pulled a rifle from the locker. On the twenty-seventh floor, he unloaded his heavy cargo, then climbed the four short flights of stairs from the lifts to the observation deck. The observation gallery was open to visitors and the gunman approached the receptionist, 47-year-old Edna Townsley, a spirited divorcée and mother of two young sons, who was working on what was normally her day off. He clubbed her with the butt of his rifle with such force that part of her skull was torn away, and dragged her behind the sofa.

At that moment, a young couple came in from the observation gallery. The girl smiled at the gunman, who smiled back. She steered her date around the dark stain that was slowly spreading across the carpet in front of the receptionist's desk. The gunman followed them back down to the lift. As they travelled innocently down in the lift car, he lugged his heavy locker up the stairs and out on to the observation gallery which ran all the way around the tower, 231 feet above ground level. From that height he could see clean across the shimmering terracotta roofs of old Austin's Spanish-style buildings. Below him the handsome white university buildings were separated by broad lawns and malls. This gave the gunman a clear field of fire across the campus below and the surrounding streets.

He assembled his equipment for what he plainly imagined would be a long siege while the lift began to climb from the ground floor up to the twenty-seventh storey again. In it were Marguerite Lamport and her husband, together with Mrs Lamport's brother, M. J. Gabour, his wife Mary and his two teenage sons, 16-year-old Mark and 19-year-old Mike, who were visiting from Texerkana, Texas.

The two boys led the way up the stairs from the lift, followed by the two women. The men dawdled behind. As Mark opened the door on to the observation deck, he was met with three shotgun blasts in quick succession. The gunman slammed the door shut. The two boys and the women spilled back down the stairs. Gabour rushed to his younger son and turned him over. He saw immediately that Mark was dead. He had been shot in the head at point-blank range. Gabour's sister Marguerite was dead too. His wife and his older son were critically injured. They were bleeding profusely from head wounds. Gabour and his brother-in-law dragged their dead and wounded back down in to the lifts.

The gunman quickly barricaded the top of the stairs with furniture and jammed the door shut with the trolley. He went over to the receptionist Mrs Townley and finished her off with a bullet through the head. Then he went out on to the gallery, which was surrounded by a chest-high parapet of limestone 18 inches thick. He positioned himself under the 'VI' of the gold-edged clock's south face and began shooting the tiny figures in the campus below.

As the lift reached the twenty-seventh floor again, two hours later, Officer Martinez said a little prayer and offered his life up to God. Immediately the lift doors opened, the officers were faced with a distraught Mr Gabour, whose wife, sister and two sons lay face up on the concrete floor.

'They've killed my family,' he cried.

Mad for revenge, he tried to wrest a gun from the officers.

As Officer Day led the weeping man away, Crum, Martinez and McCoy stepped around the bodies and pools of blood on the floor, and began to climb the stairs up to the observation deck. The door at the top of the stairs was all that stood between them and the mad killer they were about to confront.

Although he had already killed 15 innocent people and injured 31 more, the sniper was nothing like the crazed psychopath who rampaged through their adrenalin-charged imaginations. Until the night before, Charles Whitman Jr had seemed the model citizen. Ex-altar boy and US Marine, he was a broad-shouldered, blond-haired, all-American boy who was known to one and all as a loving husband and son.

Born in 1941 at Lake Worth, Florida, Whitman was the eldest of three brothers. He had been an exemplary son. Pitcher on the school's baseball team, manager of the football team and an adept pianist, he brought home good grades and earned his pocket money doing a paper round. At 12, he became an Eagle Scout, one of the youngest ever.

His father was a fanatic about guns and raised his boys knowing how to handle them. By the time Whitman enlisted in the US Marines in 1959, he was an expert marksman, scoring 215 out of a possible 250, which won him the rating of sharpshooter. He was also a keen sportsman, enjoying hunting, scuba diving and karate.

However, in the Marines, things began to go wrong. Whitman got demoted from corporal to private for the illegal possession of a pistol and was reprimanded for threatening to knock a fellow Marine's teeth out. Meanwhile the facade of his perfect, all-American family began to crack.

Charles Whitman Sr was a prominent civic leader in Lake Worth and one-time chairman of the chamber of commerce. But he was an authoritarian, a perfectionist and an unyielding disciplinarian who demanded the highest of standards from his sons. Nothing Charles Jr did was ever good enough for his father. He resigned himself to regular beatings. But what the young Whitman could not resign himself to was that his father was also a wife-beater. Whitman could not stand the sight of his mother's suffering. He withdrew into himself for long periods and bit his nails down to the quick.

After winning a Marine Corps scholarship Whitman moved to Austin and enrolled at the University of Texas to study architectural engineering.

It was in Austin that he met and married his wife, Kathy Leissner, the daughter of a rice-grower and Queen of the Fair of her hometown, Needville. They seemed to be the perfect couple – she a teacher, he the local scoutmaster. But life did not go as smoothly as the young couple had hoped. Whitman began to take his growing hostility out on his wife. He became a compulsive gambler and soon faced court martial for gambling and loan sharking. His academic work suffered and his scholarship was withdrawn. He dropped out of college and went back to finish his tour with the Marines. Then in December 1964 suddenly he quit the Corps and went back to university, determined to be a better student and a better husband. He overloaded himself with courses in an attempt to get his degree more quickly. He tried studying real estate sales part-time in case his degree course did not work out and he took on casual jobs to earn cash. Under pressure of work, he began to lose control of his temper. Fearing that he might lash out at his wife Kathy, he packed, ready to leave her – only to be talked out of it by a friend.

In March 1966, just five months before Whitman's murder spree, the long-suffering Margaret Whitman left her violent husband. Whitman was summoned home to help his mother make the break. While she packed, a Lake Worth patrol car sat outside the house. Charles Jr had called it in case his father resorted to violence. To be near to her devoted son Charles Jr, Mrs Whitman moved to Austin. Her youngest son, 17-year-old John, moved out at about the same time. Later, he was arrested for throwing a rock through a shop window. A judge ordered him to pay a $25 fine or move back in with his father. He paid the fine. Only 21-year-old Patrick, who worked in Whitman Sr's lucrative plumbing contractors' firm, stayed on with his father in the family home.

After the separation, Whitman's father kept calling Charles Jr, trying to persuade him to bring his mother home. By the end of March, this constant hassle was troubling Charles so much that he sought help from the university's resident psychiatrist, Dr Maurice Heatly. In a two-hour interview, Whitman told Dr Heatly that, like his father, he had beaten his wife a few times. He felt that something was wrong, that he did not feel himself. He said he was making an intense effort to control his temper but he feared that he might explode. He did not mention the blinding headaches that he was suffering with increasing frequency. In his notes, Dr Heatly characterised the crew-cut Whitman as a 'massive, muscular youth who seemed to be oozing with hostility'. Heatly took down only one direct quote from Whitman. He had kept on saying that he was 'thinking about going up on the tower with a deer rifle and to start shooting people'.

At the time, these ominous words did not cause the psychiatrist any concern. Students often came to his clinic talking of the tower as a site for some desperate action. Usually they threatened to throw themselves off it. Three students had killed themselves by jumping off the tower since its completion in 1937. Two others had died in accidental falls. But others said that they felt the tower loomed over them like a mystical symbol. Psychiatrists say that there is nothing unusual about threats of violence either. Dr Heatly was not unduly concerned, but recommended that the 25-year-old student come back the following week for another session. Whitman never went back. He decided to fight his problems in his own way. The result was that he declared war on the whole world.

Whatever plans Whitman made over the next four months we cannot know. But those who knew him said that in his last days his anxiety seemed to pass and he became strangely serene. On the night before the massacre, Whitman began a long rambling letter which gives us a glimpse of some of the things going through his fast-disintegrating mind. Shortly before sunset on the evening of 31 July 1966, Whitman sat down at his battered, portable typewriter in his modest yellow-brick cottage at 906 Jewell Street.

'I don't quite understand what is compelling me to type this note,' he wrote. 'I have been having fears and violent impulses. I've had some tremendous headaches. I am prepared to die. After my death, I wish an autopsy on me to be performed to see if there's any mental disorders.' Then he launched into a merciless attack on his father whom he hated 'with a mortal passion'. His mother, he regretted, had given 'the best 25 years of her life to that man'. Then he wrote: 'I intend to kill my wife after I pick her up from work. I don't want her to have to face the embarrassment that my actions will surely cause her.'

At around 7.30, he had to break off because a friend, fellow engineering student Larry Fuess, and his wife dropped round unexpectedly. They talked for a couple of hours. Fuess said later that Whitman seemed relaxed and perfectly at ease. He exhibited few of his usual signs of nervousness. 'It was almost as if he had been relieved of a tremendous problem,' Fuess said.

Life is not worth living

After they left, Whitman went back to the typewriter, noted the interruption and wrote simply: 'Life is not worth living.'

It was time to go and pick up his wife. Whitman fed the dog then climbed into his new black 1966 Chevrolet Impala and drove over to the Southwestern Bell Telephone Company where Kathy had taken a job as a telephonist during her summer vacation from teaching to augment the family income. After driving his wife back to the house, he apparently decided not to kill her immediately. Instead, he left her at home, picked up a pistol and sped across the Colorado River to his mother's fifth-floor flat at Austin's Penthouse Apartments at 1515 Guadeloupe Street. There was a brief struggle. Mrs Whitman's fingers were broken when they were slammed in a door with such force that the band of her engagement ring was driven into the flesh of her finger and the diamond was broken from its setting. Then Whitman stabbed his mother in the chest and shot her in the back of the head, killing her.

He picked up her body, put it on the bed and pulled the covers up so it looked like she was sleeping. He left a hand-written note by the body addressed 'To whom it may concern'. It read: 'I have just killed my mother. If there's a heaven she is going there. If there is not a heaven, she is out of her pain and misery. I love my mother with all my heart. The intense hatred I feel for my father is beyond all description.'

Before leaving, Whitman rearranged the rugs in his mother's apartment to cover the bloodstains on the carpet. And he pinned a note on the front door saying that his mother was ill and would not be going to work that day.

Back at Jewell Street, he added another line to his letter: '12.30 a.m. Mother already dead.' Some time after that he walked through into the room where his wife was sleeping. He stabbed her three times in the chest with a hunting knife, then pulled the bed sheet up to cover her body. He added to his letter, this time in longhand: '3.00 a.m. Wife and mother both dead.' Then he began making preparations for the day ahead.

He got out his old green Marine Corps kit-bag which had 'Lance Cpl. C. J. Whitman' stencilled on the side. Into it, he stuffed enough provisions to sustain him during a long siege – twelve tins of spam, Planter's peanuts, fruit cocktail, sandwiches, six boxes of raisins and a vacuum flask of coffee, along with jerry cans containing water and petrol, lighter fuel, matches, earplugs, a compass, rope, binoculars, a hammer, a spanner, a screwdriver, canteens, a snake-bite kit, a transistor radio, toilet paper and, in a bizarre allegiance to the cult of cleanliness, a plastic bottle of Mennen spray deodorant. He also stowed a private armoury that was enough to hold off a small army – a machete, a Bowie knife, a hatchet, a 9mm Luger pistol, a Galesi-Brescia pistol, a .357-calibre Smith and Wesson revolver, a 35mm Remington rifle and a 6mm Remington bolt-action rifle with a four-power Leupold telescopic sight. With this, experts say, a halfway decent shot can consistently hit a six-and-a-half inch circle at 300 yards. He left three more rifles and two derringers at home.

It is not known whether Whitman slept that night. But at 7.15 a.m. he turned up at the Austin Rental Equipment Service and rented a three-wheeled trolley. At 9 a.m. he called his wife's supervisor at the telephone company and said that she was too ill to work that day. Then he drove to a Davis hardware store where he bought a second-hand .30 M-1 carbine, which was standard issue in the US Army at that time. At Chuck's Gun Shop he bought some 30-shot magazines for his new carbine and several hundred rounds of ammunition. And at 9.30 a.m. he walked into Sears Roebuck's department store in Austin and bought a 12-bore shotgun, on credit.

Back at Jewell Street, he took the shotgun into the garage and began cutting down the barrel and stock. The postman, Chester Arrington, stopped by and chatted to Whitman for about 25 minutes. He was probably the last person to speak to Whitman before the massacre. Years later he recalled: 'I saw him sawing off the shotgun. I knew it was illegal. All I had to do was pick up the telephone and report him. It could have stopped him. I've always blamed myself.'

At last everything was ready. Whitman loaded his kit-bag and the last of his guns into a metal truck and loaded the locker into the boot of his car. He covered it with a blanket, then zipped a pair of grey nylon overalls over his blue jeans and white shirt and, around 10.30 a.m., set off for the university.

Nearly two-and-a-half hours later, Whitman was still fulfilling his deadly mission. Dead bodies were strewn across the streets and plazas below him and hundreds cowered from his bullets. But it could not last forever. Outside the door to the observation deck, just a few feet away, two policeman and a veteran Air Force tailgunner were determined to put an end to his psychopathic spree.

Crum, the civilian, took charge.

'Let's do this service style,' he whispered. 'I'll cover you and you cover me.'

They cleared away the barricade at the top of the stairs and, while the police on the ground intensified their fire to distract the killer, Martinez slowly pushed away the trolley that was propped against the door. Using an overturned desk as a shield, they crawled towards the observation gallery. Crum, carrying a rifle, headed west, while Martinez, with a .38 service revolver, headed eastwards around the gallery, followed by McCoy who was carrying a shotgun.

Martinez rounded one corner then, more slowly, turned on to the north side of the walkway. About fifty feet away, he saw Whitman crouched down and edging towards the corner Crum was about to come round.

But Crum heard Whitman coming and loosed off a shot. It tore a great chunk out of the parapet. Whitman turned and ran back, into the sights of Officer Martinez. Martinez, who had never fired a gun in anger before, shot – and missed. Whitman raised his carbine and fired, but he was trembling and could not keep the gun level. As he squeezed the trigger the gun jerked and the bullet screamed harmlessly over the officer's head. Martinez then emptied his remaining five rounds into the gunman. But still he would not go down. McCoy stepped forward and blasted him twice with the shotgun. Whitman hit the concrete still holding his weapon. Martinez saw that he was still moving. Grabbing the shotgun from McCoy, he ran forward, blasting Whitman at point-blank range in the head. Crum then took Whitman's green towel from his footlocker and waved it above the parapet. At last the gunman was dead.

At 1.40 p.m. two ambulance men carried Whitman's blanket-shrouded body from the tower on a canvas stretcher. The police quickly established his identity and his name was broadcast on the radio. His father rang the police department in Austin and asked them to check his son's and estranged wife's apartments. Along with the bodies of the two women and the notes he had written, Whitman left two rolls of film with the instruction to have them developed. The photographs had been taken over the previous few weeks, but only showed the killer in various ordinary domestic poses, such as snoozing on the sofa with his dog, Smokie, at his feet.

Interviewed later by the press, Whitman's father announced proudly that his son 'always was a crack shot'. In fact, he said, all of his sons were good with guns.

'I am a fanatic about guns,' he admitted. 'My boys knew all about them. I believe in that.'

Whitman had learned the lesson well. In his house, guns had hung in every room.

An autopsy later revealed that there was, as Whitman himself had suspected, something wrong with his brain. He had a tumour the size of a pecan nut in the hypothalamus, but the pathologist, Dr Coleman de Chenar, said that it was certainly not the cause of Whitman's headaches and could not have had any influence on his behaviour. The state pathologist agreed that it was benign and could not have caused Whitman any pain, but a report by the Governor of Texas said that it was malignant and would have killed Whitman within a year. The report also concluded that the tumour could have contributed to Whitman's loss of control.

A number of Dexedrine tablets – known at the time as goofballs – were also found in Whitman's possession, but physicians were not able to detect that he had taken any before he died. He may simply have laid in the stimulants to keep him alert during the long siege.

As it is, he had claimed the lives of 17 people. Thirty-one others had been injured. More were permanently scarred or disabled.

The bodies of Charles Whitman and his mother were returned together to Florida, his in a grey metal casket, hers in a green-and-white one. With hundreds of curiosity seekers gawking and jostling in the rolling, palm-fringed cemetery in West Palm Beach, mother and son were interred with full Catholic rites. The priest said that Whitman had obviously been deranged which meant he was not responsible for the sin of murder and was therefore eligible for burial in hallowed ground. The grand jury also found that Whitman was insane.

Flags were flown at half-mast on the Austin campus of the University of Texas for a week. The tower was closed to the public for a year, but re-opened in July 1967. Following a number of suicide attempts, it was closed for good in 1975.

Charles Whitman's tower-top massacre threw America into a fit of self-examination. What disturbed America so much was that the lives of so many innocent passers-by had been snuffed out randomly, for no reason. In almost every case they were unnamed and unknown to their killer, the incidental and impersonal casualties of the uncharted battlefields that existed only in his demented mind. With the massacre coming just two-and-a-half years after the assassination of President Kennedy, which had also taken place in Texas, Americans were concerned that something was going badly wrong in the land of the free.

Charles Whitman may have been unusual in having a dozen guns at his disposal, but he was by no means unique. Americans – especially

Texans – have always been gun-toting people. Guns had been used by the first settlers to protect and feed themselves and to subdue the hostile land. Later the colonists became a nation of riflemen who used the gun to win their freedom from the British in the War of Independence. Guns tamed the West and became synonymous with frontier justice. And by the 1960s, there was a massive market for guns among collectors and sportsmen. America had the largest cache of civilian handguns in the world with over 100 million in private hands. Sales were running at over a million a year by mail order alone. Another million or so were imported. But, following the assassination of President Kennedy, Americans became very conscious that there were very few legal controls over the possession of firearms. In Texas, gun laws were practically non-existent – some 72 per cent of all murders in 1965 were committed with guns. This compared with 25 per cent in New York City, where New York State's 55-year-old Sullivan Law required police permits for the possession of handguns. FBI chief J. Edgar Hoover said: 'Those who claim that the availability of firearms is not a factor in the murders in this country are not facing reality.'

American legislators were very conscious that most other countries had much stricter gun-control laws. But given America's passion for firearms, trying to ban them would be unthinkable – especially as it would curb such legitimate activities as hunting, target shooting and, in some cases, possessing a gun for self-defence. Nevertheless, in the wake of the Austin slaughter, the US Justice Department, the bar association and most American police forces felt that much tighter gun controls were called for. This prompted Connecticut Senator Thomas Dodd to propose a federal bill limiting the inter-state shipment of mail-order handguns, curbing the importing of military surplus firearms, banning over-the-counter handgun sales to out-of-state buyers and anyone under 21, and prohibiting long-arm sales to anyone under 18.

Several individual states backed the Dodd bill, as they felt it would help them enforce their own gun laws. Some proposed statutory cooling-off periods, so that buyers would have to wait a few days before they could obtain guns, and prohibiting sales to known criminals and psychotics.

Yet opposing even these trivial proposals was the influential National Rifle Association, whose 750,000 members vigorously lobbied against any gun-control legislation. Some right-wingers even claimed that gun control was a Communist plot to disarm Americans. Even ordinary citizens claimed the constitutional right to bear arms – even though, at that time, the Supreme Court denied that there was such a right. True, the Second Amendment to the American constitution mentioned the 'right of the people to keep and bear arms' but it actually read, in full: 'A well-regulated Militia being necessary to the security of a free state, the right of the people to keep and bear arms shall not be infringed.' What the Founding Fathers had in mind, the Supreme Court argued, was the collective right to bear arms, not the individual right. Since Americans already needed licences to marry, drive, run a shop or, in some states, own a dog, it was difficult to see why making them take out a licence to own a lethal weapon was any particular infringement of their liberty.

But, even under Dodd's bill, Charles Whitman would still have been able to amass his sizeable arsenal, as none of the bill's provisions applied to him.

Reacting to what he called the 'shocking tragedy' in Austin, President Johnson urged the speedy passage of the bill 'to help prevent the wrong persons from obtaining firearms'. However, no one was sure how you could recognise the 'wrong persons'.

Austin's police chief said that 'this kind of thing could have happened anywhere'. But that was no comfort. Psychiatrists began to speculate that there was something intrinsic to modern American society that created crazed killers like Whitman. *Time* magazine reported that nearly 2.5 million Americans had been treated for mental illness in hospitals and clinics that year. Almost a third of them were classified as psychotic – people who, by the minimum definition, had lost touch with reality. They lived in a world of fantasy, haunted by fears and delusions of persecution. An accidental bump on a crowded sidewalk or a passing criticism from an employer or relative could easily set any of these psychotics off.

The menace of the psychotic killer was all the more frightening because they may seem like the model citizen – until they go berserk. Many of these people have a feeling that there is a demon within themselves, said Los Angeles clinical psychiatrist Martin Grotjahn. They try to kill the demon by model behaviour. They live the opposite of what they feel. Like Whitman, they become gentle, very mild, extremely nice people who often show the need to be perfectionists.

Some psychiatrists estimated that the number of potential mass killers in the US ranged as high as one in every thousand, or at that time 200,000 people. Most of these, of course, would never carry out their murderous desires. But Houston psychiatrist C.A. Dwyer warned the American public: 'Potential killers are everywhere these days. They are driving cars, going to church with you, working with you. And you never know it until they snap.'

Potential killers are everywhere these days

Americans were warned to stay alert. They were told to watch for sudden personality changes in friends and loved ones and that special attention should be paid to habitually shy and quiet people who suddenly become aggressive and talkative – or the reverse. Other danger signs were depression and seclusion, hypersensitivity to tiny slights and insults, changes in normal patterns of eating or sleeping, uncontrolled outbursts of temper, disorganised thinking and a morbid interest in guns, knives or other instruments of destruction.

Psychiatrists were quick to point out that the appearance of any of these symptoms does not necessarily mean that someone is about to turn killer. However, those exhibiting them were in need of psychiatric help. Unfortunately, even if a dangerous psychotic – like Charles Whitman – did reach the examining room, it was by no means certain that they could be headed off. Most doctors agreed that the University of Texas psychiatrist who took no action, even after Whitman confessed his urge to climb the Austin tower and kill people several months before the actual incident took place, was not at fault. University of Chicago psychiatrist Robert S. Daniels said, 'Thousands – and I mean literally thousands – talk to doctors about having such feelings. Nearly all of them are just talking.'

Deciding who was, and who wasn't, going to follow their murderous impulses was more of an art than a science. It was also a matter of practicality. The practice of psychiatry depended on trust between patient and doctor. Psychiatrists could hardly be expected to report every threatening remark. Besides, as the New York deputy-police commissioner pointed out, 'We can't arrest people because they are ill.' New Jersey psychiatrist Henry A. Davidson added: 'We are in a situation now where there is the enormous pressure of civil rights. The idea of locking someone up on the basis of a psychiatrist's opinion that he might, in future, be violent could be repugnant. It would be a very poor way to help the vast majority of disturbed people who make threats that they will never carry out.'

However, some American states had already empowered doctors to forcibly commit any patient they thought dangerous – at least for long enough for a thorough psychiatric examination. But most states insisted that the individual commit themselves voluntarily or that their family or the courts place them in hospital care. Usually the doctor could only try and persuade the patient that voluntary commitment was in their own best interest. Unfortunately, most psychotics were not amenable to having themselves locked up and, in the 1960s, most families regarded mental illness as a shameful thing and resisted formal commitment to a mental institution until it was too late.

Medical opinion, at the time, believed that the best way of catching psychotics before they began shooting was a long-term programme of mental hygiene. They favoured more psychological testing in schools and colleges, and the spread of community clinics to give instant help to all who needed it. What was needed was a massive investment of money and manpower. Far too little was known about the psychology of the spree killer, psychiatrists conceded. The problem was they erupted infrequently – and few survived to tell the tale. Those who did, the medics said, were a vital research resource. Pilot studies of juvenile offenders in Massachusetts and Illinois at that time indicated that many potential psychotics may be identifiable, and even curable, if caught in their teens. And the medical profession had still not given up on the idea that they could find the cure to all mental illness in the chemistry of the brain. Generally, though, it was considered that there was little hope of some sort of psychiatric Geiger counter or cerebral pap smear test to spot psychotics in advance. Instead, Americans were advised to put their faith in President Johnson's Great Society and those massive welfare resources that were set to pare down the danger of sudden, irrational murder.

Whitman's murderous spree had also been seen to be associated with the Vietnam War, which was bringing true-life violence directly into America's living-rooms every night at the time. The first televised war, network coverage of Vietnam became the backdrop to the late 1960s and early 1970s. It brought with it an unprecedented tide of assassinations, urban violence and spree killings. By the end of the war, the American Army or Marine veteran had turned in the public perception from an upstanding citizen who had served his country to a degenerate butcher who might explode at any moment and kill again at the slightest excuse. This attitude was made explicit in the 1976 film *Taxi Driver*. Made just one year after the end of the war, it showed Robert De Niro as a brooding ex-Marine and Vietnam veteran Travis Bickle. The film follows the insomniac psychopath as he meticulously prepares himself to declare war on the world. It ends, predictably, in a violent bloodbath.

However, although Charles Whitman was a Marine, he was honourably discharged in 1964, a year before President Johnson committed ground troops to Vietnam. Whitman experienced none of the alienation that the veterans of that unpopular war suffered.

Two films were made about Charles Whitman. In *Targets*, made in 1968, director Peter Bogdanovich switched the action to a drive-in cinema, where a psychotic sniper picks off the innocent viewers of a horror film. *The Deadly Tower*, in 1975, gave a literal version of event, though policeman Ramiro Martinez sued the network NBC for $1 million over his unflattering portrayal. However, these films were not entirely without precedent in America. In 1952, a film called *The Sniper* had been released. It was about a youth who shot blondes. And in 1962, Ford Clark published a novel called *The Open Space*. In it, the protagonist climbs a tower in a Midwestern university and begins picking off people. As far as the police could ascertain, Whitman had neither seen the film nor read the book. The material Whitman had assembled for his murder spree remained in police custody until 1972. Then it was auctioned off to augment the fund set up to help the victims of his crimes. Whitman's guns fetched $1,500 from a dealer in Kansas, proving that the image of Charles Whitman had found a place deep in the American psyche, a chilling legacy that lasted beyond his crime and his death.

– Chapter 5 –

The Zodiac Killer

unknown

NUMBER OF VICTIMS: AS HIGH AS 40 – THE NUMBER IS UNCONFIRMED

REIGN OF TERROR: 1960s

FAVOURED METHOD OF KILLING: SHOOTING – AND HIS KILLINGS ALL HAD CONNECTIONS WITH WATER

CALLING CARD: A CIRCLE WITH A CROSS THROUGH IT

APPREHENDED: HE WAS NEVER CAUGHT OR FORMALLY IDENTIFIED

O n a chilly, moonlit night around Christmas in 1968, a teenage couple pulled up in an open space next to a pump house on Lake Herman road in the Vallejo hills overlooking San Francisco. This was the local lovers' lane and David Faraday and Bettilou Jensen were indifferent to the cold. They were so wrapped up in each other that they did not even notice when another car pulled up about ten feet away. They were rudely awoken from their amorous reverie by gunfire. One bullet smashed through the back window, showering them with glass. Another thudded into the bodywork. Bettilou threw open the passenger door and leapt out. David tried to follow. He had his hand on the door handle when the gunman leant in through the driver's window and shot him in the head. His body slumped across the front seat. Bettilou's attempt at flight was futile. As she ran screaming into the night, the gunman ran after her. She had run just thirty feet when he fired five shots into her. Then the gunman calmly walked back to his car and drove away.

A few minutes later, another car came down the quiet road. Its driver, a woman, saw Bettilou's body sprawled on the ground, but did not stop. Instead, she sped on towards the next town, Benica, to get help. On the way, she saw a blue flashing light coming towards her. It was a patrol car and she flashed her lights frantically to attract the driver's attention. The car stopped and she told the patrolmen what she had seen. They followed her back to the pump station, arriving there about three minutes later. They found Bettilou Jensen dead, but David Faraday was still alive. He was unconscious and could not help them with their enquiries. They rushed him to hospital, but he died shortly after arriving there.

There was little to go on. The victims had not been sexually assaulted, nor was anything missing. The money in David Faraday's wallet was untouched. Detective Sergeant Les Lundblatt of the Vallejo county police investigated the possibility that they had been murdered by a jealous rival. But an investigation into the victims' private lives revealed no jilted lovers or other amorous entanglements. The two teenagers were ordinary students. Their lives were an open book. And six months later, Bettilou Jensen and David Faraday were simply two more of the huge number of files of unsolved murders in the state of California.

On 4 July 1969, their killer struck again. Around midnight, at Blue Rock Park, another romantic spot just two miles from where Jensen and Faraday were slain, Mike Mageau was parked with his girlfriend, 22-year-old waitress Darlene Ferrin. They were not alone. Other cars of other courting couples were parked up there. Again Mike and Darlene were too engrossed in each other to notice when a white car pulled up beside them. It stayed there just a few minutes, then drove away. But it returned and parked on the other side of the road.

Suddenly, a powerful spotlight shone on Mike Mageau's car. A figure approached. Thinking it was the police, Mike reached for his driver's licence. As he did so, he heard gunfire and Darlene slumped down in her seat. Seconds later, a bullet tore into Mike's neck. The gunman walked calmly back to the white car, paused to fire another four or five shots at them, then sped off, leaving the smell of cordite and burning rubber behind him.

A few minutes later, a man called the Vallejo county police and reported a murder up on Columbus Parkway. He told the switchboard operator: 'You will find the kids in a brown car. They are shot with a nine millimetre Luger. I also killed those kids last year. Goodbye.'

When the police arrived, Darlene Ferrin was dead. Mike Mageau was still alive, but the bullet had passed through his tongue and he was unable to talk. However, there were some other leads. Four months earlier, Darlene's babysitter had spotted a white car parked outside Darlene's apartment. Suspicious, she asked Darlene about it. It was plain that the young waitress knew the driver. 'He's checking up on me again,' she told the babysitter. 'He doesn't want anyone to know what I saw him do. I saw him murder someone.'

The babysitter had had a good look at the man in the white car. She told the police that he was middle-aged with brown wavy hair and a round face. When Mike Mageau could talk again, he confirmed that the gunman had brown hair and a round face. But after that clues petered out.

Then, on 1 August 1969, almost two months after the shooting of Ferrin and Mageau, three local papers received hand-written letters. These began; 'DEAR EDITOR, THIS IS THE MURDERER OF THE 2 TEENAGERS LAST CHRISTMAS AT LAKE HERMAN & THE GIRL ON THE 4TH OF JULY...' The letters were printed in capital letters and contained basic errors in spelling and syntax. But the author gave details of the ammunition used and left no doubt that he was the gunman. Each letter also contained a third of a sheet of paper covered with a strange code. The killer demanded that the papers print this on the front page otherwise, the writer said, he would go on 'killing lone people in the night'. The letter was signed with another cipher – a circle with a cross inside it which looked ominously like a gunsight. All three newspapers complied and the full text of the coded message was sent to Mare Island Naval Yard where cryptographers tried to crack it. Although it was a simple substitution code, the US Navy's experts could not break it. But Dale Harden, a teacher at Alisal High School, Salinas, could. He had the simple idea of looking for a group of ciphers that might spell the word 'kill'. He found them and, after ten hours' intense work, he and his wife decoded the whole of the message.

It read: 'I like killing people because it is so much more fun than killing wild game in the forrest [sic] because man is the most dangerous of all to kill...' The killer went on to boast that he had already murdered five people in the San Francisco Bay area. He said that when he was born again in paradise, his victims would be his slaves.

The killer's cryptic message brought a tidal wave of information from the public. Over a thousand calls were received by the police. None of them led anywhere. So the killer volunteered more help. This time he gave them a name – or, at least, a nickname that would attract the attention of the headline writers. He wrote again to the newspapers, beginning: 'DEAR EDITOR, THIS IS ZODIAC SPEAKING...' Again he gave details of the slaying of Darlene Ferrin that only the killer could have known. But although this increased the killer's publicity profile, the police were no nearer to catching him.

On 27 September 1969, 20-year-old Bryan Hartnell and 22-year-old Cecelia Ann Shepard – both students at the Seventh Day Adventist's Pacific Union College nearby – went for a picnic on the shores of Lake Berryessa, some 13 miles north of Vallejo. It was a warm day. They had finished eating and were lying on a blanket kissing at around 4.30 p.m. when they noticed a man coming across the clearing towards them. He was stocky and had brown hair. He disappeared for a moment into a copse. When he emerged he was wearing a mask and carrying a gun. As he came closer, Bryan Hartnell saw that the mask had a symbol on it. It was a circle with a white cross in it. The man was not particularly threatening in his manner. His voice was soft.

'I want your money and your car keys,' he said.

Bryan explained that he only had 76 cents, but the hooded man was welcome to that. The gunman then began to chat. He explained that he was an escaped convict and that he was going to have to tie them up. He had some clothes-line with him and got Cecelia to tie up Bryan. Then he tied Cecelia up himself.

The gunman talked some more then calmly announced: 'I am going to have to stab you people.'

Bryan Hartnell begged to be stabbed first.

'I couldn't bear to see her stabbed,' he said.

The gunman calmly agreed, sank to his knees and stabbed Hartnell in the back repeatedly with a hunting knife. Hartnell was dizzy and sick, but still conscious when the masked man turned his attention to Cecelia. He was calm at first, but after the first stab he seemed to go berserk. He plunged the hunting knife into her defenceless body again and again, while she twisted and turned frantically under him in a futile attempt to escape the blows. When she finally lay still, the man grew calm again. He got up and walked over to their car. He pulled a felt-tip pen from his pocket and drew something on the door. Then he walked away.

A fisherman heard their screams and came running. Bryan and Cecelia were both still alive. The Napa Valley Police were already on their way, alerted by an anonymous phone call. A gruff man's voice had said: 'I want to report a double murder.'

He gave a precise location for where the bodies were to be found, then left the phone hanging.

Cecelia Shepard was in a coma when the police arrived. She died two days later in hospital without regaining consciousness. Bryan Hartnell recovered slowly and was able to give a full description of their attacker. But the police had already guessed who he was. The sign he had drawn on the door of their car was a circle with a cross in it. The police found the phone that the man with the gruff voice had left hanging. It was in a call box less than six blocks from the headquarters of the Napa Valley Police Department. And they managed to get a good palm print off it. Unfortunately, it matched nothing on record.

Two weeks after the stabbing, on 11 October 1969, a 14-year-old girl was looking out of the window of her home in San Francisco and witnessed a crime in progress. A cab was parked on the corner of Washington and Cherry Street and a stocky man, in the front passenger seat, was going through the pockets of the driver. She called her brothers over to watch what was happening. The man got out of the taxi, leaving the cab driver slumped across the seat. He wiped the door handle with a piece of cloth, then walked off in a northerly direction. The children called the police, but they did not give their evidence clearly enough. The telephone operator who took the call, logged at 10 p.m., noted that the suspect was an 'NMA' – negro male adult. An all-points bulletin was put out and a patrolman actually stopped a stocky man nearby and asked whether he had seen anything unusual. But as he was white, the police officer let him go.

Later a stocky man was seen running into the nearby Presidio – a military compound that contains housing and a park area. The floodlights were switched on and the area was searched by patrolmen with dogs. In the cab, the police found the taxi-driver, 29-year-old Paul Stine, dead from a gunshot wound to the head. The motive, they thought, was robbery.

Then, three days later, the *San Francisco Chronicle* received a Zodiac letter.

'THIS IS THE ZODIAC SPEAKING,' it read. 'I AM THE MURDERER OF THE TAXI DRIVER OVER BY WASHINGTON ST AND MAPLE ST [sic] LAST NIGHT, TO PROVE IT HERE IS A BLOOD STAINED PIECE OF HIS SHIRT.'

San Francisco criminologists managed to match the piece of cloth with the letter exactly with the shirt of the murdered taxi-driver. And they discovered that the bullet that had killed Stine was a .22 and fired from the same gun that had been used in the murder of Bettilou Jensen and David Faraday.

The letter went on to say: 'I AM THE SAME MAN WHO DID IN THE PEOPLE IN THE NORTH BAY AREA.

'THE S.F. POLICE COULD HAVE CAUGHT ME LAST NIGHT,' it taunted, concluding, 'SCHOOL CHILDREN MAKE NICE TARGETS. I THINK I SHALL WIPE OUT A SCHOOL BUS SOME MORNING. JUST SHOOT OUT THE TYRES AND THEN PICK OFF ALL THE KIDDIES AS THEY COME BOUNCING OUT.'

The letter was signed with a circle with a cross in it.

The description given by the children and the policeman who had stopped a stocky white male leaving the scene of the crime matched those given by Darlene Ferrin's babysitter, Mike Mageau and Bryan Hartnell. A new composite of the Zodiac Killer was drawn up and issued to the public by San Francisco Chief of Police Thomas J. Cahill. It showed a white male, 35 to 45 years old with short brown hair, possibly with a red tint. He was around five-feet-eight-inches tall, heavily built and wore glasses. The wanted poster was plastered around town.

But the Zodiac Killer's appetite for publicity was endless. At 2 a.m. on 22 October 1969, 11 days after the murder of Paul Stine, a man with a gruff voice called the police department in Oakland, which is just across the bay from San Francisco. He introduced himself as the Zodiac and said: 'I want to get in touch with F. Lee Bailey. If you can't come up with Bailey, I'll settle for Mel Belli. I want one or other of them to appear on the Channel Seven talk show. I'll make contact by telephone.'

The men he was asking for were the two top criminal lawyers in America. F. Lee Bailey has been more recently defending O. J. Simpson. But he was not available on such short notice and Melvin Belli agreed to appear on the Jim Dunbar talk show at 6.30 the next morning. The show's ratings soared as people throughout the Bay area got up the next morning and tuned in. At 7.20 a man called in and told Belli that he was the Zodiac, though he preferred to be called Sam. He said: 'I'm sick. I have headaches.'

But the two police switchboard operators who talked to the Zodiac when he reported the murders said his voice was that of an older man. The mystery caller was eventually traced to Napa State Hospital and proved to be a mental patient.

The real Zodiac continued his correspondence. He wrote to Inspector David Toschi of the San Francisco homicide squad threatening to commit more murders. In another letter, he claimed to have killed seven people – two more than the official Zodiac body count so far. Later he claimed to have killed ten, taunting the San Francisco Police Department with the scoreline: 'ZODIAC 10, SFPD 0.' He gave cryptic clues to his name and fantasised about blowing up school children with a bomb.

The following Christmas, Melvin Belli received a card saying: 'DEAR MELVIN, THIS IS THE ZODIAC SPEAKING. I WISH YOU A HAPPY

CHRISTMAS. THE ONE THING I ASK OF YOU IS THIS, PLEASE HELP ME... I AM AFRAID I WILL LOSE CONTROL AND TAKE MY NINTH AND POSSIBLE TENTH VICTIM.' Another piece of Paul Stine's bloodstained shirt was enclosed and forensic handwriting experts feared that the Zodiac's mental state was deteriorating.

On 24 July 1970, the Zodiac Killer wrote a letter which spoke of 'THE WOEMAN [sic] AND HER BABY THAT I GAVE A RATHER INTERESTING RIDE FOR A COUPLE OF HOWERS ONE EVENING A FEW MONTHS BACK THAT ENDED IN MY BURNING HER CAR WHERE I FOUND THEM.' The woman was Kathleen Jones of Vallejo. On the evening of 17 March 1970, she had been driving in the area when a white Chevrolet pulled alongside her. The driver indicated that there was something wrong with her rear wheel. She pulled over and the other driver stopped. He was a 'clean-shaven and neatly dressed man'. He said that the wheel had been wobbling and

You know I am going to kill you

offered to tighten the wheel nuts for her. But when she pulled away, the wheel he had said he had fixed came off altogether. The driver of the Chevrolet then offered her a lift to a nearby service station, but drove straight past it. When she pointed this out, the man said, in a chillingly calm voice: 'You know I am going to kill you.'

But Kathleen Jones kept her head. When he slowed on the curve of a freeway ramp, she jumped from the car with her baby in her arms. Then she ran and hid in an irrigation ditch. He stopped and, with a flashlight from the trunk of his car, started searching for her. He was approaching the ditch when he was caught in the headlights of a truck and ran off. An hour later, she made her way to a police station to report what had happened to her. When she looked up and saw the Zodiac's wanted poster, she identified him as the man who had threatened to kill her. And when the police drove her back to her car, they found it burnt out. It seemed he had returned and set it alight.

Despite the new leads Kathleen Johns provided, the police got no nearer to catching the Zodiac Killer. Police in Vallejo believed that the man they were after was now the driver of a new green Ford. He had stopped and watched a Highway Patrolman across the freeway. When the Highway Patrolman decided to ask him what he was doing and cut around through an underpass, he found the green Ford was gone. It was now sitting on the other side of the freeway where the squad car had been moments before. This cat and mouse game was played every day for two weeks.

Detective Sergeant Les Lundblatt became convinced that the Zodiac Killer was a man named Andy Walker. He had known Darlene Ferrin and Darlene's sister identified him as the man who had waited outside Darlene's apartment in a white car. He also bore a resemblance to the description of the man seen near Lake Berrylessa when Cecelia Shepard was stabbed to death. And he had studied codes in the military. However, his fingerprints did not match the one left in Paul Stine's cab and his handwriting did not match the Zodiac's notes. But the police discovered that Walker was ambidextrous and believed that the murder of Paul Stine had been planned so meticulously that the Zodiac may have used the severed finger of a victim they did not know about. He was also known to suffer from bad headaches and he got on badly with women at work.

The police decided that they had to get his palm prints to see if they matched those on the telephone that had been left dangling after the Paul Stine killing. An undercover policeman asked Walker to help him carry a goldfish bowl. Walker obliged, but the palm prints he left were smudged. Walker realised what was going on and a judge issued a court order forcing the police to stop harassing him.

Zodiac letters threatening more murders were received. Some of them were authenticated, but they rendered few new clues. The only thing that detectives could be sure of was that the Zodiac was a fan of Gilbert and Sullivan. He taunted with a parody of 'The Lord High Executioner' listing those people he intended to kill – and used the refrain 'titwillo, titwillo, titwillo'. And there were no letters or criminal activity that could have been ascribed to the Zodiac Killer during the entire run of the *Mikado* in San Francisco's Presentation Theatre.

There may have been more Zodiac murders, too. On 21 May 1970, the naked body of Marie Antoinette Anstey was found just off a quiet country road in Lake County. Traces of mescaline were found in her body. She had been hit over the head and drowned. Her clothes were never found. The murder of Marie Antoinette Anstey followed the pattern of the Zodiac killings. It took place at a weekend, in the same general area around Vallejo, and near a body of water. Although she was naked, there were no signs that she had been sexually molested.

The Zodiac had some curious connection with the water. All the names of all murder scenes had same association with water – even Washington Street. In one of the Zodiac letters, he claimed that the body count would have been higher if he had not been 'swamped by the rain we had a while back'. The police deduced that he lived in a low-lying area, susceptible to flooding. Perhaps he had a basement where he kept the equipment to make the long-threatened bomb.

A K-Mart store in Santa Rosa, California, was evacuated after a bomb threat by a man identifying himself as the Zodiac Killer. Two months later, the Zodiac wrote another letter to the *San Francisco Chronicle* claiming to have killed twelve people and enclosing the map with an X marking the peak of Mount Diablo – the Devil's Mountain – in Contra Costa Country across the bay from San Francisco. From there, an observer could see the entire panorama of the area where the murders had taken place. But when detectives checked it out more closely, the spot marked was within the compound of a Naval Relay Station, where only service personnel with security clearance could go.

The letters continued, demanding that people in the San Francisco area wear lapel badges with the Zodiac symbol on it. When they did not, he threatened to kill Paul Avery, the *Chronicle*'s crime writer who had been investigating the story. Journalists, including Paul Avery, began wearing badges saying 'I am not Paul Avery'. But Avery, who was a licensed private eye and a former war correspondent in Vietnam, took to carrying a .38 and put in regular practice at the police firing range.

An anonymous correspondent tied the Zodiac slayings to the unsolved murder of Cheri Jo Bates, a college girl in Riverside, California, on

Hallowe'en 1966. The police could not rule out a connection, but could not prove a concrete link either. But when Paul Avery checked it out he discovered that the police had received what they considered to be a crank letter about the murder, five months after the killing. It was signed with the letter Z.

Cheri Jo Bates was an 18-year-old freshman, who had been stabbed to death after leaving the college library one evening. In a series of typewritten letters, the killer gave details of the murder only he could have known. He also said that there would be more and talked of a 'game' he was playing. But there were also hand-written letters, where the handwriting matched the Zodiac's and Avery managed to persuade the police to re-open the Bates case in the light of the Zodiac murders.

During 1971, there were a number of murders that could have been committed by the Zodiac. Letters purporting to come from him confessed to them. But he could easily have been claiming credit for other people's handiwork. However, on 7 April 1972, 33-year-old Isobel Watson, who worked as a legal secretary in San Francisco, alighted from the bus at around 9 p.m. in Tamalpais Valley and began walking home up Pine Hill. Seemingly out of nowhere, a white Chevrolet swerved across the road at her. The car stopped. The driver apologised and offered to give her a lift home. When Mrs Watson declined, he pulled a knife on her and stabbed her in the back. Her screams alerted the neighbours. The man ran back to his car and sped off. Mrs Watson recovered and gave a description: her assailant was a white man in his early forties, around five foot nine inches and he wore black-rimmed reading glasses. The police said that there was a better than fifty-fifty chance that this was the Zodiac Killer.

As time went on, other detectives dropped out of the case, leaving only Inspector David Toschi. The FBI looked at the files, but even they could take the case no further.

The correspondence from the Zodiac ceased for nearly four years. Though psychologists believed that he was the type who might commit suicide, Toschi did not believe he was dead. Toschi reasoned that the Zodiac got his kicks from the publicity surrounding the killings, rather than the killings themselves. Surely he would have left a note, or some clue in his room, that he was the Zodiac. Then on 25 April 1978, Toschi got confirmation. The *Chronicle* received a new letter from him. This time it mentioned Toschi by name. And the author wanted the people of San Francisco to know he was back. This gave the police a new opportunity to catch him.

Robert Graysmith, author of the book *Zodiac*, deduced that the killer was a film buff. In one of his cryptograms he mentions 'the most dangerous game' which is the title of a film. In another, he calls himself 'the Red Phantom', the title of another film. And he frequently mentions going to the cinema to see *The Exorcist* or *Badlands*, a fictionalised account of the murderous spree of Nebraskan killer Charles Starkweather. The police used this information and the Zodiac Killer's obvious love of publicity to try and trap him. When a film about the Zodiac killings was shown in San Francisco a suggestions box was left in the lobby of the cinema. The audience were asked to drop a note of any information or theories they may have in it. The box was huge and a detective was hidden inside it. He read every entry by torchlight as it fell through the slot. If any looked like they came from the Zodiac Killer, he was to raise the alarm. None did.

The Oakland police thought that they had captured the Zodiac Killer. He was a Vietnam veteran who had seen the film three times and had been apprehended in the lavatory at the cinema masturbating after a particularly violent scene. The Oakland PD was soon proved wrong. His handwriting did not match the Zodiac's. Soon there was a welter of recrimination. Toschi was transferred out of homicide after baseless accusations that he had forged the Zodiac letters for self-promotion. The police in the Bay area began to believe that the Zodiac Killer was either dead or in prison outside the state for another crime. Or it could have been, after the close call following the killing of Paul Stine, that he figured that his luck was running out.

But Robert Graysmith was not convinced. He managed to connect the Zodiac killings with the unsolved murder of 14 young girls, usually students or hitch-hikers in the Santa Rosa area in the early 1970s. Most of them were found nude, their clothes were missing but largely they had not been sexually molested. Each of them had been killed in different ways, as if the murderer was experimenting to find out which way was best. Graysmith reckons that the Zodiac's body count could be as high as 40.

The Zodiac's symbol, a cross in a circle, Graysmith believes, is not a stylised gunsight but the projectionist's guide seen on the lead-in to a film. Through a cinema in San Francisco which has the constellations painted on the ceiling he traced a promising suspect. The man, Graysmith was told, filmed some of the murders and kept the film in a booby-trapped film can.

Another Graysmith suspect was a former boyfriend of Darlene Ferrin's. He had also been a resident of Riverside when Cheri Jo Bates had been murdered. He lived with his mother, who he loathed, and dissected small mammals as a hobby. During the crucial 1975–78 period when the Zodiac Killer was quiet, he was in a mental hospital after being charged with child molestation at a school where he worked.

Although he had two promising candidates Graysmith could not pin the Zodiac murders on either of them. He published the story of his investigation in 1985.

But then, in 1990, a series of strange murders began in New York. The perpetrator claimed to be the Zodiac. The killer's description does not match those given by the witnesses in California. But a man can change a lot in twenty years.

– Chapter 6 –

The Family

Charles Manson

ACCOMPLICES: SUSAN ATKINS, LESLIE VAN HOUTTEN, TEX WATSON, PATRICIA KRENWINKEL

NATIONALITY: AMERICAN

BORN: 1934

NUMBER OF VICTIMS: 8

FAVOURED METHOD OF KILLING: STABBING, SHOOTING

DOWNFALL: THEY WERE CAUGHT BECAUSE SUSAN ATKINS BOASTED ABOUT HER CRIMES

FINAL NOTE: 'FROM THE WORLD OF DARKNESS I DID LOOSE DEMONS AND DEVILS IN THE POWER OF SCORPIONS TO TORMENT'

Charles Manson was born in 1934 in Cincinnati, Ohio, the illegitimate son of a teenage prostitute. Unable to support herself and her son, even through prostitution, his mother left him with her mother in McMechen, West Virginia. Later, he was sent to the famous orphans home, Boys' Town in Nebraska but he was kicked out for his surly manner and constant thieving. He escaped 18 times from Indiana Boys' School and served four years in a federal reformatory in Utah after being arrested for theft.

In November 1954, he was released. He married Rosalie Jean Willis before being arrested for transporting stolen cars across a state line and sentenced to three years in Terminal Island Federal Prison near Los Angeles. Rosalie divorced Manson after his arrest.

Out again in 1958, Manson became a pimp and was arrested repeatedly under the Mann Act for transporting women across state lines for immoral purposes. He started forging cheques. When he was caught, he was sentenced to ten years in the federal penitentiary on McNeil Island in Washington state.

Being small, just five foot two, he had a hard time in prison. He was raped repeatedly by the other prisoners, many of whom were black. This left him with a lifelong racial chip on his shoulder.

To survive in prison, Manson became shifty, cunning and manipulative. This set him in good stead when he was released in 1967. He soon discovered that he could use the manipulative powers he had learnt in jail on the long-haired flower children that inhabited Southern California. With his hypnotic stare, his Bohemian lifestyle and the strange meaningless phrases he babbled, he was the perfect hippy guru. His contempt for authority and convention made him a focus of the counter-culture and he soon developed a penchant for the middle-class girls who had dropped out of mainstream society according to the fashion of the times.

Manson travelled with an entourage of hangers-on, known as the Family. They comprised young women – who were all his lovers – and docile males who would do anything he told them to. They numbered as many as thirty at one time.

One typical recruit was Patricia Krenwinkel. She was a former Girl Scout from a normal middle-class family. Her expensive education earned her a good job at a big insurance company in Los Angeles. She met Manson on Manhattan Beach when she was 21 and abandoned everything for him. She ditched her car and walked out of her job without even bothering to pick up her last paycheque. She moved in with the Family on the Spahn Ranch, a collection of broken-down shacks in the dusty east corner of the Simi Valley where they hung out.

Leslie Van Houten was just 19 when she had dropped out of school. She lived on the streets on a perpetual acid trip until she met Manson. Twenty-year-old Linda Kasabian left her husband and two children and stole $5,000 from a friend to join the Family. She too began to see her seamy life through a constant haze of LSD.

Susan Atkins was a 21-year-old topless dancer and bar-room hustler. A practising devil worshipper, she became Manson's closest aide. But, like the others, she had to share his sexual favours. Manson quenched his insatiable sexual appetite with his female followers, one or two at a time – or even with all of them together. He knew the power of sex and drugs. When, for a short while in the 1950s, he had been a pimp, he had fallen in love with his main girl, who had dumped him. Then he had picked up two girls – Mary and Darlene – and had slept with them on a rota basis. Soon he had them in his thrall. With the girls in the Family, he used LSD and orgies to control them. He would choreograph his sexual activities with his followers, artistically positioning their naked bodies. He also promised each girl a baby in return for their devotion, while Susan used the situation to plant her Satanist ideas into their receptive minds.

One of the few men in the commune was 23-year-old former high-school football star from Farmersville, Texas, Charles 'Tex' Watson. He had once been an honours student, but in Manson's hands he had become a mindless automaton.

Surrounded by these compliant sycophants, the drug-addled Manson began to enjoy huge delusions, fuelled by Susan Atkins' studies of Satanism. She convinced him that his own name, Manson, was significant. Manson, or Man-son, meant Son of Man, or Christ, in her twisted logic. He was also the devil, Susan Atkins said.

The lyrics of the Beatles' songs were also dragged into Manson's growing delusions. He was blissfully unaware that a helter skelter was a harmless British funfair ride and interpreted the track 'Helter Skelter' on the Beatles' *White Album* as heralding the beginning of what he saw as an inevitable race war. The blacks would be wiped out, along with the pigs – the police, authority figures, the rich and the famous, and what Manson called 'movie people'.

Manson fancied himself as something of a popstar himself and took one of his feeble compositions to successful West Coast musician Gary Hinman. Manson also learned that Hinman had recently inherited

$20,000. He sent Susan Atkins and Bob Beausoleil – another Family hanger-on – to steal it and to kill Hinman for refusing to put Manson at the top of the charts, where he believed he belonged. They held Hinman hostage for two days and ransacked the house. The money was nowhere to be found. Out of frustration, they stabbed him to death. Then devil-worshipper Susan Atkins dipped her finger in Hinman's blood and wrote 'political piggie' on the wall.

The police found Beausoleil's fingerprints in the house and tracked him down. They found the knife that killed Hinman and a T-shirt drenched in Hinman's blood in Beausoleil's car. He was convicted of murder and went to jail – without implicating Atkins or Manson.

Next Manson tried to get his composition recorded by Doris Day's son, Terry Melcher. Melcher was a big player in the music industry and refused to take Manson's material further. Meanwhile Manson's followers formed a death squad. They dressed in black and trained themselves in the arts of breaking and entering abandoned buildings. These exercises were known as 'creepy crawlies'. They were told that they should kill anyone who stood in their way.

On 8 August 1969, Manson's death squad was dispatched to Melcher's remote home on Cielo Drive in Benedict Canyon in the Hollywood Hills. Melcher had moved, but this did not matter to Manson. The people he saw going into the house were 'movie types'. Their slaughter would act as a warning.

The house at the end of Cielo Drive was indeed occupied by 'movie people'. It had been rented by film director Roman Polanski, who was away shooting a film in London. But his wife, film star Sharon Tate, who was eight months pregnant, was at home. Coffee heiress Abigail Folger, and her boyfriend Polish writer Voyteck Frykowski were visiting. So was Sharon Tate's friend, celebrity hairdresser Jay Sebring.

Manson ordered Tex Watson, Susan Atkins, Patricia Krenwinkel and Linda Kasabian to kill them. They were armed with a .22 revolver, a knife and a length of rope. Kasabian lost her nerve at the last minute and stayed outside. When Tex Watson, Susan Atkins and Patricia Krenwinkel pushed open the wrought-iron gates, they bumped into 18-year-old

Steven Parent, who had been visiting the caretaker. He begged for his life. Watson shot him four times.

Inside the house, Manson's disciplines told Sharon Tate and her guests that the house was simply being robbed and no harm would

There were 51 stab wounds on his body

come to them. They were to be tied up, but Jay Sebring broke free. He was shot down before he could escape. Fearing they were all going to be killed, Voyteck Frykowski attacked Watson, who beat him to the ground with the pistol butt. In a frenzy, the girls stabbed him to death. There were 51 stab wounds on his body.

Abigail Folger also made a break for it. But Krenwinkel caught up with her halfway across the lawn. She knocked her to the ground and Watson stabbed her to death.

Sharon Tate begged for the life of her unborn child. But Susan Atkins showed no mercy. She stabbed her 16 times. Tate's mutilated body was tied to Sebring's corpse. The killers spread an American flag across the couch and wrote the word 'pig' on the front door in Sharon Tate's blood. They changed their bloody clothes, collected their weapons and made their way back to the Spahn Ranch.

Manson got high on marijuana and read the reports of the murders in the newspapers as if they were reviews. To celebrate this great victory, he had an orgy with his female followers. But soon he craved more blood.

On 10 August, Manson randomly selected a house in the Silver Lake area and broke in. Forty-four-year-old grocery-store owner Leno LaBianca and his 38-year-old wife Rosemary, who ran a fashionable dress shop, awoke to find Manson holding a gun to their faces. He tied them up, telling them they would not be harmed. He only intended to rob them.

He took LaBianca's wallet and went outside to the car where the rest of his followers, including 23-year-old Steve Grogan, were waiting. Manson sent Tex Watson, Leslie Van Houten and Patricia Krenwinkel back into the LaBiancas' house. He said that he was going to the house next door to murder its occupants. Instead, he drove home.

Watson did as he was told. He dragged Leno LaBianca into the living-room, stabbed him to death and left the knife sticking out of his throat. Meanwhile, Van Houten and Krenwinkel stabbed the helpless Mrs LaBianca as they chanted a murderous mantra. They used their victim's blood to write more revolutionary slogans on the walls. Then the three killers took a shower together.

The killers thought of their senseless slayings as a joke. They also expected them to set off 'helter skelter', the great revolutionary race war. When it did not, they knew they were in danger and the Family began to break up.

Susan Atkins turned back to prostitution to support herself. She was arrested and, in prison, she boasted to another inmate about the killings. When the police questioned her, she blamed Manson.

On 15 October 1969, Manson was arrested and charged with murder. Basking in publicity, Manson portrayed himself as the baddest man on Earth and boasted that he had been responsible for 35 other murders. But at his trial he pointed out a simple truth.

'I've killed no one,' he told the jury. 'I've ordered no one to be killed. These children who come to you with their knives, they're your children. I didn't teach them – you did.'

It did not make any difference. He, Beausoleil, Atkins, Krenwinkel, Van Houten, Watson and Grogan were all sentenced to death in the gas chamber. But before the sentence could be carried out, the death penalty was abolished in California. Manson and his followers had their sentences commuted to life imprisonment and they are now eligible for parole. So far, only Steven Grogan has been granted it.

Leslie Van Houten, Susan Atkins and Patricia Krenwinkel have all got skilful lawyers working on legal loopholes. Susan Atkins became a born-again Christian and like Leslie Van Houten she became a model prisoner, although she was denied parole for the eleventh time in 2005. At the California Institute for Women in Frontera, Van Houten, who was denied parole in 2004, graduated with degrees in literature and psychology. She could also argue that she did not actually kill anybody.

She stabbed Mrs LaBianca, but only after she was dead. Even Vincent Bugliosi conceded that the three women will be released eventually.

Tex Watson has less of a chance. He was doing well when he found God and became assistant pastor at the California Men's Colony at San Luis Obispo. But he made Bruce Davis, another Family member, as his assistant, and Stephen Kay, a Los Angeles County district attorney who worked as Vincent Bugliosi's assistant during the trial, suspected he was trying to build himself a powerbase in prison. Watson was denied parole in 2005 and is now working, inside, as a motor mechanic.

Former Family member Lynette Fromme made a half-hearted attempt to get Manson out in 1975 when she pulled a gun on US President Gerald Ford. But she did not pull the trigger and succeeded only in putting Manson back in the headlines again.

Manson constantly asks for parole. He does it, not because he has a reasonable chance of getting out, but because it gains him publicity. He revels in his image as the 'baddest man on Earth'.

Kay keeps an eye on the parole hearings and turns up to oppose any release. In 1981, at a parole hearing, Manson said that Kay would be murdered in the car park as he left. But he was present again, alive and well, for the next parole board hearing.

The following year, Manson was transferred to a maximum security cell at Vacaville prison after the authorities learned he was planning an escape by hot-air balloon. A ballooning catalogue, a rope, a hacksaw and a container of flammable liquid were found in the jail.

At one parole board hearing, Manson was asked why he unravelled his socks and used the yarn to make into woollen scorpions. He rose from his seat and said quite seriously: 'From the world of darkness I did loose demons and devils in the power of scorpions to torment.'

Parole was refused.

In 1986, Manson's parole request was opposed by California's governor George Deukmejian. In response, Manson read a 20-page hand-written statement which was described, by those who heard it, as 'bizarre and rambling'. Three years later he refused to appear before the parole board because he was made to wear manacles. These, he said, made the board think he was dangerous.

In 1992, his hearing was held within hours of the first execution held in California for over a decade. Of course, Manson's death sentence cannot be reinstated. Nevertheless, Manson did not do his chances of getting parole much good when he told the parole board: 'There's no one as bad as me. I am everywhere. I am down in San Diego Zoo. I am in your children. Someone had to be insane. We can't all be good guys. They've tried to kill me thirty or forty times in prison. They've poured fire over me. They haven't found anyone badder than me because there is no one as bad as me – and that's a fact.'

The truth is, Manson will never be allowed out.

− Chapter 7 −

The Moors Murderers

Ian Brady
and Myra Hindley

NATIONALITY: SCOTTISH

NUMBER OF VICTIMS: 5 KILLED

REIGN OF TERROR: 1963–65

FAVOURED METHOD OF KILLING: TORTURE, SEXUAL PERVERSION, STRANGULATION

Moors murderers Ian Brady and Myra Hindley's bizarre and deviant sexual relationship drove them to torture and murder defenceless children for pleasure in a case that appalled the world. When 19-year-old Myra Hindley met Ian Brady in January 1961 he was already deeply disturbed. He was 21 years old and worked as a stock clerk at Millwards, a chemical company in Manchester, but his mind was full of sadistic fantasies. He had a collection of Nazi memorabilia and recordings of Nazi rallies. In his lunch hour, he read *Mein Kampf* and studied German grammar. He believed in the rightness of the Nazi cause and regretted only that he could not join in its sadistic excesses. Myra Hindley had problems of her own. When she was 15, her boyfriend had died. She could not sleep for days afterwards and eventually turned to the Catholic Church for consolation. She was known as a loner and a daydreamer although at school it was noted that she was tough, aggressive and rather masculine, enjoying contact sports and judo. But that hardly made her suited to working life in 1950s Britain. After a series of menial jobs, she became a typist at Millwards, where she met Brady. He impressed her immediately. Most of the men she knew she considered immature. But Brady was well-dressed and rode a motorbike. Everything about him fascinated her. 'Ian wore a black shirt today and looked smashing… l love him,' she confided to her diary. For nearly a year Brady took no notice of her. 'The pig. He didn't even look at me today,' she wrote more than once. Finally, in December 1961, he asked her out. 'Eureka!' her diary says. 'Today we have our first date. We are going to the cinema.' The film was *Judgment at Nuremberg*.

Soon Hindley had surrendered her virginity to Brady. She was madly in love with him and was writing schoolgirlishly: 'I hope Ian and I love each other all our lives and get married and are happy ever after.' But their relationship was far more sophisticated than that. Hindley was Brady's love slave. He talked to her of sexual perversions and lent her books on Nazi atrocities. They took pornographic photographs of each other and kept them in a scrapbook. Some showed the weals of a whip across her buttocks.

Hindley gave up babysitting and going to church. Within six months, Brady had moved in with Hindley who lived (with her dog) in her grandmother's house on the outskirts of Manchester. A frail woman, Hindley's grandmother spent most of her time in bed, giving them the run of the place. Brady persuaded Hindley to bleach her hair a Teutonic blonde and dressed her in leather skirts and high-heeled boots. He called her Myra Hess – or Hessie – after sadistic concentration camp guard Irma Grese.

Hindley became hard and cruel, doing anything Brady asked. She did not even balk at procuring children for him to abuse, torture and kill. The first victim was 16-year-old Pauline Reade who disappeared on her way to a dance on 12 July 1963. Somehow they managed to persuade her to walk up to the nearby Saddleworth Moor, an isolated, windswept part of the Peak Districk National Park, where they killed and buried her in a shallow grave.

Four months later, Hindley hired a car and abducted 12-year-old John Kilbride. When she returned the car, it was covered in peaty mud from the moors. Brady and Hindley laughed when they read about the massive police operation to find the missing boy.

In May 1964, Hindley bought a car of her own, a white Mini van. The following month, 12-year-old Keith Bennett went missing. He too was buried on Saddleworth Moor. At Brady's behest, Hindley joined a local gun club and bought pistols for them both. They would go up to the moors for practice. While they were there they would visit the graves of their victims. They would photograph each other kneeling on them.

Murder is a hobby and a supreme pleasure

On 26 December 1964, they abducted 10-year-old Lesley Ann Downey. This time they were determined to hurt their defenceless victim as much as possible. They forced her to pose nude for pornographic photographs. Then they tortured her, recording her screams, before strangling her and burying her with the others on Saddleworth Moor.

Even this did not satisfy the depraved Brady. He wanted to extend his evil empire. He aimed to recruit Myra's teenage brother-in-law, David Smith. Brady began to systematically corrupt Smith. He showed the youth his guns and talked to him about robbing a bank. He lent him books about the Marquis de Sade and got him to copy out quotations. 'Murder is a hobby and a supreme pleasure' and 'People are like maggots, small, blind, worthless fish-bait' Smith wrote in an exercise book under Brady's guidance.

Brady believed he could lure anyone into his world of brutality and murder. He bragged to Smith about the murders he had already committed, saying he had photographs to prove it. They were drinking at the time and Smith thought Brady was joking. Brady decided to prove what he was saying – and ensnare Smith into his vicious schemes by making him a party to murder. On 6 October 1965 Brady and Hindley picked up 17-year-old homosexual Edward Evans in a pub in Manchester and took him home. Smith had been invited to visit around midnight.

He was in the kitchen when he heard a cry from the next room. Then Hindley called to him: 'Help him, Dave.' Smith rushed through into the living-room to find Evans in a chair with Brady astride him. Brady had an axe in his hands and was smashing it down on the boy's head. He hit him again and again – at least 14 times. 'That's it, it's the messiest,' Brady said with some satisfaction. 'Usually it takes only one blow.'

He handed the axe to the dumbstruck Smith. This was a simple attempt to incriminate Smith by making him put his fingerprints on the murder weapon. Although Smith was terrified by what he had seen, he helped clean up the blood, while Brady and Hindley wrapped the body in a plastic sheet. The couple made jokes about the murder as they carried the corpse upstairs to a bedroom. Hindley made a pot of tea and they all sat down.

'You should have seen the look on his face,' said Hindley, flushed with excitement, and she started reminiscing about the previous murders. Smith could not believe all this was happening, but he realised that if he showed any sign of disgust or outrage he would be their next victim. After a decent interval, he made his excuses and left. When he got back to his flat, he was violently ill.

He told his wife and she urged him to go to the police. Armed with a knife and a screwdriver, they went out to a phonebox at dawn and reported the murder. A police car picked up Smith and his wife and, at the station, the terrified 17-year-old told his lurid story to unbelieving policemen. At 8.40 a.m., the police dropped round to Hindley's house to check Smith's story out. To their horror, they found Edward Evans's battered body in the back bedroom. Brady admitted killing Evans, but said it had happened during an argument and tried to implicate Smith. Hindley only said: 'My story is the same at Ian's... Whatever he did, I did.'

The only time she showed any emotion was when she was told that her dog had died. 'You fucking murderers,' she screamed at the police. The police found a detailed plan that Brady had drawn up for the removal from the house of all clues to Evans's murder. One of the items mentioned was, curiously, Hindley's prayer book. When the police examined the prayer book, they found a left luggage ticket from

Manchester station stuck down the spine. At the left luggage office, they found two suitcases which contained books on sexual perversion, coshes and pictures of Lesley Ann Downey naked and gagged. There was also the tape of her screams, which was later played to the stunned court-room at Chester Assizes. Other photographs showed Hindley posing beside graves on Saddleworth Moor. These helped the police locate the bodies of Lesley Ann Downey and John Kilbride. At the trial the true, horrific, sexual nature of the crimes was revealed. The pathologist disclosed that Edward Evans's fly had been undone and he had found dog hairs around Evans's anus. John Kilbride's body was found with his trousers and underpants around his knees. Hindley, it seemed, got turned on by watching Brady perform homosexual acts on his victims. Later Brady let it slip that both he and Hindley had been naked during the nude photographic sessions with Lesley Ann Downey. But otherwise they refused to talk. They were sentenced to life. Brady did not bother to appeal. Hindley did, but her appeal was rejected. They were also refused permission to see each other, though they were allowed to write. Brady has shown no contrition in prison and has refused to be broken. He saw himself as a martyr in his own perverted cause. Gradually, he went insane. Hindley eventually broke down and petitioned to be released. When that was refused, a warder, who was Hindley's lesbian lover, organised an escape attempt. It failed and Hindley was sentenced to an additional year in jail. She took an open university degree and gave additional information on the whereabouts of the victims' graves in a bid for mercy. But Brady countered her every move by revealing more of her involvement in the crimes. He saw any attempt on her part to go free as disloyalty. 'The weight of our crimes justifies permanent imprisonment,' Brady told the Parole Board in 1982. 'I will not wish to be free in 1985 or even 2005.' He got his wish. Though he made several attempts to starve himself Brady was still incarcerated in 2005. Hindley died in jail in 2002.

– Chapter 8 –

Ted Bundy

Ted Bundy

NATIONALITY: AMERICAN

BORN: 1946

NUMBER OF VICTIMS: 20 KILLED

FAVOURED METHOD OF KILLING: RAPE, STRANGULATION

REIGN OF TERROR: 1970S

DEFENCE: CONDUCTED HIS OWN DEFENCE AND TRIED TO CHARM THE JURY

EXECUTED: 24TH JANUARY 1989

Ted Bundy had the power to charm women. Many of them paid with their lives. He claimed his sexual impulses were so strong that there was no way that he could control them. He later maintained that during his first attacks he had to wrestle with his conscience. But soon he began to desensitise himself. He claimed not to have tortured his victims unnecessarily, but said that he had to kill them after he had raped them to prevent them identifying him.

Bundy had been a compulsive masturbator from an early age and later became obsessed by sadistic pornography. After glimpsing a girl undressing through a window, he also became a compulsive Peeping Tom. His long-time girlfriend Meg Anders described how he would tie her up with stockings before anal sex. This sex game stopped when he almost strangled her. For years they maintained a more or less normal sexual relationship, while Bundy exercised his craving for total control with anonymous victims, whom he often strangled during the sexual act.

His attitude to sex was often ambivalent. Although he desired the bodies of attractive young women, he would leave their vaginas stuffed with twigs and dirt and sometimes sodomise them with objects such as aerosol cans.

Some of the bodies, though partly decomposed, had freshly-washed hair and newly-applied make-up, indicating that he had kept them for necrophilia. In only one case did he admit to deliberately terrorising his victims. He kidnapped two girls at the same time so that he could rape each of them in front of the other, before killing them.

Bundy's first victim was Sharon Clarke of Seattle. He had broken into her apartment while she was asleep and smashed her around the head with a metal rod. She suffered a shattered skull, but survived. She could not identify her attacker and no motivation for the attack has been given.

Then young women began to disappear from the University of Washington campus nearby. Six disappeared within seven months. At the Lake Sammanish resort in Washington State, a number of young women reported being approached by a young man calling himself Ted. He had his arm in a sling and asked them to help get his sailing boat off his car. But in the car park they found that there was no boat on the car. Ted then said that they would have to go to his house to get it. Sensibly, most declined. Janice Ott seems to have agreed to go with him. She disappeared. A few hours later, Denise Naslund also disappeared from the same area. She had been seen in the company of a good-looking, dark-haired young man who fitted Ted Bundy's description. The remains of Janice Ott, Denise Naslund and another unidentified young woman were later found on wasteland, where their bodies had been eaten and scattered by animals.

Other witnesses came forward from the University of Washington, saying that they had seen a man wearing a sling and some other bodies were found, again disposed of on waste ground.

The police had two suspects. Ex-convict Gary Taylor had been picked up by the Seattle police for abducting women under false pretences. And park attendant Warren Forrest picked up a young woman who consented to pose for him. He took her to a secluded part of the park, tied her up and stripped her naked. He taped her mouth and fired darts at her breasts. Then he raped her, strangled her and left her for dead. But she survived and identified her attacker. Both were in custody though, and the attacks continued. Bundy's girlfriend, who was beginning to suspect something

Then he raped her, strangled her and left her for dead

was up, called anonymously, giving his name, but it disappeared among the thousands of other leads the police had to follow up.

Bundy began to travel further afield. On 2 October 1974 he abducted Nancy Wilcox after she left an all-night party in Salt Lake City. In Midvale on 18 October, he raped and strangled Melissa Smith, the daughter of the local police chief. Her body was found in the Wasatch Mountains. He took Laura Aimee from a Hallowe'en party in Orem, Utah. Her naked body was found at the bottom of a canyon.

In Salt Lake City a week later, he approached a girl named Carol DaRonch. Bundy pretended to be a detective and asked her the licence number of her car. Someone had tried to break into it, he said. He asked her to accompany him to the precinct to see the suspect. She got into his car, but once they were in a quiet street he handcuffed her.

She began to scream. He put a gun to her head. She managed to get out of the door and Bundy chased after her with a crowbar. He took a swing at her skull, but she managed to grab the bar. A car was coming down the street. Carol jumped in front of it, forcing it to stop. She jumped in and the car drove away.

Carol gave a good description to the police, but Bundy continued undeterred. He tried to pick up a pretty young French teacher outside her high school. She declined to go with him. But Debbie Kent did. She disappeared from a school playground where a key to a pair of handcuffs was later found.

The following January in Snowmass Village, a Colorado ski resort, Dr Raymond Gadowsky found that his fiancée, Caryn Campbell, was missing from her room. A month later, her naked body was found out in the snow. She had been raped and her skull had been smashed in. Julie Cunningham vanished from nearby Vail and the remains of Susan Rancourt and Brenda Bell were also found on Taylor Mountain.

The body of Melanie Cooley was found only ten miles from her home. Unlike the other victims, she was still clothed, though her jeans had been undone, convincing the police that the motive was sexual.

The Colorado attacks continued with Nancy Baird who disappeared from a petrol station and Shelley Robertson whose naked body was found down a mine shaft.

A Salt Lake City patrol man was cruising an area of the city that had recently suffered a spate of burglaries. He noticed Bundy's car driving slowly and indicated that he should pull over. Instead, Bundy sped off. The patrolman gave chase and caught up with him. In his car, they found maps and brochures of Colorado. Some coincided with the places girls had disappeared.

Forensic experts found a hair in Bundy's car that matched that of Melissa Smith. A witness also recognised Bundy from Snowmass Village. He was charged and extradited to Colorado to stand trial. However, few people could believe that such an intelligent and personable young man could be responsible for these terrible sex attacks, even though Carol DaRonch picked him out of a line-up.

Bundy was given permission to conduct his own defence. He was even allowed to use the law library to research. There he managed to give his guard the slip, jumped from a window and escaped. He was recaptured a week later.

Bundy still protested his innocence and managed to prolong the pre-trial hearings with a number of skilful legal stalling manoeuvres. In the time he gained, he lost weight and cut a small hole under the light fitting in the ceiling of his cell. He squeezed through the one-foot-square hole he had made and got clean away.

He travelled around America before settling in Tallahassee, Florida, a few blocks from the sorority houses of Florida State University. One evening, Nita Neary saw a man lurking in front of her sorority house. She was about to phone the police when a fellow student, Karen Chandler, staggered from her room with blood streaming from her head. She was screaming that she and her roommate, Kathy Kleiner, had just been attacked by a madman. Both Margaret Bown and Lisa Levy had been attacked sexually – Margaret had been strangled with her own pantyhose and Bundy had bitten one of Lisa's nipples off and left teeth marks in her buttocks before beating her around the head. She died on the way to hospital. In another building, Cheryl Thomas had also been viciously attacked, but she survived.

The police had only a sketchy description of the attacker. But Bundy had plainly got a taste for killing again. While making his getaway, he abducted 12-year-old Kimberley Leach, sexually assaulted her, strangled her, mutilated her sexual organs and dumped her body in the Suwannee River Park.

Bundy was now short of money. He stole some credit cards and a car, and sneaked out of his apartment where he owed back rent. But the stolen car was a give-away. He was stopped by a motorcycle cop and arrested. At the police station, he admitted that he was Ted Bundy and that he was wanted by the Colorado police.

The Florida police began to tie him in with the Tallahassee attack. When they tried to take an impression of his teeth, he went berserk. It took six men to hold his jaw open. The impression matched the teeth marks on Lisa Levy's buttocks.

Again Bundy conducted his own defence, skilfully using the law to prolong the court case and his personality to charm the jury. But the evidence of the teeth marks was too strong. He was found guilty of murder and sentenced to death. On death row, Bundy made a detailed confession. He also received sacks full of post from young women whose letters dwelt on cruel and painful ways to make love. Even on death row he had not lost his charm. At 7 a.m. on 24 January 1989, Bundy went to the electric chair. He is said to have died with a smile on his face.

– Chapter 9 –

The Yorkshire Ripper

Peter Sutcliffe

NATIONALITY: ENGLISH

REIGN OF TERROR: 1975–81

NUMBER OF VICTIMS: 13 KILLED, 7 INJURED

FAVOURED METHOD OF KILLING: HAMMER BLOWS TO THE HEAD

STATED MOTIVE: HAD BEEN ACTING ON INSTRUCTIONS FROM GOD TO 'CLEAN THE STREETS' OF PROSTITUTES.

Nearly ninety years after the notorious Jack the Ripper finished his killing spree in the East End of London, the Yorkshire Ripper picked up where he left off. In a reign of terror spanning nearly six years, the Yorkshire Ripper managed to elude the biggest police squad that has ever assembled in the UK to catch one man. By the time he was caught, 20 women had been savagely attacked, 13 brutally murdered and a whole community was virtually under siege.

It started on 30 October 1975 when a Leeds milkman on his rounds saw a shapeless bundle in a bleak recreation ground. With Bonfire Night just a week away, he thought it was only a Guy. But he went over to investigate anyway. He found a woman sprawled on the ground, her hair matted with blood, her body exposed. Her jacket and blouse had been torn open, her bra pulled up. Her slacks had been pulled down below her knees and in her chest and stomach there were 14 stab wounds.

The milkman didn't see the massive wound on the back of her head that had actually caused her death. The victim had been attacked from behind. Two vicious blows had been delivered by a heavy, hammer-like implement, smashing her skull. The stab wounds were inflicted after she was dead.

The body belonged to a 28-year-old mother of three, Wilma McCann. She regularly hitch-hiked home after nights on the town. She died just 100 yards from her home, a council house in Scott Hall Avenue. Post-mortem blood tests showed that she had consumed 12 to 14 measures of spirits on the night of her death, which would have rendered her incapable of defending herself.

Although her clothes had been interfered with, her knickers were still in place and she had not been raped. There seemed to be no overt sexual motive for her murder. Her purse was missing. So, in the absence of any other motive, the police treated her killing as a callous by-product of robbery.

This changed when a second killing occurred in the area of Chapeltown, the red-light district of Leeds, three months later. Not all the women who worked there were professional prostitutes. Some housewives sold sex for a little extra cash. Others, such as 42-year-old Emily Jackson, were enthusiastic amateurs who did it primarily for fun. She lived with her husband and three children in the respectable Leeds suburb of Churwell. On 20 January 1976, Emily and her husband went to the Gaiety pub on Roundhay Road, the venue for the Chapeltown irregulars and their prospective clientele. Emily left her husband in the main lounge and went hunting for business. An hour later, she was seen getting into a Land-Rover in the car park. At closing time, her husband drank up and took a taxi home alone. His wife, he thought, had found a client who wanted her for the night.

Emily Jackson's body was found the next morning huddled under a coat on open ground. Like Wilma McCann, her breasts were exposed and her knickers left on. Again, she had been killed by two massive blows to the head with a heavy hammer. Her neck, breasts and stomach had also been stabbed – this time over fifty times. Her back had been gouged with a Phillips screwdriver and the impression of a heavy-ribbed Wellington boot was stamped on her right thigh.

The post-mortem indicated that Emily Jackson had had sex before the attack, not necessarily with the murderer. Once again, there seemed to be no real motive. And the killer had left only one real clue: he had size-seven shoes.

Over a year later, on 5 February 1977, 28-year-old part-time prostitute Irene Richardson left her tawdry rooming house in Chapeltown at 11.30 p.m. to go dancing. The following morning, a jogger in Soldier's Field, a public playing-field just a short car ride from Chapeltown, saw a body slumped on the ground and stopped to see what the matter was. It was Irene Richardson. She lay face down. Three massive blows had shattered her skull. Her skirt and tights were torn off. Her coat was draped over her buttocks and her calf-length boots had been removed from her feet and laid neatly across her thighs. Again, her neck and torso were studded with knife wounds. The post-mortem indicated that she had not had sex and had died only half an hour after leaving her lodgings.

After the murder of Irene Richardson, the police were able to link the three cases. They were plainly the work of a serial killer and the parallel with the Jack the Ripper case quickly sprang into the public imagination. The murderer of Wilma McCann, Emily Jackson and Irene Richardson soon became known as the Yorkshire Ripper.

The girls of Chapeltown heeded the warning. They moved in droves to Manchester, London and Glasgow. Those who could not travel so far from home began plying their trade in nearby Bradford. But the next victim, Patricia 'Tina' Atkinson, was a Bradford girl. She lived just around the corner from the thriving red-light district in Oak Lane. On 23 April 1977, she went to her local pub, The Carlisle, for a drink with her friends. She reeled out just before closing time. When she was not seen the next day, people assumed she was at home, sleeping it off.

The following evening, friends dropped round and found the door to her flat unlocked. Inside, they found her dead on her bed covered with blankets. She had been attacked as she came into the flat. Four hammer blows had smashed into the back of her head. She had been flung on the bed and her clothes pulled off. She had been stabbed in the stomach seven times and the left side of her body had been slashed to ribbons. There was a size-seven Wellington boot print on the sheet.

The man the footprint belonged to was Peter Sutcliffe. Like Jack the Ripper before him, he seems to have been on a moral crusade to rid the streets of prostitutes.

The eldest of John and Kathleen Sutcliffe's six children, he was born in Bingley, a town just six miles north of Bradford. He had been a timid child and inscrutable young man, who was always regarded as being somehow different. He was small and weedy. Bullied at school, he clung to his mother's skirts.

His younger brothers inherited their father's appetite for life, the opposite sex and the consumption of large quantities of beer. Peter liked none of these things. Although he took no interest in girls, he spent hours preening himself in the bathroom. He later took up body-building.

Leaving school at 15, he took a temporary job as a grave-digger at a cemetery in Bingley. He regularly joked about having 'thousands of people below me where I work now'. He developed a macabre sense of humour during his three years there. Once he pretended to be a corpse. He lay down on a slab, threw a shroud over himself and started making moaning noises when his workmates appeared. They called him 'Jesus' because of his beard.

At his trial Sutcliffe claimed that he had heard the voice of God coming from a cross-shaped headstone while he was digging a grave. The voice told him to go out on to the streets and kill prostitutes.

Despite Peter Sutcliffe's youthful good looks, girls were not attracted to him. His first proper girlfriend, Sonia, was a 16-year-old schoolgirl when he met her in the Royal Standard, his local pub. He was 24. Sonia suffered the same introversion as Peter. On Sundays, they would sit in the front room, lost in their own conversation. Sonia would only speak to other members of the Sutcliffe family when it was absolutely unavoidable.

A devout Catholic, Peter was devastated when it was discovered that his mother was having an affair with a neighbour, a local policeman.

His father arranged for the children, including Peter and bride-to-be Sonia, to be present at a Bingley hotel for a humiliating confrontation. His mother arrived in the bar believing she was meeting her boyfriend, only to be greeted by her husband and children. He forced her to show the family the new nightdress she had bought for the occasion. This was particularly painful for Peter who had discovered earlier that Sonia also had a secret boyfriend.

Later that year, 1969, Sutcliffe carried out his first known attack. He hit a Bradford prostitute over the head with a stone in a sock following a row over a ten-pound note. Psychiatrists later said that the discovery of his mother's affair triggered his psychosis.

Sonia knew nothing of this and on 10 August 1974, after an eight-year courtship, she and Peter were married. They spent the first three years of their married life living with Sonia's parents, then they moved to a large detached house in Heaton, a middle-class suburb of Bradford, which they kept immaculate.

On the evening of Saturday, 25 June 1977, Peter dropped his wife off at the Sherrington nursing home where she worked nights. With his neighbours Ronnie and Peter Barker, he went on a pub crawl around Bradford, ending up at the Dog in the Pound. At closing time, they went to get some fish and chips.

It was well past midnight when he dropped the Barker brothers at their front door. But instead of parking his white Ford Corsair outside his house, Sutcliffe drove off down the main road towards Leeds. At around 2 a.m., he saw a lone girl wearing a gingham skirt in the street light of Chapeltown Road. As she passed the Hayfield pub and turned left down Reginald Terrace, Sutcliffe parked his car, got out and began to follow her down the quiet side street.

The girl's body was found lying by a wall the next morning by a group of children on their way into the adventure playground in Reginald Terrace. She had been struck on the back of the head, then dragged 20 yards and hit twice more. She was also stabbed once in the back and repeatedly through the chest. The trademarks were unmistakable.

However, the victim was not a prostitute. Jayne McDonald was 16, had just left school and was working in the shoe department of a local supermarket. On the night of her death, she had been out with friends in Leeds. When she was attacked, she was on her way back to her parents' home, which was just a few hundred yards from where her body was found.

The murder of a teenage girl gave the investigation new impetus. By September, the police had interviewed almost 700 residents in the area and taken 3,500 statements, many of them from prostitutes who worked in the area.

Two weeks after the killing of Jayne McDonald, the Ripper savagely attacked Maureen Long on some waste ground near her home in Bradford. By some miracle she survived, but the description of her assailant was too hazy to help the inquiry.

The staff of the investigation was increased to 304 full-time officers who had soon interviewed 175,000 people, taken 12,500 statements and checked 10,000 vehicles. The problem was that they no idea of the type of man they were looking for. Certainly no one would have suspected Peter Sutcliffe. The 3l-year-old was a polite and mild-mannered neighbour, a hard-working long-distance lorry driver and trusted employee, a good son and a loyal husband. He was the sort of man who did jobs around the house or tinkered with his car at weekends. Nothing about him suggested that he was a mass murderer.

Those who knew him would even have been surprised if they had seen him out picking up prostitutes. But that's what he did, regularly. On Saturday, 1 October 1977, Jean Jordan climbed into Sutcliffe's new red Ford Corsair near her home in Moss Side, Manchester. She took £5 in advance and directed him to some open land two miles away that was used by prostitutes with their clients. They were a few yards away from the car when Sutcliffe smashed a hammer down on to her skull. He hit her again and again, 11 times in all. He dragged her body into some bushes, but another car arrived and he had to make a quick getaway.

As he drove back to Bradford, Sutcliffe realised that he had left a vital clue on the body. The £5 note he had given Jean Jordan was brand new. It had come directly from his wage packet and could tie him to the dead girl.

For eight long days, he waited nervously. In that time, there was nothing in the press about the body being found. So he risked returning to Moss Side to find the note. Despite a frantic search, he could not find Jean Jordan's handbag. In frustration, he started attacking her body with a broken pane of glass. He even tried to cut off the head to remove his hammer blow signature. But the glass was not sharp enough to sever the spine. In the end, he gave up, kicked the body several times and drove home.

The following day, an allotment owner found Jean Jordan's naked body. The damage to her head made her unrecognisable and there was no evidence to identify her among her scattered clothing She was eventually identified from a fingerprint on a lemonade bottle she had handled before leaving home for the last time.

The police also found the five-pound note. They set about tracing it. In three months they interviewed 5,000 men. One of them was Peter Sutcliffe. But after leaving Sutcliffe's well-appointed house, detectives filed a short report which left him free to go about his gruesome business.

Sutcliffe's next victim was 18-year-old Helen Rytka, who shared a miserable room by a flyover in Huddersfield with her twin sister Rita. The two of them worked as a pair in the red-light district around busy Great Northern Street. They concentrated on the car trade.

The Yorkshire Ripper murders scared them, so they had devised a system which they thought would keep them safe. They based themselves outside a public lavatory. When they were picked up separately, they took the number of the client's car. They each gave their client precisely twenty minutes and then returned to the toilet at a set time. But their system went terribly wrong.

On the snowy night of Tuesday 31 January 1978, Helen arrived back at the rendezvous five minutes early. At 9.25 p.m., a bearded man in a red Ford Corsair offered her the chance of a quick fiver. She thought she could perform her services quickly and make it back to the rendezvous before Rita returned. She could not. Rita never saw her again.

Helen took her client to nearby Garrard's timber yard. There were two men there, so he could not kill her straight away. Instead, Sutcliffe had to have sexual intercourse with her in the back of the car. When they were finished, the men were gone. As she got out of the back seat to return to the front of the car, Sutcliffe swung at her with his hammer. He missed and hit the door of the car. His second blow struck her on the head. Then he hit her five more times. The walls of the foreman's shed a few feet away were splattered with blood.

The walls of the foreman's shed a few feet away were splattered with blood

Sutcliffe dragged Helen's body into a woodpile and hid it there. Her bra and black polo-neck sweater were pushed up above her breasts. Her socks were left on, but the rest of her clothes were scattered over a wide area. Her black lace panties were found the next day by a lorry driver, pinned to the shed door.

Back at the lavatory, Rita was desperately worried, but fear of the police prevented her from reporting her sister's disappearance for three days. A police Alsatian found the hidden body. It had been horribly mutilated. There were three gaping wounds in the chest where she had been stabbed repeatedly.

The Ripper's latest victim had disappeared from a busy street. Over a hundred passers-by were traced, and all but three cars and one stocky, fair-haired man were eliminated. The police appealed on the radio to any wife, mother or girlfriend who suspected that they were living with the Ripper. No one came forward.

A few weeks later, a passer-by spotted an arm sticking out from under an overturned sofa on wasteland in Bradford's red-light district. At first he thought it was a tailor's dummy but the putrid aroma soon sent him rushing to a telephone.

The body was that of 22-year-old Yvonne Pearson. She was a high-class prostitute, who serviced a rich businessman trade in most of Britain's cities. She had been killed two months earlier, ten days before Helen Rytka. The killing bore all the hallmarks of the Ripper. A hammer blow to the head had smashed her skull. Her bra and jumper were pulled up exposing her breasts, and her chest had been jumped on repeatedly. Her black flared slacks had been pulled down. Horsehair from the sofa was stuffed in her mouth.

Yvonne Pearson had spoken of her fear of the Ripper only days before she disappeared. On the night of her death, she had left her two daughters with a neighbour. Soon after 9.30 p.m., she was seen climbing into a car driven by a bearded man with black, piercing eyes. On the wasteland in nearby Arthington Street, he killed her with a club hammer. Then he dragged her body to the abandoned sofa and jumped on her until her ribs cracked.

Although he had hidden her body, the killer seemed concerned that it had not been found and returned to make it more visible. He tucked a copy of the *Daily Mirror*, from four weeks after her death, under her arm.

Two months after Yvonne Pearson's body was found, the Yorkshire Ripper attacked 41-year-old Vera Millward. The Spanish-born mother of seven children, Vera had come to England after the war as a domestic help. She lived with a Jamaican and had resorted to prostitution in Manchester's Moss Side to help support her family. On the night of Tuesday, 16 May, she went out to get painkillers from the hospital for her chronic stomach pains. She died in a well-lit part of the grounds of Manchester Royal Infirmary. Sutcliffe hit her three times on the head with a hammer and then slashed her across the stomach. Her body was discovered by a gardener the next morning on a rubbish pile in the corner of the car park.

Three months after Vera Millward's death, the police visited Sutcliffe again because his car registration number had cropped up during special checks in Leeds and Bradford. They returned to question him about the tyres on his car. They were looking for treads that matched tracks at the scene of Irene Richardson's murder, 21 months earlier.

As always, Sutcliffe's was helpful and unruffled, giving them absolutely no reason to suspect him. They never even asked Sutcliffe for his blood group – the Ripper's was rare – or his shoe size which was unusually small for a man.

Suddenly the Ripper's killing spree stopped. For 11 months he dropped out of sight. The police believed that he had committed suicide, taking his identity with him to the grave. This man was eerily similar to the disappearance of Jack the Ripper 90 years before.

But Sutcliffe was not dead. Nor could he contain his desire to murder. On the night of Wednesday, 4 April 1979, he drove to Halifax. Around midnight, he got out of his car and accosted 19-year-old Josephine Whitaker as she walked across Savile Park playing fields. They spoke briefly. As they moved away from the street lamps, he smashed the back of her head with a hammer and dragged her body into the shadows. Her body was found the next morning.

Like Jayne MacDonald, Josephine Whitaker was not a prostitute. She lived at home with her family and worked as a clerk in the headquarters of the Halifax Building Society. Now no woman felt safe on the streets after dark.

Two weeks before Josephine Whitaker died, a letter arrived at the police station. It was postmarked Sunderland, 23 March 1979. Handwriting experts confirmed that it came from the same person that had sent two previous letters purporting to come from the Yorkshire Ripper. This one mentioned that Vera Millward had stayed in hospital. The police believed, wrongly, that this information could only have come from Vera herself. On this basis they leapt to the conclusion that the writer of the three letters was indeed the Ripper.

The letter said that the next victim would not be in Bradford's Chapeltown district as it was 'too bloody hot there' because of the efforts of 'curserred coppers'. This odd misspelling so closely aped the original Ripper's notes that it should have rang warning bells.

Traces of engineering oil had been found on one of the letters. Similar traces were found on Josephine Whitaker's body. The police called a press conference. The public was asked to come forward with any information they had about anybody who might have been in Sunderland on the days the letters were posted. The response was overwhelming, but all it added up to was more useless information to be checked, analysed and filed.

Then, on the morning of 18 June 1979, two months after Josephine Whitaker's death, a buff-coloured envelope arrived. It was addressed in the same handwriting and contained a cassette tape. On it, there was a 257-word message in a broad Geordie accent.

A huge publicity campaign was mounted. The public could phone in and listen to the 'Geordie Ripper Tape', in the hope that someone might recognise the voice. Within a few days, more than 50,000 people had called.

Language experts confirmed the accent as genuine Wearside, and pinned it down to Castletown, a small, tightly-knit suburb of Sunderland. Eleven detectives were installed in a Sunderland hotel and 100 officers combed the town. Only 4,000 people lived in Castletown, but the police could not find their man. The letters and tape turned out to be a hoax and in October 2005 a Sunderland man was charged with perverting the course of justice.

In July 1979, Detective-Constable Laptew visited Sutcliffe. His car had been spotted in the red-light district of Bradford on 36 separate occasions. This time Laptew felt suspicious of Sutcliffe but, because all eyes were focused on the Geordie tape, his report was not followed up and Sutcliffe went back to Bradford for his eleventh victim.

He stabbed her eight times, stuffed her body into a dustbin and slung an old carpet over it

On Saturday, 1 September 1979, Sutcliffe cruised the streets around Little Horton, a residential area. At about 1 a.m., he saw Barbara Leach, a student, moving away from a group of friends outside the Mannville Arms. Just 200 yards from the pub, he attacked Barbara Leach and dragged her body into a backyard. He stabbed her eight times, stuffed her body into a dustbin and slung an old carpet over it. It was found the following afternoon.

Two high-ranking officers from Scotland Yard were sent to Yorkshire but got nowhere. A taskforce from Manchester reviewed the £5-note inquiry. They narrowed the field down to 270 suspects, but could get no further.

Like everyone else in Yorkshire, Sutcliffe spoke to family and friends about the Ripper. He would make a point of picking up Sonia from work to protect her and told a workmate: 'Whoever is doing all these murders has a lot to answer for.' Once his colleagues at the depot made a bet that he was the Ripper – but Sutcliffe just laughed and said nothing.

The Ripper took another break of nearly a year. Then on Thursday, 18 August 1980, he struck for the twelfth time. The victim was Marguerite Walls, a 47-year-old civil servant. She was working late at the Department of Education and Science in Leeds, tidying up loose ends before going on a ten-day holiday. She left at 10 p.m. to walk home. Her body was found two days later, under a mound of grass clippings in the garden of a magistrate's house. She had been bludgeoned and strangled, but her body had not been mutilated so the police did not realise that she was one of the Ripper's victims.

Three months later, Sutcliffe had just finished eating a chicken dinner when he saw Jacqueline Hill, a language student at the University of Leeds, get off the bus outside a Kentucky Fried Chicken outlet. His fingers were still greasy from his supper when he viciously struck her down. He dragged her body to the waste ground behind the shops and attacked it savagely. Death had struck Jacqueline so suddenly that one of her eyes had remained open. Sutcliffe stabbed it repeatedly with a rusty Phillips screwdriver specially sharpened into a fine point.

The Home Office appointed a special squad to solve the case. But six weeks after Jacqueline Hill's murder, it reached the same conclusion as the West Yorkshire force – it had no idea how to crack the case. What was needed was a little bit of luck.

On 2 January 1981, Sergeant Robert Ring and Police Constable Robert Hydes started their evening shift by cruising along Melbourne Avenue in Sheffield's red-light district. They saw Olivia Reivers climbing into a Rover V8 3500 and decided to investigate. The driver – a bearded man – identified himself as Peter Williams. He said he wanted no trouble. Then he scrambled out of the car and asked if he could relieve himself. He went over to the bushes lining the street and, while pretending to take a pee, dropped his ball-peen hammer and sharp knife which he kept in a special pocket of his car coat. The police did not notice this as Olivia Reivers was remonstrating loudly with the men who had just saved her life, complaining that they were ruining her livelihood.

But by the time the man had strolled back to his car, the police had discovered that the number plates were false. He was taken to the police station where he admitted his name was Peter William Sutcliffe.

During his interview, Sutcliffe said his main worry was that the police would tell his wife that he had been picked up a prostitute. Otherwise, he was calm and forthcoming. He readily admitted that he had stolen the number plates from a scrapyard in Dewsbury. The police even let him go to the lavatory alone, where he hid a second knife in the cistern.

There was no real reason to suspect Sutcliffe, but the police had so little to go on that, when any man was caught with a prostitute, his details had to be forwarded to the West Yorkshire Police before he could be released. Sutcliffe was locked up for the night. The next morning he was taken, unprotesting, to Dewsbury Police Station.

There, Sutcliffe was a chatty, eager interviewee. In passing, he mentioned that he had been interviewed by the Ripper Squad about the £5 note and that he had also visited Bradford's red-light district.

Dewsbury police called the Ripper Squad in Leeds. Detective Sergeant Des O'Boyle discovered that Sutcliffe's name had come up several times in the course of the investigation. He drove to Dewsbury. When he called his boss, Detective Inspector John Boyle, in Leeds that evening, he told Boyle that Sutcliffe was blood group B – the rare blood group the police knew the Ripper had. Sutcliffe was locked in his cell for a second night.

Meanwhile, Sergeant Ring heard one of his colleagues casually mention that the man he had arrested was being interviewed by detectives from the Ripper Squad. Ring rushed back to Melbourne Avenue. Hidden in the bushes there, he found a ball-peen hammer and a knife.

Sonia Sutcliffe was questioned and the house was searched. Then, early on Sunday afternoon, Boyle told Sutcliffe that they had found a hammer and knife in Sheffield. Sutcliffe, who had been talkative up to this point, fell silent.

'I think you're in trouble, serious trouble,' said Boyle.

Sutcliffe finally spoke. 'I think you are leading up to the Yorkshire Ripper,' he said.

Boyle nodded.

'Well,' Sutcliffe said, 'that's me.'

Sutcliffe's confession took almost 17 hours to complete. He told them of his first killing in 1969 but at that time, he mentioned nothing about hearing a voice from God.

Sixteen weeks later, Sutcliffe stood trial at the Old Bailey. The Crown Prosecution, defence counsel and Attorney General Sir Michael Havers agreed that Sutcliffe was mentally ill, suffering from paranoid schizophrenia. But the judge would have none of this. He told both counsels that the jury would listen to the evidence and decide whether Sutcliffe was a murderer or a mad man.

Sutcliffe pleaded guilty to manslaughter. He was calm and self-assured, even managing a laugh when he recalled that during his questioning about the size-seven Wellington boot imprinted on Emily Jackson's thigh and Tina Atkinson's bed sheet – the policeman interviewing him had not noticed he was wearing the boots. He also claimed that he had been acting on instructions from God to 'clean the streets' of prostitutes.

The jury would have none of it. They found him guilty of 13 murders and he was sentenced to life imprisonment, with a recommendation that he should serve at least 30 years.

– Chapter 10 –

Son of Sam

David Berkowitz

NATIONALITY: AMERICAN

BORN: 1953

NUMBER OF VICTIMS: 6 KILLED

FAVOURED METHOD OF KILLING: SHOOTING

REIGN OF TERROR: 1976–1977

MOTIVE: CLAIMED THE DEMONS AND THE DOGS MADE HIM DO IT

IN THE END: NOT ALL THE SON OF SAM SLAYINGS CAN BE ATTRIBUTED TO DAVID BERKOWITZ

At 1 a.m. on 29 July 1976, 19-year-old Jody Valente and 18-year-old Donna Lauria were sitting in Jody's car outside Donna's home in the Bronx, New York. It was a hot summer night and they were discussing their boyfriends. Then Donna said goodnight and opened the door to get out.

A young man was standing a few feet away. He was holding a brown paper sack. As the car door opened, he reached into the sack, pulled out a gun and dropped to a crouching position.

'What does this guy want?' said Donna, rather alarmed.

Before the words were out of her mouth a bullet struck her in the side of the neck. A second bullet smashed the window in the door. A third smashed her elbow as she raised her hands to protect her face. Fatally wounded, she tumbled out of the car on to the sidewalk. The killer then shot Jody in the thigh. She fell forward on to the car's horn which sounded and the killer ran away.

Donna's father, Mike Lauria, was taking the family's dog for a walk and was halfway down the stairs when he heard the shots. He ran the rest of the way. Jody was still conscious, though hysterical. In the ambulance, Mike Lauria begged his daughter not to die. It was too late. When Donna reached the hospital, she was pronounced DOA – dead on arrival. Jody was treated for hysteria, but nevertheless gave the police a good description of their assailant. He was a young white male, about 30 years old, clean shaven with dark curly hair. He was not a rejected boyfriend. In fact, Jody had never seen him before. The only other clue to his identity was a yellow car parked near Jody's which was gone by the time the police arrived. But New York is full of yellow cars.

The car in question actually belonged to David Berkowitz. In the days leading up to the murder, he had been looking for a job. But he had spent the nights, he said, 'Looking for a victim, waiting for a signal.' Demon voices inside him told him to kill. Even though the Devil was on his side, he was not sure that he could be successful.

'I never thought I could kill her,' he said of Donna Lauria. 'I just fired the gun, you know, at the car, at the windshield. I never knew she was shot.'

But the police were not looking for a madman driven by demons. They had another theory altogether. As the North Bronx, where the Laurias lived, was a predominantly Italian area, the police immediately suspected Mafia involvement. Perhaps a hit had gone wrong – a case of mistaken identity. However, the Mafia are usually scrupulous when it comes to contract killings. Women and children are out of bounds. Besides, ballistics tests showed that the murder weapon was a Charter Arms, five-round, .44 Bulldog revolver. It had a powerful recoil and was grossly inaccurate at distances of more than a few metres – hardly a hit-man's weapon. But still, it was no Saturday-night special. It is the weapon for a man who seriously wants to kill. A .44 Bulldog can blow a large hole in a door at close range.

The other side of the East River from the Bronx lies the borough of Queens. It is a comfortable middle-class area. Eighteen-year-old student Rosemary Keenan attended Queens College there. Twelve weeks after the murder of Donna Lauria, she went to a bar in Flushing, the area of Queens which was considered a 'posh' part of New York. There she met 20-year-old record salesman Carl Denaro who was enjoying his last few days of freedom before joining the Air Force. Rosemary and Carl left together in Rosemary's red Volkswagen. They were parked, talking, when a man crept up on them. He had a .44 Bulldog handgun tucked in his belt. He may have thought Carl, who was sitting in the passenger seat, was a woman because he had long brown hair. He pulled out his gun and fired five times through the passenger window. But his shooting was wildly inaccurate. Only one bullet found its mark. As Carl threw himself forward to protect himself from flying glass, the bullet clipped the back of his head, knocking away part of the skull. Carl Denaro was lucky – he didn't suffer any brain damage and after two months in hospital, he recovered completely. However, the metal plate in his head ended his career in the Air Force before it had begun.

On the evening of 27 November 1976, two schoolgirls, 16-year-old Donna DeMasi and her 18-year-old friend Joanne Lomino were sitting on the front porch of Joanne's home on 262nd Street in Queens. At the end of the conversation, they said goodnight and Joanne stood up and reached in her handbag for her front door keys. It was then that the two girls noticed a man walking down the other side of the road. He was acting rather suspiciously. When he saw them he suddenly changed direction. After crossing the street at the corner, he came over to them as if he was going to ask for directions.

'Say, can you tell me how to get to…?' he said, then he pulled a gun from his waistband and began firing.

The two girls fled toward the front door, Joanne frantically searching for her keys. The first bullet hit Joanne in the back. The second hit Donna in the neck. They stumbled into the bushes as the gunman loosed off the remaining three shots – all of which missed. He ran off down the street and was spotted by a neighbour, with the gun still in his hand.

The two wounded girls were rushed to Long Island Jewish Hospital, where Donna was found not to be badly injured. In three weeks, she made a full recovery. But Joanne was not so lucky. The bullet had smashed her spinal cord. She was paralysed from the waist down and would spend the rest of her life in a wheelchair. The neighbour who had spotted the gunman making his escape gave the police a description. One key feature he mentioned was the young man's dark curly hair. Despite the girls' claim that he had long fair hair, this tied the shooting of Donna DeMasi and Joanne Lomino to the man who had killed Donna Lauria and wounded Jody Valente.

On 29 January 1977, 30-year-old John Diel and his 26-year-old girlfriend, Christine Freund, went to see the film *Rocky* in Queens. Afterwards they went for dinner at the Wine Gallery in Austin Street, where they discussed their forthcoming engagement. Soon after midnight, the couple walked the several blocks to where their Pontiac Firebird was parked. It was cold outside and their breath fogged the windows. They were eager to get home but stopped for a moment and kissed. Then John turned the key in the ignition. But before he could pull away he heard the blast of gunfire. The passenger window shattered and Christine slumped forward, bleeding. She died a few hours later in St John's Hospital of bullet wounds to the right temple and the neck. She had never even seen her killer. But he had seen her – and so had the demons within him. Berkowitz later claimed that he had heard voices commanding him to 'get her, get her and kill her'. After firing three shots and realising that he had hit her, he felt calm again.

I satisfied the demon's lust

'The voices stopped,' he said. 'I satisfied the demon's lust.'

After the murder of Christine Freund, Berkowitz completely gave in to the impulse to kill. After all, he was getting his reward by all the publicity he was getting. 'I had finally convinced myself that I was good to do it, and that the public wanted me to kill,' Berkowitz said later.

Six weeks later, on 8 March 1977, Virginia Voskerichian, a 19-year-old Armenian student, left Columbia University in Manhattan after her day's study and set off home to Forest Hills, Queens. Around 7.30

p.m., she was nearing her home on Exeter Street. A young man was approaching her on the sidewalk and she, politely, stepped out of his way. But he pulled a gun and shoved it in her face. As he fired she raised her books in a vain attempt to protect herself. The bullet tore through them and entered through her upper lip, smashing out several teeth and lodging in her brain. Virginia collapsed in the bushes at the side of the street and died instantly. A witness saw a young man running away. This description was of an 18-year-old man, five feet eight inches tall, and there was no dark curly hair to be seen. The killer was wearing a ski mask.

Berkowitz was almost caught that day. Minutes after the murder of Virginia Voskerichian, the police put out a 'Code 44'. Two police officers were assigned to the south end of the Bronx with orders to stop all cars containing a single white man. Berkowitz drove up to the checkpoint with his .44 Bulldog loaded and lying in plain view on the passenger seat of his Ford Galaxie. He was third in line when the police called off the search and he could not believe his luck when he watched the officers walk away.

However, the New York Police Department was on his trail. Their ballistics lab ascertained that the bullet had come from a .44 Bulldog handgun. That, in turn, tied it to the murder of Donna Lauria and the shootings of Jody Valente, Carl Denaro, Donna DeMasi, Joanne Lomino and Christine Freund. However, apart from the mention of dark curly hair by Jody Valente and the neighbour in the DeMasi/Lomino case, the descriptions of the gunman varied so widely that no one in the NYPD had yet concluded that the four shootings were the job of a single individual.

On the afternoon of 10 March 1977, a press conference was held at One Police Plaza, a 13-storey red stone building that is New York's equivalent of London's New Scotland Yard. Police Commissioner Mike Codd stood with some trepidation before New York's hard-bitten crime reporters. As he read his carefully-prepared statement, he began to have an inkling that he was unleashing a wave of hysteria that would engulf the city. He started by saying that the murder of Donna Lauria, nine months before, was linked to the killing of Virginia Voskerichian, a mere two days ago. In both cases, the killer had used a .44 Bulldog revolver which had also been used in three other incidents. Worse, the killer chose his victims completely at random. Reporters pushed for other information. Commissioner Codd said that the police were looking for a Caucasian male, about six feet tall, medium build, 25 to 30 years old, with dark hair. Next day, the '.44 killer' made the headlines.

The man in charge of the investigation was Deputy Inspector Timothy J. Dowd. He had been one of New York's finest since 1940. By 1973, he had worked his way up to the rank of deputy inspector at a major metropolitan precinct, but the then commissioner, David Crawley, announced a get-tough programme. He said that Dowd and 14 other senior officers had been underperforming and demoted them. Dowd fought the case and a year later it was Crawley who found himself demoted. Michael Codd took over as police commissioner and Dowd was restored to his former rank. But even then it was not plain sailing. As a test, Dowd was put in charge of an investigation in Chinatown. He was to break a secret society called The Flying Dragon and it was generally thought that no westerner could penetrate the Chinese crime syndicates. However, in 1977, Dowd announced that the leader of The Flying Dragons had been arrested for the murder of the leader of the rival gang, The Ghost Shadows. Under Dowd was Chief of Detectives John Keenan who had a special reason for wanting to capture the .44 killer. His daughter was Rosemary Keenan, the girl in the car with Carl Denaro when he was shot in the head.

'I know he was aiming for her,' Keenan said. 'So let's just say I put a little more than I had to into this case.'

The police realised that their chances of catching a lone, seemingly motiveless killer on the streets of New York were remote. So they announced 'Operation Omega' and asked for the help of every New Yorker. Tip-offs jammed the police switchboards. Dowd and the Omega team followed up 250–300 leads a day. There was some speculation that the .44 killer could be the 'Westchester Dartman' who had wounded 23 women in Westchester County just north of the Bronx between February

1975 and May 1976. He prowled the area at night and fired inch-long darts at women through ground floor windows, wounding them in the head, neck or chest. He was never caught.

As the investigation got under way, Berkowitz took pity on the police. He decided he would give them a few clues to juggle with, so he wrote them a letter. It took him two days to complete. Then he had to deliver it. But dropping it in a mail box and letting the postal service handle it was too mundane.

Another young couple went to the cinema in New York on the night of 16 April 1977. They were 18-year-old Valentina Suriani and her boyfriend, 20-year-old Alexander Esau. After they had seen the film, they went on to a party. Around 3 a.m., they were parked in a borrowed Mercury Montego outside Valentina's apartment building in the North Bronx, only three blocks from where Donna Lauria had been killed. Valentina was sitting on Alexander's lap with her legs stretched out across the passenger seat and they were enjoying a prolonged series of goodnight kisses when bullets shattered the passenger window. Two hit Valentina's head, killing her instantly. Another two hit Alexander Esau in the top of the head as he dived across the seat towards the passenger door. He died two hours later.

When the police arrived, they found a white envelope in the middle of the road by the car. It was addressed to Captain Joe Borelli, Timothy Dowd's second-in-command. The letter was all in capitals and full of spelling mistakes. It appeared to be the work of a madman. The writer claimed that he had been ordered to kill by his father, who was a vampire. His father's name, the writer said, was Sam – hence the killer's macabre sobriquet 'Son of Sam'. In the letter, he professed to love the people of Queens, but said he intended to kill more of them – particularly the women, which he spelt as if it rhymed with 'demon'. The writer signed off with the words:

YOURS IN MURDER, MR. MONSTER

'I SAY GOODBYE AND GOODNIGHT. POLICE:
LET ME HAUNT YOU WITH THESE WORDS; I'LL BE BACK!
I'LL BE BACK! TO BE INTERPRETED AS – BANG BANG, BANG,

BANG, BANK, BANG – UGH!! YOURS IN MURDER, MR. MONSTER.'

By the time the letter reached the police labs, eight policemen had handled it. Only tiny traces of the writer's fingerprints remained. He appeared to have held the letter by the tips of his fingers and there was not enough of a print on the paper to identify the sender. Consequently, the police kept the existence of the letter secret. But they showed a copy to celebrated New York columnist Jimmy Breslin, who dropped hints about the letter in his column in the *New York Daily News*.

On 1 June 1977, Breslin himself received a letter. It had been posted two days before in Englewood, New Jersey, just over the George Washington Bridge from Manhattan. Although the *Daily News* was then the biggest selling newspaper in America – its offices on 42nd Street double as those of the *Daily Planet* in *Superman* films – it held back publication of the full letter for six days, instead reproducing it in four parts to give the public a taste of what was to come and to heighten anticipation: on 3 June 1977, they ran the front page headline: 'THE .44 CALIBER KILLER NEW NOTE: CAN'T STOP KILLING'. The next day, they ran: '.44 KILLER: I AM NOT ASLEEP'. By Sunday, they were running: 'BRESLIN TO .44 KILLER: GIVE UP! IT'S THE ONLY WAY OUT'. This edition sold out within an hour of going on sale. So the presses kept rolling. By the end of the day, the *Daily News* had sold 1,116,000 copies – a record that would be beaten only on the day Berkowitz was arrested. The editors assumed that interest had peaked and reproduced the letter in full in the Monday edition. Like the Zodiac Killer's letters, it was written all in capital letters and was as rambling and incoherent as the letter he had sent before to the police. It signed off:

'NOT KNOWING WHAT THE FUTURE HOLDS I SHALL SAY FAREWELL AND I WILL SEE YOU AT THE NEXT JOB, OR SHOULD I SAY YOU WILL SEE MY HANDIWORK AT THE NEXT JOB? REMEMBER MS. LAURIA. THANK YOU. IN THEIR BLOOD AND FROM THE GUTTER, "SAM'S CREATION" .44.'

Then there was a long postscript:

'HERE ARE SOME NAMES TO HELP YOU ALONG. FORWARD THEM TO THE INSPECTOR FOR USE BY THE NCIC: "THE DUKE OF DEATH". "THE WICKED KING WICKER", "THE TWENTY TWO DISCIPLES OF HELL", JOHN "WHEATIES" – RAPIST AND SUFFOCATER OF YOUNG GIRLS.

PS: J.B. PLEASE INFORM ALL THE DETECTIVES WORKING THE SLAYINGS TO REMAIN.'

At the police's request, this last page was withheld from publication. The reason they gave was that they wanted the NCIC – the National Crime Information Center – kept secret. But the .44 killer certainly knew about it. Perhaps the real reason was the satanic undertones in the list of pseudonyms he gave. The 'Wicked King Wicker' was presumed to be 'wicca'. The 'Twenty-Two Disciples of Hell' sounded like some satanic organisation. John 'Wheaties' was supposed to be a 'rapist and suffocater of young girls'. The police could find no trace of him. In fact, none of the names were much help to the Omega team or the NCIC. Nor were they any use to Jimmy Breslin who now began calling the .44 killer, the 'Son of Sam'.

Seventeen-year-old Bronx schoolgirl Judy Placido went to the same school as Valentina Suriani and had been to her funeral. Three weeks after the Breslin letter appeared, on 25 June, she celebrated her graduation from high school at a discotheque called Elephas in Queens. There she met a handsome young man called Salvatore Lupo, who worked in a petrol station. They hit it off immediately and went outside to a car for some privacy. As Salvatore slipped his arm around Judy's shoulders, they discussed the Son of Sam killings. At that moment, their lurid speculation turned into murderous reality. A .44 bullet smashed through the passenger window, passed through Salvatore's wrist and into Judy's neck. A second bullet hit her in the head, but miraculously failed to penetrate her skull. A third bullet entered her right shoulder. Terrified, Salvatore threw open the car door and ran back to the discotheque for help. But it was too late. The shooting was over and the attacker had fled. Although she had been hit three times, Judy was quite unaware that she had been shot. She was shocked to see in the rear-view mirror that her face was covered with blood. She too jumped out of the car and headed for the disco, but she only made it a few yards before she collapsed. Salvatore suffered a shattered wrist and cuts from the flying glass. And in hospital, it was found that Judy had unbelievably escaped without serious injury.

Nevertheless, the city was in panic. Takings at discotheques and restaurants – particularly in Queens – fell off, while newspaper circulations soared. Not only did they have the gory details of the latest shooting to relay, they could speculate about the next killing.

In the Son of Sam's letter to Jimmy Breslin, he had written: 'TELL ME JIM, WHAT WILL YOU HAVE FOR JULY TWENTY-NINTH?' That was the date of the first murder. Was he planning to celebrate the killing of Donna Lauria with another murder? New York's English-born Mayor Abraham Beame could not wait to find out. He was running for re-election. He quickly announced that even more officers were being seconded to the Omega investigation. Overnight it became the largest single operation in the history of the New York Police Department. Two hundred men were on the case. They recruited from precincts in every borough of the city. The investigation cost more than $90,000 a day to run. Volunteers like Donna Lauria's father, Mike, manned special Son of Sam patrols and the number of calls to Omega's hotline, which started at 250 a day, peaked at 5,000 a day. A team of psychiatrists tried to come up with some sort of profile of the killer. The best they could come up with was that he was 'neurotic, schizophrenic and paranoid'. This description was duly released by the police. It did not help anyone to identify the gunman.

Fortunately, 29 July passed without incident. But two days later, with a sense of relief, two sisters from Brooklyn, 15-year-old Ricki Moskowitz and 20-year-old Stacy, decided to go out. In a Brooklyn restaurant, they were approached by a handsome young man who introduced himself as Bobby Violante. The next day, Bobby and Stacy went to see the film *New York, New York*. Afterwards, they went to dinner, then headed off to a quiet place where they could be alone. They drove to a secluded spot on Shore Parkway near Coney Island, South Brooklyn, which was used as an urban lovers' lane. They felt safe enough there. So far there had been no Son-of-Sam killings in the borough of Brooklyn and the nearest shooting had taken place 22 miles away in Queens. What they did not know was that, a week before, a man claiming to be the Son of Sam had phoned the Coney Island Precinct and said that he would strike next in that area. Extra patrol cars were assigned to Brooklyn and Coney Island. Shore Parkway was being patrolled regularly.

Bobby Violante and Stacy Moskowitz pulled up under a street lamp, the only available parking spot. There was a full moon that night. It was not dark enough for what they had in mind, so the two of them went for a walk in the park nearby. They walked over a bridge and spent a few minutes playing on the swings. Near the public toilets they noticed a man in jeans, who they described as a 'hippy type', leaning against a wall. He was not there when they walked back to the car. Back in the car, they kissed. Stacy suggested that they move on, but Bobby wanted one more kiss. It was a mistake. While they were embracing, Bobby Violante took two bullets in the face, blinding him and exploding his eardrums. He could neither see nor hear, but he felt Stacy jerk violently in his arms, then collapse forward. He feared she was dead. Bobby threw himself against the car horn, fumbled at the car door, cried for help, then collapsed on the pavement.

In the car in front, Tommy Zaino had seen the shooting in his rear-view mirror. He had watched as a man approached the car from behind and pull out a gun. From a crouching position, he had fired four shots through the open passenger window. When his girlfriend, Debbie Crescendo, heard the shooting, she said 'What's that?'

'Get down,' he said. 'I think it's the Son of Sam.'

Zaino watched as the gunman ran towards the park. He looked at his watch. It was exactly 2.35 a.m. A patrol car was just five blocks away at the time.

Stacy Moskowitz was still conscious when the ambulance arrived. One bullet had grazed her scalp, but the other had lodged in the back of her brain. She died 38 hours later. Bobby Violante survived, but his sight could not be restored.

Tommy Zaino gave a good description of the killer. He was stocky with stringy, fair hair. This matched the description given by Donna DeMasi and Joanne Lomino, but not the one of the dark curly-haired man described by Jody Valente and the neighbour in the DeMasi/ Lomino case. The police wondered whether he was wearing a wig. A beautician and her boyfriend were seated by the entrance to the park when they heard the shots. They saw a man wearing a denim jacket and what they took to be a cheap nylon wig. He jumped into a light-coloured car and drove off, as if he had just robbed a bank. A young girl on a bicycle identified the car as a yellow Volkswagen. A nurse who looked out of the window when she heard the shots, also said that she had seen a yellow VW. It almost collided with another car at the first intersection and the driver was so incensed that he gave chase, only to lose the car after a couple of blocks. The yellow VW's driver, he said, had stringy brown hair.

But an even more vital witness took a little longer to come forward. She was Mrs Cacilia Davis, a 49-year-old widow, who had been out with a male friend. They had returned to her apartment, two blocks from the park, at around 2 a.m. They sat and talked for a few minutes but, as they had been forced to double park, they kept an eye open for other cars. A little way ahead, Mrs Davis saw a police car and two patrolmen writing out parking tickets. Some way behind was a yellow Ford Galaxie. It was parked by a fire hydrant and a few minutes before an officer from the patrol car had given it a ticket. A young man with dark hair walked up to the Galaxie and irritably pulled the parking ticket from the windscreen.

Mrs Davis invited her friend in for coffee. He declined, saying that it was 2.20 a.m. already. At that moment, the police car pulled off. So did the Galaxie, but it could not get past Mrs Davis' friend's car. The man in the Galaxie impatiently honked the horn. Mrs Davis hurriedly got out and her friend pulled off. The Galaxie followed, passing him quickly and speeding after the police car. Minutes later, Mrs Davis went out to take her dog for a walk in the park. She noticed Tommy Zaino's car, Bobby Violante's car and a VW van. On her way home, she saw a man with dark hair and a blue denim jacket striding across the road from the cars. He glared at her and he was walking with his right arm stiff, as if something was concealed up his sleeve. He also looked rather like the man with the Ford Galaxie she had seen earlier. Mrs Davis did not come forward with this information immediately though. She realised that if the man she had seen was the Son of Sam, she was in danger. He could easily identify her and he knew where she lived. Two days after the shooting, Mrs Davis told two close friends what she had seen. They realised that she might have a vital clue and urged her to call the police. Eventually, her friends called the police on her behalf. Detective Joseph Strano visited her and took her statement. It caused hardly a ripple. Tommy Zaino, the best witness to the shooting, had seen a man with fair hair, not dark. And the driver of the Ford Galaxie had left the scene of the crime before the shooting.

But Mrs Davis now felt that she had risked her life to come forward and would not be ignored. She threatened to go, anonymously, to the newspapers with her story. To humour her, Detective Strano interviewed her again, bringing along a police artist to make a sketch of the man. He also took her on a shopping expedition to see if she could pick out a similar denim jacket. But still nothing got done. The problem with her story was that the local police had not issued any parking tickets in that area that night. But the police cars patrolling the area had been seconded in from other boroughs. It was ten days before four missing tickets turned up. Three of the cars were quickly eliminated. The fourth, a yellow Galaxie, number 561-XLB, belonged to a David Berkowitz of 35 Pine Street, Yonkers, a suburban area just north of the Bronx. Detective James Justus called Yonkers police headquarters. Switchboard operator Wheat Carr answered. Justus said that he was working on the Son-of-Sam case and that he was checking on David Berkowitz. The woman shouted, 'Oh, no.'

Not only did she know David Berkowitz, she had suspected that he was the Son of Sam for some time.

It had begun the previous year when her father began to receive anonymous letters complaining about his dog. In October, a petrol bomb had been thrown through the window of the Carr's house at

316 Warburton Avenue, Yonkers. A neighbour had also been receiving anonymous letters and abusive phone calls and on Christmas Eve 1976, someone had fired a number of shots through their window and killed their Alsatian. Then on 27 April 1977, someone entered the Carr's backyard and shot their black labrador, Harvey. On 10 June 1977, Wheat's father Sam Carr had received a phone call from a man named Jack Cassaras who lived in New Rochelle, out on Long Island Sound. Mr Cassaras wanted to know why Mr Carr had sent him a get well card. The card said that Mr Cassaras had fallen off a roof but he had never even been on a roof. Mr Carr had no explanation and invited Mr Cassaras over to discuss the matter. The drive took about twenty minutes. Sam Carr examined the card. Strangely, it had a picture of an Alsatian on it and Mr Carr told Cassaras about the bizarre things that had been happening. Mr Cassaras drove home even more puzzled, but his son thought that he had the answer. The year before, the Cassaras family had rented out a room above their garage to a David Berkowitz. He had complained about the Cassarases' Alsatian. After a few weeks, he had left suddenly without collecting the deposit of $200. When Mrs Cassaras looked David Berkowitz up in the telephone directory, she found that he now lived at 35 Pine Street, Yonkers. She rang Sam Carr and asked him whether Pine Street was near them. It was right around the corner. Mr Carr was convinced that David Berkowitz was responsible for the harassment they had suffered and went to the police. However, the police explained that they could take the matter no further without more concrete evidence.

Another of Berkowitz's neighbours, Craig Glassman, had also been receiving abusive letters. He lived in the apartment underneath Berkowitz. But he was a police officer and when, a week after the Moskowitz murder, rubbish was piled against Glassman's front door and set on fire, he reported it. That was 6 August 1977. He also showed detectives two anonymous letters he had received. They accused Glassman of being a spy planted there by Sam Carr. Glassman and the Carrs were part of a black magic sect out to get him, the author alleged. The detective who examined the letters recognised the handwriting. It belonged to another man he was investigating – David Berkowitz.

However, Berkowitz was not the only suspect in the Son-of-Sam slayings. New York has a rich supply of paranoid schizophrenics. Besides, Berkowitz did not fit the description given by Tommy Zaino. Nor did he drive a yellow VW. So it was not until 10 August 1977 that Omega detectives John Longo and Ed Zigo went to Yonkers to check Berkowitz out. Zigo spotted Berkowitz's Ford Galaxie parked outside the apartment block in Pine Street. There was a bag on the back seat with a rifle butt protruding from it. In New York, possessing a rifle did not even require

I am Sam a licence. Nevertheless, Zigo forced open the car. Inside he found another, more formidable weapon, a Commando Mark III semi-automatic. Then in the glove compartment, he found a letter addressed to the head of Operation Omega, Deputy Inspector Timothy Dowd. It said that the next shooting would be in Long Island. Detective Zigo phoned into Operation Omega and told Sergeant James Shea, 'I think we've got him.'

Police from all over the city were brought in. They staked out the car for six hours until Berkowitz turned up. He was a stocky man with a round cherubic face and dark hair. When he got into the driver's seat, he found himself looking down the barrel of a police revolver.

'Freeze!' yelled Detective William Gardella. 'Police!'

Berkowitz simply smiled.

Detective John Falotico opened the passenger door, held his .38 to Berkowitz's head and told him to get out. When he put his hands on the roof, Falotico asked, 'Who are you?' Berkowitz answered, 'I am Sam.'

At One Police Plaza, Berkowitz confessed to the shootings and the anonymous letters. He also admitted that his crime spree had begun on Christmas Eve 1975. About seven o'clock he had driven to the Co-op City in the Bronx, where his adoptive father lived. He saw a young Hispanic woman leaving a store and followed her. He pulled a knife and stabbed her in the back. She did not realise what had happened, turned, screamed and grabbed his wrist. He ran away. But on his way home, he followed 15-year-old Michelle Forman and stabbed her in the back and head. She fell screaming on the sidewalk. Again Berkowitz fled. Somehow she managed to stagger to the apartment block where her parents lived. They rushed her to hospital where they found that she had a collapsed lung. Her other injuries were superficial and she only spent a week in hospital. His first victim did not even report the attack and was never identified. These early attacks convinced Berkowitz that he needed a gun. A friend called Billy Dan Parka bought him a .44 Bulldog revolver in Houston, Texas, for $130. Under interrogation, Berkowitz explained that he had been ordered to commit the murders by Sam Carr, via Carr's demon dog Harvey. Other demon voices accompanied him when he was stalking his victims. Berkowitz was so forthcoming that his complete confession took only half an hour.

Further enquiries revealed that Richard David Berkowitz had been an illegitimate child who had been given up for adoption as a baby. His natural mother, Betty Broder, was Jewish. At 19, she married Tony Falco, an Italian-American. He left her for another woman six years later. She began an affair with real estate agent Joseph Kleinman, a married man, in 1947. She got pregnant by him, but when she told him that she was going to have a child, he said she had better get rid of it, if she wanted to go on seeing him. The child was born on 1 June 1953 and was adopted immediately by a Jewish couple, Pearl and Nathan Berkowitz, who were unable to have children of their own. They named him David. But in 1967, when David was just 14, Pearl Berkowitz succumbed to cancer. He was deeply upset at this new loss.

Two years later, Nathan decided to move to Co-op City in the Bronx, a middle-class suburb. But the area was deteriorating and gangs of youths soon began terrorising the neighbourhood. David's school grades plunged and he seemed to lose any sense of direction. He was shy and found himself a victim of bullying, though others saw him as spoilt and something of a bully himself. He was big for his age, strong and an excellent baseball player. But he liked to play with kids younger than himself. His biggest problem was with girls. One friend remembers Berkowitz asking him if he wanted to join the 'girl-haters club'. He only ever dated one girl in Co-op City, Iris Gerhardt. She liked his warm and obliging nature, but the relationship was never consummated. While Berkowitz remained chaste, almost everyone else seemed not to be and this provided his motive.

'After a while, at Co-op City, there wasn't one girl who was a virgin,' he said resentfully.

In prison, Berkowitz wrote: 'I must slay women for revenge purposes to get back at them for all the suffering they caused me.'

His friends also started smoking marijuana but, again, Berkowitz was too inhibited to join in.

Things got worse in 1971 when his father remarried. Berkowitz resented his stepmother and stepsister, and decided to join the army. But that did not last long. Home again in 1974, Berkowitz had rejected Judaism and become a Baptist. Nathan Berkowitz remembers his son standing in front of the mirror beating his head with his fists. Things became so uncomfortable in the Berkowitz household that David moved out to take a drab one-room apartment at 2151 Barnes Avenue in the Bronx. By this time Nathan became convinced that his son needed psychiatric help. But Nathan and his new family were moving to Florida and nothing was done. With his father gone, another door closed for Berkowitz.

He had known from the age of seven that he had been adopted. Isolated, he tried to trace his real family. It took a year. Through the Bureau of Records, he discovered that his real name was Richard Falco and he came from Brooklyn. Using an old telephone directory, he managed to trace his mother and an elder sister. He dropped a card in his mother's mailbox and, a few days later, she called him. The reunion was emotional. He also met his 37-year-old sister and became a regular visitor to the house where she lived with her husband and children. At last, he had found a family and, at last, Berkowitz was happy. Or so it seemed.

In the first half of 1976, his visits to his real mother and sister became increasingly rare. He complained of headaches. In February, he moved into the room above the Cassarases' garage out in New Rochelle. Two months later, he moved suddenly to Pine Street, Yonkers. And in July, he killed Donna Lauria.

After a year-long killing spree the police at last had Berkowitz under lock and key. He pleaded guilty to all six charges of murder and was sentenced to 365 years in prison. One of the Omega team, Sergeant Joseph Coffey, who had conducted the initial interrogation, said: 'I feel sorry for him. The man is a fucking vegetable.'

However, not everyone was satisfied. Investigative journalist Maury Terry spotted a number of inconsistencies in Berkowitz's story. Berkowitz claimed that he had acted alone. But he simply could not have been responsible for the Violante-Moskowitz shooting if Tommy Zaino's description was accurate. Even if he had been wearing a wig, he was not tall enough. And if he was the man Mrs Cacilia Davis had seen outside her apartment building, only minutes before the shootings, he could not have got to Violante's car on Shore Parkway in time. Terry interviewed Zaino and Davis. Both confirmed their original accounts. When Davis went through her story again, Terry realised that it was unlikely that, if Berkowitz had been carrying a .44 Bulldog revolver already connected to a number of murders, he would have sped off after a police car, honking his horn late at night. Maybe, as Berkowitz said, 'The demons were protecting me, I had nothing to fear from the police.' Terry tracked down the witnesses who said that they had seen a fair-haired man in a yellow VW. All of them stuck to their stories. They could have been mistaken. But their descriptions seemed to match those given by the two schoolgirls who had been shot in Queens. Terry concluded that Berkowitz had a fair-haired accomplice.

Another inconsistency was Berkowitz's pseudonym 'Son of Sam'. His real father's name was Tony, and his adoptive father's name was Nathan. The only Sam in the case was Sam Carr, who Berkowitz claimed had given him orders to kill via the demon dog Harvey. However, although the Carr house was visible from Berkowitz's sixth floor apartment, they had never met. Carr confirmed that the first time he had even heard Berkowitz's name was when Mrs Cassaras called and told him about their former lodger. So why was Berkowitz so obsessed with Carr? Sam Carr did, in fact, have two sons, John and Michael. Both of them hated their father. Carr's daughter was called Wheat and John Carr was nicknamed 'Wheaties'. Then Terry remembered 'John "Wheaties", rapist and suffocater of young girls' in the Son of Sam's letter to Jimmy Breslin. John 'Wheaties' Carr was tall, with long stringy fair hair. While Terry tried to trace John Carr, he became interested in some of the Satanic clues in the Breslin letter. He was also concerned about Berkowitz's seeming obsession with dogs. He did discover that in Walden, New York, about an hour's drive from Yonkers, 85 Dobermans and Alsatians had been found skinned during the year of the Son-of-Sam killings. More dead dogs had been found in a wooded area of Untermeyer Park in Yonkers. A local teenager said that devil-worshippers held ceremonies there. Could Berkowitz have been involved in a satanic cult? The police dismissed the idea.

In October 1978, when Terry eventually traced John Carr, it was too late to ask him about any of this. He had been shot dead in the small town of Minot, North Dakota. His body had been found in the bedroom of his girlfriend Linda O'Connor, with a bullet through the roof of the mouth and rifle beside the body. The coroner's verdict was suicide, but the police believed he had been murdered.

John Carr had been born in Yonkers, New York, on 12 October 1946 – he shared a birthday with the self-styled 'wickedest man in the world' the Satanist Aleister Crowley. After leaving Catholic school, Carr joined the US Air Force. He was stationed in Korea and served for 12 years. In 1972, he returned to the US and was stationed in Minot, North Dakota. He was discharged in 1976, allegedly for drug addiction. In 1976 and 1977, he went to hospital three times with overdoses and had a reputation as a drug dealer and a heavy drinker. He was in New York for probably five of the eight Son-of-Sam attacks, including the shootings of Donna DeMasi and Joanne Lomino, and he closely resembled the descriptions they had given.

In late January 1978, Carr drove the 1,500 miles from Minot to New York, saying he was going to stay for a long time. But within two weeks, he called his girlfriend and told her that the police were after him. On 14 February, he flew back to Minot. He rented a post office box, opened a bank account and enquired about the continued payment of a disability allowance he received for a service injury, hardly the actions of a man contemplating suicide. Two days later he was dead.

Mysteriously, on the skirting board by the body, the letters 'S.S.N.Y.C.' had been scrawled in blood. A man who has blown the top of his head off with a rifle bullet seldom has time to write things in his own blood. Terry deduced that Carr had been beaten to the ground by his assailants, then his killer, or killers, had gone to search for his gun, leaving Carr time to write his message before he was killed. The letters 'S.S.N.Y.C.', Terry concluded, stood for 'Son of Sam, New York City'. Carr also had the figures '666' written in blood on his hand. 666 was the number of the Beast in the Book of Revelations and was used as a Satanic pseudonym by Aleister Crowley. The police in Minot had also discovered that Carr was connected with a number of local occult groups and his girlfriend said that when Carr had seen news of Berkowitz's arrest for the Son-of-Sam shootings on the TV, he had said, 'Oh shit'.

Up to this point Terry had been dismissed as a conspiracy theorist. But John Santucci, the District Attorney of Queens, began to believe there was something to Terry's investigation. He re-opened the case. It was soon discovered that, far from being the classic psychotic loner, Berkowitz had a wide circle of friends. Chief among them was John 'Wheaties' Carr's brother Michael. In 1975, the year before the killings started, when Berkowitz was living in his drab one-room apartment in Barnes Avenue, he met Michael, a young drug addict who had been hanging about outside the apartment block. He invited Berkowitz to a party. The guests included John Carr and other members of The Twenty-Two Disciples of Hell, the Satanic group Berkowitz referred to in his letter to Breslin. In due course, Berkowitz moved to Yonkers, to within 200 yards of Sam Carr's house where Michael Carr then lived. Michael Carr had since moved out and, by the time he could be traced, he, too, was dead. In the early hours of 4 October 1979, Michael Carr's car ran into a street lamp at 75 miles an hour as he drove towards Manhattan. There were no skid marks and his sister, Wheat, was convinced that he had been forced off the road or that one of his tyres had been shot out.

The most unexpected witness in Santucci's new investigation was Berkowitz himself. In February 1979, he had called a press conference and announced that his story about Sam Carr's dog and demon voices had been concocted in the hope that he would be able to enter a plea of insanity. But court-appointed psychiatrists had declared him sane. Now, a year after being incarcerated in Attica Correctional Facility, he said that he had bought his .44 knowing exactly what he intended to do. He wanted to kill women because of his disappointments with sex.

In prison, Berkowitz had become a prolific letter writer. In them, he described how he had stage dressed his apartment to back his insanity plea. A week before his arrest, he had stripped his apartment of an expensive Japanese stereo system, a dinner service, a bureau, sofa and bed. These had been loaded into a van and dumped in front of a Salvation Army warehouse in Mount Vernon. Berkowitz specified the location of the garage he had rented the van from, the cost of the rental and the location of the warehouse – all of which checked out. He had also vandalised his apartment, knocking a hole in a wall so violently that it had cracked the plaster in a neighbour's flat. He had also covered the walls with ravings. This was all true. In a letter to a priest in California, Berkowitz wrote:

'I really don't know how to begin this letter, but at one time I was a member of an occult group. Being sworn to secrecy or face death, I cannot reveal the name of this group, nor do I wish to. The group contained a mixture of Satanic practices which included the teachings of Aleister Crowley and Eliphaz Levi. It was (and still is) blood orientated, and I am certain you know what I mean. The Coven's doctrines are a blend of ancient Druidism, the teachings of the Secret Order of the Golden Dawn, Black Magick, and a host of other unlawful and obnoxious practices. These people will stop at nothing, including murder. They had no fear of man-made laws or the Ten Commandments.'

None of the other members of The Twenty-Two Disciples of Hell were found. But the postman who delivered letters to the Pine Street district of Yonkers killed himself. He was a young married man named Andrew Dupay. In the month before Berkowitz was arrested, he was noticeably worried. Then on 20 September 1977, five weeks after

Berkowitz's arrest, he and his wife were bathing their two baby daughters when Dupay excused himself, went down to the basement and blew his head off with a shotgun. A neighbour said that Dupay had said that he had learned something on his rounds that had frightened him. One of Terry's informants said that Dupay knew both Carr and Berkowitz and had killed himself because threats had been made against his family.

Berkowitz made other disturbing references in his letters. Shortly after the Son-of-Sam shootings had begun, he applied for a job in a dog pound. The pay was not good, but Berkowitz said that 'there was another way in which I was getting paid. Somebody needed dogs. I guess you understand what I'm trying to say.' Terry's investigation again proved that Berkowitz was telling the truth.

Then Berkowitz dropped a bombshell. He ripped a chapter out of a standard work on Satanism and witchcraft. It concerned the satanic practices of Charles Manson and his Family. Then he wrote a note in the margin, saying: 'Call the Santa Clara Sheriff's office. Please ask the sheriffs what happened to Arlis Perry.' He went on to say that Perry had been 'hunted, stalked and slain. Followed to California. Stanford Univ'.

Stanford University is in Santa Clara County. A 19-year-old student called Arlis Perry was horribly murdered in the church in Stanford University at midnight on October 1974. She had only been in California for a few weeks. Her body was naked from the waist down. Her legs were spread and a 30-inch altar candle had been rammed into her vagina. Her arms were crossed over her chest and another candle was between her breasts. Her jeans lay inverted over her legs. She had been beaten, strangled and stabbed behind the ear with an ice pick. Little of this was made public until 1988, but Berkowitz knew details about the murder that had been withheld. He even cut out a picture from the paper that he said resembled Arlis Perry. The only picture of her that appeared in the newspapers showed how she looked in her school days. The picture that Berkowitz selected looked much more like Arlis Perry the night she died. At the very least, he had seen a picture of the murder, performed, Terry maintains, by the California satanic group associated with Charles

Manson. Berkowitz said that Arlis Perry had once been a member of the group but had tried to leave.

Terry also noted that some of the Son-of-Sam killings had been performed with a ruthless efficiency. Others were inept and bungled. Terry concluded that Berkowitz had only committed three of the Son-of-Sam killings – those of Donna Lauria, Valentina Suriani and Alexander Esau. Donna Lauria had been killed, Terry says, because she knew about the coven. Christine Freund died because she had offended one of the members. Terry believes that the killer in the balaclava was actually a woman, who was a member of the coven. According to Terry, Stacy Moskowitz was killed by John Carr and Berkowitz was there because the killing was being filmed as a 'snuff movie'. That is why the killer had picked out the car under the street lamp. Tommy Zaino and his girlfriend Debbie Crescendo were lucky. They had been parked under the street lamp but had moved to a darker spot just before Stacy Moskowitz and Bobby Violante drove up.

On 10 July 1979, Berkowitz was slashed with a razor by another inmate in the cell-block reserved for high risk prisoners. The cut ran from the left-hand side of his throat to the back of his neck. It needed 56 stitches and nearly killed him. He would not say who had attacked him. He later said that it was an attempt by a Satanic group to make him live up to his vow of silence. Maury Terry claimed that the leader of satanic cult was Roy Alexander Radin, a tycoon who earned his money in show business. He moved to California in 1982. But by the time Terry had tracked him down, yet again, it was too late. Radin had been murdered on Friday, 13 May 1983. His body was found dumped in Death Valley – Charles Manson's old stamping ground. A defaced bible was found nearby.

Berkowitz became a born-again Christian in 1987 and works as a chaplain in prison. In March 2002, he wrote to New York governor George Pataki asking that his parole hearing be canceled, stating he didn't want to be released. In June 2004, he was denied parole again, even though he had made it clear that he would refuse it.

– Chapter 11 –

Dennis Nilsen

Dennis Nilsen

NATIONALITY: SCOTTISH

BORN: 1945

NUMBER OF VICTIMS: 6 KILLED

FAVOURED METHOD OF KILLING: STRANGULATION

REIGN OF TERROR: 1978–83

MOTIVE: KEPT THE BODIES OF HIS VICTIMS

IN THE END: FEELS NO REMORSE FOR HIS VICTIMS OR THEIR FAMILIES

Dennis Nilsen was born in Fraserburgh, a small town on the bleak north-east coast of Scotland, on 23 November 1945. His father was a Norwegian soldier who had escaped to Scotland after the German invasion of his homeland in 1940 and married Betty Whyte, a local girl, in 1942. The marriage did not work out and Betty continued to live with her parents. A few years later, the marriage ended in divorce.

Dennis grew up with his mother, elder brother and younger sister, but the strongest influence on his young life were his stern and pious grandparents. Their Christian faith was so strict that they banned alcohol from the house, and the radio and the cinema were considered instruments of the Devil. Nilsen's grandmother would not even cook on the Lord's day and their Sunday dinner had to be prepared the day before.

As a boy Dennis Nilsen was sullen and intensely withdrawn. The only person who could penetrate his private world was his grandfather,

Andrew Whyte. A fisherman, he was Nilsen's hero. He would regale the little boy with tales of the sea and his ancestors lost beneath its churning waves.

When Andrew Whyte died of a heart attack at sea in 1951, he was brought home and laid out on the dining room table. Dennis was invited to come and see his granddad's body. At the age of six, he got his first glimpse of a corpse. From that moment, the images of death and love fused in his mind.

He left school at 15 and joined the army. After basic training he was sent to the catering corps. There he was taught how to sharpen knives – and how to dissect a carcass. During his life in the army, Nilsen only had one close friend, who he would persuade to pose for photographs, sprawled on the ground as if he had just been killed in battle.

One night in Aden, Nilsen was drunk and fell asleep in the back of a cab. When he awoke he found himself naked, locked in the boot. When the Arab cab driver returned, Nilsen played dead. Then as the driver man-handled him out of the boot, Nilsen grabbed a jack handle and beat him around the head. Nilsen never knew whether he had killed the man or not. But the incident had a profound effect on him. Afterwards he had nightmares of being raped, tortured and mutilated.

After 11 years in the army, Nilsen left and joined the police force. His training included a mortuary visit, where recently qualified constables were initiated in the gruesome habit of viewing the dead. But Nilsen was not repelled. He found the partially dissected corpses fascinating.

Nilsen did well in the police, but his private life was gradually disintegrating. Death became an obsession. He would pretend to be a corpse himself, masturbating in front of a mirror with blue paint smeared on his lips and his skin whitened with talcum powder.

Since his teens, he had been aware of his attraction towards other men, but in the army and in the police force he had somehow managed to repress it.

Eleven months after he joined the police, he was on the beat when he caught two men committing an act of gross indecency in a parked car.

Aware of his own inclinations, he could not bring himself to arrest them and he decided to resign.

He went to work interviewing applicants at the Jobcentre in London's Charing Cross Road. There he became branch secretary of the civil service union and developed increasingly radical political views. Nevertheless his work was good enough to earn him promotion to executive officer at the Jobcentre in Kentish Town, north London.

Despite his professional progress, Nilsen was lonely and yearned for a lasting relationship. In 1975, he met a young man called David Gallichen outside a pub. They moved into a flat at 195 Melrose Avenue together, with a cat and a dog called Bleep. Gallichen, or Twinkle as Nilsen called him, stayed at home and decorated the flat while Nilsen went to work. They made home films together and spent a lot of time drinking and talking. But the relationship was not destined to last. Gallichen moved out in 1977 and Nilsen was plunged back into a life of loneliness.

On New Year's Eve 1978, Nilsen met a teenage Irish boy in a pub and invited him back to Melrose Avenue. They were too drunk to have sex. When Nilsen woke in the morning, the boy was lying fast asleep beside him. He was afraid that when the boy woke up he would leave – and Nilsen wanted him to stay.

Their clothes were thrown together in a heap on the floor. Nilsen lent over and grabbed his tie. Then he put the tie around the boy's neck and pulled. The boy woke immediately and began to struggle. They rolled onto the floor, but Nilsen kept pulling on the tie.

After about a minute, the boy's body went limp but he was still breathing. Nilsen went to the kitchen and filled a bucket with water. He brought the bucket back and held the boy's head under water until he drowned. Now he had to stay.

Nilsen carried the dead boy into the bathroom and gave him a bath. He dried the corpse lovingly, then dressed it in clean socks and underpants. For a while, he just lay in bed holding the dead boy, then he put him on the floor and he went to sleep.

The following day, he planned to hide the body under the floor, but *rigor mortis* had stiffened the joints, making it hard to handle. So he left the body out while he went to work. After a few days, when the corpse had loosened up, Nilsen undressed it again and washed it. This time he masturbated beside it and found he could not stop playing with it and admiring it.

Nilsen expected to be arrested at any moment, even while he played with the corpse. But no one came. It seemed no one had missed the dead boy. After a week living happily with the corpse, Nilsen hid it under the floorboards. Seven months later he cut the body up and burnt it in the garden.

Nilsen's unexpected experience of murder frightened him. He was determined it would not happen again and decided to give up drinking. But Nilsen was lonely. He liked to go to pubs to meet people and talk to them. Soon he slipped off the wagon.

Nearly a year later, on 3 December 1979, Nilsen met Kenneth Ockenden, a Canadian tourist, in a pub in Soho. Nilsen had taken leave from work that afternoon and took Ockenden on a sight-seeing tour of London. Ockenden agreed to go back to Nilsen's flat for something to eat. After a visit to the off-licence, they sat in front of the television eating ham, eggs and chips and drinking beer, whisky and rum.

As the evening wore on, disturbing feelings began to grow inside Nilsen. He liked Ockenden, but realised that he would soon be leaving and going back to Canada. A feeling of desolation crept over him. It was the same feeling he had had when he killed the Irish boy.

Late that night, when they were both very drunk, Ockenden was listening to music through earphones. Nilsen put the flex of the earphones around Ockenden's neck and dragged him struggling across the floor. When he was dead, Nilsen took the earphones off and put them on himself. He poured himself another drink and listened to records.

In the early hours, he stripped the corpse and carried it over his shoulder into the bathroom, where he washed it. When the body was clean and dry, he put it on the bed and went to sleep next to it.

In the morning, he put the body in a cupboard and went to work. That evening, he took the body out and dressed it in clean socks, underpants and vest. He took some photographs of it, then lay it next to him on the bed. For the next two weeks, Nilsen would watch TV in the evening with Ockenden's body propped up in an armchair next to him. Last thing at night, he would undress it, wrap it in the curtains and place the body under the floorboards.

As Ockenden had gone missing from a hotel, his disappearance made the news for a few days. Again Nilsen was convinced that he was about to be arrested at any moment. Several people in the pub, on the bus, at the sights they had visited and even in the local off-licence had seen them together. But still there was no knock on the door. From then on Nilsen felt that he could pursue his murderous hobby unfettered.

Although plenty of people visited the flat in Melrose Avenue and emerged alive, Nilsen now began to deliberately seek out victims. He would go to pubs where lonely young homosexuals hung out. He would buy them drinks, offer advice and invite them back to his flat for something to eat. Many accepted.

One of them was Martin Duffey. After a disturbed childhood, he ran away from home and ended up in London, sleeping in railway stations. He went back to Nilsen's flat and, after two cans of beer, crawled into bed. When he was asleep, Nilsen strangled him. While he was still barely alive, Nilsen dragged his unconscious body into the kitchen, filled the sink with water and held his head under for four minutes.

Nilsen then went through the standard procedure of stripping and bathing the corpse, then he took it to bed. He talked to it, complimenting Duffey on his body. He kissed it all over and masturbated over it. Nilsen kept the body in a cupboard for a few days. When it started to swell up, he put it under the floorboards.

Twenty-seven-year old Billy Sutherland died because he was a nuisance. Nilsen didn't fancy him, but after meeting him on a pub crawl Sutherland followed him home. Nilsen vaguely remembered strangling him. There was certainly a dead body in the flat in the morning.

Nilsen did not even know some of his victims by name. He was not much interested in them – only their bodies, their dead bodies. The murder routine was always much the same. That part was mechanical.

But once they were dead, they really turned him on. Touching the corpse would give him an erection.

Nilsen would never think of his victims' bodies lying around his flat while he was out at work. But in the evening when he got home, he could not help playing with them. He was thrilled to own their beautiful bodies and was fascinated by the mystery of death. He would hold the corpse in a passionate embrace and talk to it, and when he was finished with it he would stuff it back under the floorboards.

Some of his murders were terrifyingly casual. Nilsen found one victim, 24-year-old Malcolm Barlow, collapsed on the pavement in Melrose Avenue. Barlow was an epileptic and said that the pills he was taking made his legs give way. Nilsen carried him home and called an ambulance. When he was released from hospital the next day, Barlow returned to Nilsen's flat where Nilsen prepared a meal. Barlow began drinking, even though Nilsen warned him not to mix alcohol with the new pills he had been prescribed. When Barlow collapsed, Nilsen could not be bothered to call the ambulance again and strangled him, then carried on drinking until bedtime. It was full of corpses under the floorboards, so the next morning Nilsen stuffed Barlow's body in the cupboard under the sink. Now that he had completely run out of storage space, Nilsen decided it was time to move.

There were six corpses under the floor, and several others had been dissected and stored in suitcases. After a stiff drink, Nilsen pulled up the floorboards and began cutting up the corpses. He put the internal organs in plastic bags, emptying them out in the garden. Birds and rats did the rest. The other body parts were wrapped in carpet and put on a bonfire in the garden. A car tyre was put on top to disguise the smell.

At the end of 1981 Nilsen moved to a small attic flat at 23 Cranley Gardens. This was a deliberate attempt to stop his murderous career. He could not kill people, he thought, if he had no floorboards to hide them under and no garden to burn them in. He had several casual encounters at his new flat, picking men up at night and letting them go in the morning, unmolested. This made him elated. He thought he had finally broken the cycle.

But then John Howlett, or Guardsman John as Nilsen called him, came back to Cranley Gardens with him and Nilsen could not help himself. He strangled Howlett with a strap and drowned him. A few days later, he strangled another man, Graham Allen.

The death of his final victim, Stephen Sinclair, upset Nilsen. Sinclair was a drifter and a drug addict. When they met, Nilsen felt sorry for him and bought him a hamburger. Back at Cranley Gardens, he slumped in a chair in a stupor and Nilsen decided to relieve him of the pain of his miserable life. He got a piece of string from the kitchen, but it was not long enough. Then he got his one and only remaining tie and choked the life out of his unconscious victim.

Killing in Cranley Gardens presented Nilsen with a problem. He was forced to dispose of the bodies by dissecting them, boiling the flesh from the bones, dicing up the remains and flushing them down the toilet.

He thought the substance he had found was human flesh

Unfortunately, the sewage system in Muswell Hill were not built to handle dissected corpses.

The drains at 23 Cranley Gardens had been blocked for five days on 8 February 1983 when Dyno-Rod sent Michael Cattran to investigate. He quickly determined that the problem was not inside, but outside the house. At the side of the house, he found the manhole that led to the sewers. He removed the cover and climbed in.

At the bottom of the access shaft, he found a glutinous grey sludge. The smell was awful. As he examined it, more sludge came out of the pipe that led from the house. He called his manager and told him that he thought the substance he had found was human flesh.

Next morning, Cattran and his boss returned to the manhole, but the sludge had vanished. No amount of rainfall could have flushed it through. Someone had been down there and removed it.

Cattran put his hand inside the pipe that connected to the house and pulled out some more meat and four small bones. One of the tenants in the house said that they had heard footsteps on the stairs in the night and suspected that the man who lived in the attic flat had been down to the manhole. They called the police.

Detective Chief Inspector Peter Jay took the flesh and bones to Charing Cross Hospital. A pathologist there confirmed that the flesh was, indeed, human.

The tenant of the attic flat was out at work when Jay got back to Cranley Gardens. At 5.40 p.m. that day, Nilsen returned. Inspector Jay met him at the front door and introduced himself. He said he had come about the drains. Nilsen remarked that it was odd that the police should be interested in drains. When Nilsen let him into the flat, Jay said that the drains contained human remains.

'Good grief! How awful,' Nilsen exclaimed.

Jay told him to stop messing about.

'Where's the rest of the body?' he asked.

After a short pause, Nilsen said: 'In two plastic bags in the wardrobe next door. I'll show you.'

He showed Chief Inspector Jay the wardrobe. The smell coming from it confirmed what he was saying.

'I'll tell you everything,' Nilsen said. 'I want to get it off my chest, not here but at the police station.'

The police could scarcely believe their ears when Nilsen admitted killing 15 or 16 men. In the wardrobe in Nilsen's flat, the police found two large, black bin-liners. In one, they found a shopping bag containing the left side of a man's chest, including the arm. A second bag contained the right side of a chest and arm. In a third, there was a torso with no arms, legs or head. A fourth was full of human offal. The unbearable stench indicated that the bags had evidently been closed for some time and the contents had rotted.

In the second bin-liner, there were two heads – one with the flesh boiled away, the other largely intact – and another torso. The arms were still attached, but the hands were missing. One of the heads belonged to Stephen Sinclair. Nilsen had severed it only four days earlier and had started simmering it in a pot on the kitchen stove.

Under a drawer in the bathroom, the police found Sinclair's pelvis and legs. In a tea chest in Nilsen's bedroom, there was another torso, a skull and more bones.

The police also examined the gardens at 195 Melrose Avenue. They found human ash and enough fragments of bone to determine that at least eight people, probably more, had been cremated there.

Nilsen was eventually charged with six counts of murder and two of attempted murder. His solicitor had one simple question for Nilsen: 'Why?'

'I'm hoping you will tell me that,' Nilsen said.

Nilsen intended to plead guilty, sparing the jury and the victims' families the details of the horrendous crimes. Instead, his solicitor persuaded him to claim 'diminished responsibility'.

One of the most extraordinary witnesses at the trial was Carl Stottor. Nilsen had tried to strangle him three times, but somehow his frail body had clung to life. Nilsen had then dragged him to the bath and held him under water. Stottor had found the strength to push himself up three times and beg for mercy. But Nilsen pushed him down again. Thinking he was dead, Nilsen took Stottor's body back into the bedroom and smoked a cigarette. Then Bleep, Nilsen's dog, began to lick Stottor's face and the young man began to revive. Nilsen could easily have snuffed out his life then and there. Instead, he rubbed Stottor's legs to stimulate his circulation. He wrapped him with blankets and nursed him back to life. When he was well again, Nilsen walked him to the tube station and wished him luck.

Nilsen had left another survivor to testify against him. Paul Nobbs had slept at Cranley Gardens one night and woke at 2 a.m., with a splitting headache. When he woke again in the morning, he found red marks around his neck. Nilsen advised him to see a doctor. At the hospital, Nobbs was told that he had been half strangled. He assumed that his attacker had been Nilsen, but did not report the assault to the police, assuming they would dismiss the attack as a homosexual squabble.

In November 1983, Nilsen was convicted of the attempted murder of Stottor and Nobbs, plus the actual murder of six others. He was sentenced to life imprisonment with the recommendation that he serve at least 25 years.

He says he does not lose sleep over what he has done, or have nightmares about it. Nor does he have any tears for his victims or their relatives.

– Chapter 12 –

The Dingo Case

Lindy Chamberlain, Michael Chamberlain

NATIONALITY: AUSTRALIAN

NUMBER OF VICTIMS: 1

DEFENCE: BOTH LINDY AND MICHAEL CLAIMED THAT THEY WERE INNOCENT AND THAT A DINGO TOOK THEIR BABY DAUGHTER

S eventh Day Adventism is an apocalyptic religion. It was founded in the nineteenth century by former US Army officer William Miller. From his studies of the book of Daniel and the Book of Revelations, he worked out that Christ would make his Second Coming between 21 March 1843 and 21 March 1844. When Christ did not turn up between the appointed dates, Miller came up with a second date of 22 October 1844. His 100,000 followers, many of whom had sold up all their worldly goods, waited all night but Christ and his fiery conflagration did not turn up then either. This is known among Adventists as the 'Great Disappointment'. Miller himself was so disappointed he died four years later.

In 1845, the Adventists got together to figure out what to do next. The Mutual Conference of Adventists decided that Miller had indeed got the date right, but that his interpretation was off. In fact, God started 'cleansing the heavenly sanctuary' on that date – in other words, he was spring-cleaning heaven ready for the righteous to turn up. After that he would have to go through all the names in the Book of Life and investigate all the sins listed. Only after that would he make his judgement and send Christ back to Earth to separate the righteous from the wicked. So he could be some time yet. Meanwhile those Adventists who had already died were in a state of 'conditional immorality' awaiting the judgement when they would either be extinguished with the wicked or live forever on Earth under Christ's millennial reign. Seventh Day Adventists also believed that celebrating the Sabbath as God ordained on the seventh day – that is, Saturday – rather than the first day – Sunday – would help speed the Second Coming. Refusing to work on Saturdays means that Seventh Day Adventists suffer some job discrimination. One of the original Adventists who had suffered the Great Disappointment, Ellen Hamond White, found she had been given the gift of prophecy and was told by God to take the church to Australia, which she did in 1894. She introduced dietary laws that discourage the eating of meat and the intake of intoxicants. This leaves Seventh Day Adventists somewhat marginalised in the land of steaks, barbies and Fosters and was, no doubt, a contributing factor in the famous 'Dingo Baby Case'.

In August 1980, 32-year-old Lindy Chamberlain and her 36-year-old husband Michael, a Seventh Day Adventist parson, were on a camping holiday near Ayers Rock in central Australia when a dingo entered their tents and dragged away their baby, nine-week-old Azaria. Despite an extensive search, no trace of the baby could be found. At an inquest, the coroner ruled that the Chamberlains were not to blame and took the unprecedented step of allowing the TV cameras into his courtroom to broadcast their innocence. However, Ayers Rock is sacred to the Aborigines. At the base of it is the Cave of Fertility, said to be the birth passage of the world. The Rock is also a place of death, a burial ground guarded by stone warriors as the ancient ancestors sleep. The Australian public were intrigued by the child's name Azaria. It had an Old Testament ring to it and rumours circulated that it meant 'blood sacrifice'. The talk of Australian dinner tables was that

Azaria was the product of an adulterous affair and had been killed in a bizarre religious rite at Ayers Rock. But search as they may, the newspapers could not find a single shred of evidence to that effect. However, the police did not give up. They contacted a forensic scientist in England, who had never even seen a dingo. He claimed that a dingo could not possibly make off with a child – despite the fact that 27 attacks had been reported in the area, several on the night that baby Azaria went missing. The finding of the first inquest was quashed. A second inquest recommended that Lindy and Michael Chamberlain be sent for trial. The trial of the Chamberlains' case was unique in the annals of modern murder trials. Here was a prosecution case where there

The dingo is innocent

was no body, no murder weapon, no eyewitness and no motive. In their opening statement, the Crown admitted that it was not even going to suggest a motive. But what prosecuting counsel Ian Barker QC did say attacked the very core of the defence case. 'The dingo story was a fanciful lie, calculated to conceal the truth,' he said.

Outside the court building, pretty girls wore T-shirts emblazoned with the slogan: 'The dingo is innocent.' The trial turned into a battle between forensic scientists. The defence effectively shredded the prosecution case. Their cross-examination of the prosecution's witnesses demonstrated that the 'experts' were mistaken and incompetent. Even the judge in his summing up said that the jury must allow for the possibility that a dingo had indeed taken the baby. The jury was out for just three hours. When they filed back, they found Lindy Chamberlain guilty of murder and Michael Chamberlain of being an accessory.

The next morning, the judge sentenced Michael to 18 months' hard labour, but under his powers as a judge in the Northern Territory, he was able to suspend this sentence and bound Michael over for three years on a bond of AU$500. With Lindy though, he had no choice. For murder a life sentence of hard labour was mandatory. How did the jury make such a heinous mistake? An anonymous juryman explained later why they had reached such an astounding decision. 'It really came down to whether you believed it was the dingo or not,' he said. Plainly, the jury did not. Lindy, who was eight months pregnant during the trial, went straight to Berrimah jail in Darwin where, less than three weeks later, she gave birth to a second daughter, Kahlia. The baby was taken from her after four hours and given into the care of Michael.

The defence were so shocked by the unexpected guilty verdict, they were ill-prepared for an appeal. There was little more they could say when the Federal Appeal Court convened in Sydney in February 1983. After a month's hearing and two months' deliberation, the three appeal judges unanimously rejected the appeal. In a final appeal to the High Court of Australia, the judges let the judgement of the lower courts stand on a majority verdict of two to one. Lindy turned to her faith and accepted that she would be spending the rest of her life in prison. But Michael resigned the priesthood.

A crisis of faith was rumoured. Many felt that if they had been through what Michael had been through they would have been atheists by then. But letters of support still poured in. Pleas for Lindy's release appeared in the press. A film was made showing two versions of the story – the prosecution's and the Chamberlains'. Somehow they could not get the Crown's case to hang together dramatically. A prison psychologist who examined Lindy publicly proclaimed that he found himself unable to account for any 'criminal behaviour on her part'. Newspapers employed their own analysts, handwriting experts and the like, who all proclaimed Lindy innocent. Prominent scientists protested at the interpretation of the forensic evidence. A petition was organised. The Plea of Justice Committee was formed and travelled the country, campaigning on Lindy's behalf.

Then, in February 1986, David Brett, a British tourist who was climbing on Ayers Rock, slipped and fell to his death. When it was found, his body had been partially eaten by dingos. Near his body a baby's jacket was found. It was identified as Azaria's. Organic material that could have been the remains of Azaria's body was also found. This was all consistent with a dingo taking the baby. That should have been an end to it, but there were rumours that Brett had Azaria's name tattooed on his arm. His mother believes that both her son and baby

Azaria were victims of black magic. His parting words when he left Britain, she said, were: 'If anything happens to me, I have been made a sacrifice.' Nevertheless Lindy was granted parole and was released. T-shirts began appearinginAustraliabearingtheslogan:'Watchout,Kahlia–Mummy'shome.' A judicial inquiry set up under Federal judge Mr Justice Trevor Morling in 1988 exonerated the Chamberlains. His 380-page report blamed erroneous and unreliable forensic evidence.

– Chapter 13 –

The Night Stalker

Richard Ramirez

REIGN OF TERROR: 1984–86

NUMBER OF VICTIMS: 28

FAVOURED METHOD OF KILLING: RAPE, STRANGULATION, STABBING, SHOOTING, BEATING

PSEUDONYM: WOULD HAVE PREFERRED THE NAME 'THE NIGHT PROWLER'

CALLING CARD: AN INVERTED PENTAGRAM

FINAL NOTE: 'I AM BEYOND YOUR EXPERIENCE. I AM BEYOND GOOD AND EVIL'

Devil worshipper Richard Ramirez was the Night Stalker who terrorised Los Angeles for two years in the 1980s. A scrawled pentagram – a Satanic symbol – was his calling card and he made his victims declare their love of Satan before he slaughtered them.

The Night Stalker's murder career began ordinarily enough. On the night of 28 June 1984, the mutilated body of 79-year-old Jennie Vincow was found spread-eagled on the bed of her one-bedroom apartment in the Eagle Rock district of Los Angeles. She had been raped and her throat had been slashed so violently that she had almost been decapitated. There was blood on the walls of the bedroom and bathroom and her flat had been ransacked. But in LA, it was just another murder.

Nine months later he attacked again. Maria Hernandez had just parked her car in her garage in the Rosemead suburb of Los Angeles and was walking towards her apartment, when she heard footsteps behind her. She turned to be confronted by a man with a gun. He shot her but, miraculously, the bullet ricocheted off her car keys and hit her with only a glancing blow.

Even so, the impact of the bullet was enough to knock her to the ground. The gunman stepped over her, giving her a vicious kicking, and made his way into her apartment. From inside, Maria heard a gunshot. She staggered to her feet, only to be confronted by the gunman running from the house.

'Please don't shoot me again,' she begged. The gunman froze, then took to his heels.

Inside the apartment Maria Hernandez found her boyfriend, 34-year-old Hawaiian-born Dayle Okazaki, lying on the kitchen floor, dead. He had been shot through the head.

There was only one clue to the murder. Maria said that the gunman had worn a baseball cap with the AC/DC logo on the front. The Australian heavy metal band AC/DC had recently released an album called *Highway to Hell*. On it, there was track called 'Night Prowler'. This was the *nom d'assassin* Ramirez preferred. He was annoyed that the newspapers insisted on calling him the Night Stalker.

That night, his lust for blood had not nearly been satisfied. Less than an hour later, on his way home, Ramirez pulled 30-year-old Taiwanese law student Tsai Lian Yu from her car and shot her repeatedly. She died before the ambulance arrived.

Ten days later, Ramirez entered the home of Vincent and Maxine Zazzara, half a mile from the San Gabriel freeway. Maxine was a successful lawyer and Vincent had just fulfilled a lifetime ambition to open his own pizzeria. Both of them were shot at point-blank range and Maxine Zazzara's naked body was mutilated after death. Ramirez stabbed her repeatedly, making a pattern of a large ragged T. He also gouged her eyes out. The bodies were found by their son Peter, when he called in at the house the next day.

On 14 May 1985, Ramirez broke into the home of William and Lillie Doi. He shot 66-year-old William in the head while he lay sleeping. His wife, 63-year-old Lillie who was in bed next to him, was beaten repeatedly around the head until she told the intruder where the valuables were hidden. Then he handcuffed her and ransacked the house. Later he returned to rape her.

A fortnight later, Carol Kyle was awoken in her Burbank flat by a torch shining in her eyes. A man pointed a gun at her and dragged her out of bed. In the next room, Carol's terrified 12-year-old son was handcuffed and locked in a cupboard. His mother was then raped. Even then, she was sympathetic.

'You must have had a very unhappy life to have done this to me,' she said.

Ramirez shrugged off her sympathy.

'I don't know why I'm letting you live,' he spat. 'I've killed people before.'

> **You must have had a very unhappy life to have done this to me**

He ransacked the apartment for valuables. Satisfied with the jewellery he found, he went away, leaving both Carol and her son alive.

Around the same time, two elderly women, 83-year-old Mabel Bell and her 80-year-old sister Florence Long, an invalid, were attacked in their home in the suburb of Monrovia. On 1 June, Carlos Venezuala, a gardener who did chores for the sisters, dropped round. The house was unusually silent and he let himself in. He found Florence lying on her bed in a coma. There was a huge wound over her ear and a bloodstained hammer was lying on the dressing table. Mabel was lying barely conscious on her bedroom floor in a pool of her own blood. Both women had been beaten with the hammer. They had been cut and tortured. There were even signs that Ramirez had tried to rape the older sister Mabel. The police concluded that the two sisters had been left that way for two days.

The house had been ransacked but this time, the attacker had left some clues. Along with the hammer, he had left a half-eaten banana on the dining table. He had also left what was to become his trademark – an inverted pentagram, the encircled five-point star that is used in witchcraft. One was scrawled in lipstick on Mabel's thigh. Another was drawn on Florence's bedroom wall.

Six weeks after the attack Mabel Bell died. But Florence eventually regained consciousness and survived.

Then the Night Stalker's onslaught began in earnest. On the night of 27 June 1985, Ramirez slashed the throat of 32-year-old Patty Elaine Higgins in her home in Arcadia. The same fate befell Mary Louise Cannon five days later. Three days after that, again in Arcadia, Ramirez savagely beat 16-year-old Whitney Bennett with a crowbar. She survived.

On 7 July, Ramirez turned his attention back to Monterey Park, where Tsai Lian Yu and the Dois had been attacked. Sixty-one-year-old Joyce Lucille Nelson was found beaten to death in her home and 63-year-old Sophie Dickmann was raped and robbed in her apartment

On 20 July, Ramirez murdered 66-year-old Maxson Knciding and his 64-year-old wife Lela in their Glendale home, then went on to murder 32-year-old Chainarong Khovananth at his home in Sun Valley. After shooting him as he lay asleep in his bed, Ramirez raped and beat Chainarong's 29-year-old wife Somkid. He forced her to perform oral sex on him and stole $30,000 in cash and jewellery. Then he forced her to swear in Satan's name that she would not cry out. After that he raped her eight-year-old son.

The police were aware that they had a serial killer on their hands but the problem was that he had no clear modus operandi. He killed with guns, hammers and knifes. He raped young and old, both children and women, orally, anally and genitally. Sometimes he mutilated the bodies after death, sometimes he didn't. In a moment of dark humour the LAPD quipped that he was an equal-opportunity monster.

But some patterns were emerging. The killer stalked quiet suburbs away from the city's main centres of crime where homeowners were less security conscious. He tended to pick houses painted in beige or pastel yellow. They were usually close to a freeway, making his escape easier. Entry was usually through an open window or an unlocked door. Although burglary was one of his motives, rape and sheer brutality seemed to figure highly. Pentagrams and other satanic symbols were also commonly left by the killer.

On the night 5 August, postal worker Virginia Petersen was awoken by the sound of an intruder. She sat up in bed and cried out: 'Who are you? What do you want?'

The burglar laughed, then shot her in the face. The bullet entered the cheek just below her eye and went clean through the back of her head. Miraculously, she survived.

Her husband Christopher, who was lying beside her, was woken by the shot. He leapt to his wife's defence. This earned him a bullet in the temple. But Christopher Petersen was a tough guy, a truck driver. It took more than one small-calibre bullet to put him down. He dived out of bed and chased his attacker. The intruder was unprepared for this. He panicked and ran.

Christopher Petersen also survived the ordeal, though he has suffered partial memory loss and has had to live ever since with a bullet lodged in his brain. But, for the second time, the Night Stalker had been put to flight.

It did not end his violent rampage though. Three days later, he shot another 35-year-old Asian man and beat and raped his 28-year-old wife. Again she was forced to swear by Satan that she would not cry out, but this time he left their two young children unharmed, though their three-year-old son Amez was tied up.

By this time, public terror was at fever pitch in Los Angeles. In the affluent suburbs, locksmiths and burglar alarm salesmen were doing a roaring trade. Gun shops quickly sold out and local residents set up neighbourhood watch committees.

So Ramirez took a vacation. He travelled north to San Francisco. There on the night of 17 August, he attacked 66-year-old Asian accountant Peter Pan and his 64-year-old wife Barbara in their home in the suburb of Lake Merced. Both were shot through the head. An inverted pentagram was painted in lipstick on the bedroom wall, and under it, Ramirez wrote 'Jack the Knife'. At first, the police thought it was a copycat killing.

But the bullets that he killed the couple with matched the small calibre rounds found in the Los Angeles' murders.

A week later, Ramirez travelled 50 miles south of Los Angeles to the small town of Mission Viego. He shot 29-year-old computer engineer William Carns three times in the head and raped his fiancée Inez Erickson, also 29, twice.

'You know who I am, don't you,' Ramirez taunted. 'I'm the one they're writing about in the newspapers and on TV.'

He also forced Inez to say 'I love Satan' during her ordeal.

William Carns survived the shooting, but suffered permanent brain damage and the couple never married. However, Inez provided a vital clue. She spotted Ramirez's rusty, old orange Toyota after he left the house. This would put an end to the reign of the Night Stalker.

A sharp-eyed kid, James Romero III, had also spotted the orange Toyota as it cruised the area and had noted down its licence-plate number. The police put out an all-points bulletin. Two days later, the car was found in a car park of Los Angeles' Rampart suburb.

When examining the car, forensic scientists used a new technique. They put a dab of Superglue in a saucer in the car and sealed the doors and window. Fumes from the Superglue would react with moisture in any fingerprints and then turn them white. The interior of the car was then scanned using a laser. This technique should pick up any fingerprints, including those that the culprit had tried to wipe off.

The scan yielded one fingerprint. It was computer matched to that of 25-year-old Richard Ramirez, who had been arrested three times for marijuana possession in El Paso. Soon Ramirez's photograph was on the front page of every newspaper in California.

Ramirez was quite unaware of this when he stepped down from the Greyhound bus at Los Angeles' main bus station. He had been out in Phoenix, Arizona, to score some cocaine and was high. He had killed several people and felt good. Surely by now he must be Satan's favourite son.

He went to a drugstore to buy himself a Pepsi. Then at the checkout desk he saw his own face splashed across the Spanish language paper

La Opinion. The checkout clerk recognised him too, so did the other customers. Ramirez made a run for it.

In the street, someone cried out: 'It's the Night Stalker.' Soon he heard the wail of police sirens behind him. He knocked on a door. Bonnie Navarro opened it. Ramirez shouted 'Help me!' in Spanish. She slammed the door in his face.

On the next block, he tried to pull a woman from her car, but bystanders rushed to her rescue. Ramirez jumped a fence into a backyard where Luis Muñoz was cooking a barbecue. He hit Ramirez with his tongs. In the next garden, he tried to steal a red 1966 Mustang, but 56-year-old Faustin Pinon, who was working on the transmission, grabbed him in a headlock. Ramirez broke free, but across the street 55-year-old construction worker Jose Burgoin heard Pinon's shouts. He picked up a steel rod and hit Ramirez with it.

I love to kill people. I love watching them die

Ramirez stumbled on but Burgoin soon caught up with him. This time he clubbed him to the ground.

In the nick of time, Deputy Sheriff Andres Ramirez pulled up in a patrol car.

'Save me!' yelled the Night Stalker.

As his namesake handcuffed him, Ramirez said: 'Thank God you came. I am the one you want. Save me before they kill me.'

Only the arrival of more police patrol cars prevented the angry mob taking the law into their own hands. Even at the police station, a crowd gathered, calling for him to be lynched.

Ramirez showed no contrition. He told the police: 'I love to kill people. I love watching them die. I would shoot them in the head and they would wiggle and squirm all over the place, and then just stop. Or I would cut them with a knife and watch their faces turn real white. I love all that blood. I told one lady one time to give me all her money. She said no. So I cut her and pulled her eyes out.'

In court, Ramirez made Satanic signs and even appeared with the inverted pentagram scratched in his palm. He told the judge: 'You maggots make me sick. Hypocrites one and all. You don't understand me. You are not expected to. You are not capable of it. I am beyond your experience. I am beyond good and evil.'

Ramirez was found guilty on 63 counts, including 13 murders. He was sentenced to death penalties on 19 counts and over 100 years' imprisonment. On death row, many women wrote to him, sending provocative pictures, pledging undying love and proposing marriage. When Ramirez accepted divorcée Christine Lee over nude model Kelly Marquez, it made headlines.

Christine, a mother of two, bombarded Ramirez with pin-up pictures of herself and visited him over 150 times. She was undaunted by the fact that her fiancé was a perverted killer, declaring, 'We really love each other and that's all that matters. From the moment I saw him in prison, I knew he was special. I couldn't believe he was the evil monster people were calling him. He's always been sweet and kind to me.'

But it did not work out. In October 1996, in a simple ceremony in San Quentin, Ramirez married Doreen Lioy, a 41-year-old freelance magazine editor with an IQ of 152.

'The facts of his case ultimately will confirm that Richard is a wrongly convicted man,' she said. 'I believe fervently that his innocence will be proven to the world.'

Nevertheless, Richard Ramirez remains on death row.

– Chapter 14 –

Hungerford

Michael Ryan

NATIONALITY: ENGLISH

NUMBER OF VICTIMS: 16 KILLED

FAVOURED METHOD OF KILLING: SHOOTING

FINAL ACT: SHOT HIMSELF IN HIS SCHOOL

REIGN OF TERROR: 20 AUGUST 1987

On **19 August 1987**, 33-year-old Susan Godfrey took her two children for a picnic in Savernake Forest, 10 miles from the drowsy village of Hungerford in Berkshire. It was around 12.30 p.m. They had finished eating and Mrs Godfrey was strapping four-year-old Hannah and two-year-old James into the back of the family car when a man dressed in black appeared.

Incongruously for the Berkshire countryside, he was carrying a Chinese-made AK47 – a Kalashnikov assault rifle more usually seen in the hands of Third World guerrillas. He took the car keys from the dashboard of the black Nissan and forced Mrs Godfrey to come with him. Less than a hundred yards from the car he emptied the entire magazine of the Kalashnikov – 15 high-velocity rounds – into her back at point-blank range. The children were later found wandering the forest.

There seems to have been no motive for this savage murder. Mrs Godfrey was not sexually assaulted and there seems to have been no connection between her and her murderer – 27-year-old Michael Ryan – before her death. There is no evidence that Ryan had trailed the family.

He had been in the forest, armed, since the mid-morning. The police could only speculate that she had surprised him during target practice. A local boy had heard a burst of semi-automatic fire from the forest at around 10.30 that morning.

But one senseless act of violence was not enough for the lonely and deluded Ryan. He drove his D-registered Vauxhall Astra back down the A4 towards his home in Hungerford.

Hungerford is an ancient market town with a population of less than five thousand. The broad main street is dominated by the Bear Hotel and the redbrick clock-tower that tolls out the hours with a long, flat note. Hungerford was granted a charter by John of Gaunt, whose name is commemorated by a pub in the town and the secondary school Michael Ryan attended. The charter allows the owner of three cottages the freedom of the town. This brings with it grazing and fishing rights – the nearby River Kennet is well stocked with trout and grayling. The owner also has to hold office on 'Tutty' (Tithing) Day and act as ale-taster, Constable and Tutty Man, parading through the streets in morning dress, kissing maidens and throwing oranges and pennies to the children.

The summer in Hungerford is quiet and still, though in August the sky is occasionally darkened by smoke from the burning stubble. The redbrick villas of the old town are a symbol of stability in the changing English countryside. The only lurking sense of fear emanates from the dark Victorian mental asylum that stands across the cattle grid on the Common. On the back road from Hungerford to Lambourn there is a monument half-buried in the hedgerow. It commemorates the death of two policemen who were murdered there by a gang of robbers in 1870. It was Hungerford's only previous experience of public slaughter.

On the way back to Hungerford, Ryan stopped at the Golden Arrow filling station in Froxfield, Wiltshire. It was 12.45 p.m. The cashier, mother-of-three Kabaub Dean, recognised Ryan. He stopped there for petrol every other day, normally paying by credit card but never passing the time of day.

Today was somehow different. Mrs Dean noticed Ryan was hanging around nervously. He appeared to be waiting for another customer to leave. Then she saw him fiddling about with something in the boot of his car. Suddenly he pulled a gun out and started shooting at her. The glass window of her booth shattered and she was showered with glass. She dived for cover.

She begged for her life as he stood over her

Ryan approached as she lay helpless under the counter. She begged for her life as he stood over her. Coldly he took aim and – at point-blank range – he pulled the trigger.

Mrs Dean heard the click of an empty gun chamber. Ryan had run out of ammunition. He pulled the trigger again and again. Mrs Dean heard four or five clicks. Then Ryan walked back to his car and drove away.

His next stop was Number Four, South View in Hungerford where he lived with his mother. There he had built up a fearsome arsenal. In a steel cabinet bolted to the wall of the house he kept at least one shotgun, two rifles, the 7.62mm Kalashnikov, three handguns including a 9mm pistol and an American-made M-l carbine and 50 rounds of ammunition which he had bought for £150 at the Wiltshire Shooting Centre just eight days before the incident.

Ryan had joined the shooting centre only three weeks before that. There he was known as 'polite' and 'unremarkable'. Those who got to know him better found him articulate, especially about his favourite subject – guns. He could reel off a detailed history of the M-l and its use in World War Two and the Korean War. He had been practising with the M-l on the club's shooting range the day before the massacre.

Little is known about what occurred between Ryan and his mother when he got home. But it is known that less than twenty minutes after the shooting at the petrol station, Ryan shot his mother. Her body was found lying in the road outside the house. Ryan then set the house on fire. The blaze quickly spread to the three adjoining houses in the terrace.

A neighbour, Jack Gibbs, was the next to die. He was in the kitchen of his home when Ryan began his murderous assault. Sixty-six-year-old Mr Gibbs threw himself across his 63-year-old, wheelchair-bound wife, Myrtle Gibbs, to protect her from the burst of semi-automatic fire from Ryan's Kalashnikov. Four high-powered bullets passed through his body, fatally wounding his wife. She died in Princess Margaret Hospital, Swindon, the next day.

Then Ryan shot neighbours Sheila Mason and her 70-year-old father Roland as they rushed from their home at Number Six. He gunned down 84-year-old retired shopkeeper Abdur Khan who used to wander the streets of Hungerford from his home in Fairview Road, talking to anyone he met.

Ryan shot at passing cars, killing George White from Newbury who happened to be driving through Hungerford. Ian Playle, the 34-year-old chief clerk of West Berkshire Magistrates' Court, was driving down the A338 through the village with his wife Elizabeth, his six-year-old son Mark and their 18-month-old baby daughter Elizabeth when Ryan sprayed their car with bullets. Mr Playle was hit several times and died later at the John Radcliffe Hospital in Oxford.

As Ryan roamed the village where he had lived his entire life the death toll mounted. Ken Clements was killed as he walked down a footpath at the end of South View. Douglas Wainwright and his wife were shot in their car on Priory Avenue. Taxi-driver Marcus Barnard was on his way home to his wife and month-old baby when he was shot. Eric Vardy was also found dead in his car in Priory Road.

Ryan's last victim was Sandra Hill. She was also shot in her car on Priory Road. She was rushed to the local doctor's surgery, but it was too late. She died shortly after arrival.

In less than an hour and a half, Ryan's murderous rampage left 15 dead and more wounded. But the police would soon be closing in on the quiet Berkshire village whose name would soon be synonymous with mindless murder.

At 12.40 p.m. Mrs Kabaub Dean, the cashier at the Golden Arrow service station, had called the police. But she thought the shooting incident was just a robbery until much later when she heard about the bloodletting in Hungerford on the radio. Five minutes after her call the

Wiltshire police alerted the neighbouring Thames Valley force assuming that Ryan would have moved into their jurisdiction.

At 12.47 p.m. the Thames Valley police got their first 999 call from Hungerford. The caller reported a shooting in South View, the street where Ryan lived with his mother. Shortly after 1 p.m. Police Constable Roger Brereton arrived in South View. At 1.05 p.m. he radioed the message: 'Eighteen. One-oh-nine. One-oh-nine.' It was the code for 'urgent assistance required, I have been shot'. No more was heard from him. His body was later recovered from his police car near Ryan's house. He had been shot in the back. He left a wife and two teenage sons.

By 2 p.m. the killing had stopped. Then the caretaker at John O'Gaunt Secondary School reported seeing a man enter the school building at around 1.52 p.m.

Michael Ryan had attended the school ten years before. It had done little for him academically. He had remained in the C-stream for pupils of below average achievement. The headmaster David Lee could not recall him. Lyn Rowlands, who had been classmates with Ryan at Hungerford County Primary School and John O'Gaunt Secondary School, said that he never seemed a very happy child. He was always on his own, always on the sidelines. Other children would try to include him in their games, but he was always moody and sulky. Eventually people left him to his own devices. But she did not remember him ever being nasty in any way. He was not the kind of boy who got involved in fights. He was very introverted and 'a bit of a mystery'.

Another of his schoolmates, Andy Purfitt, told much the same story – that Ryan was a loner. He never mixed with anyone and did not play football with the other boys. But Purfitt remembers that Ryan was picked on by the other children a lot. As if to compensate for this bullying, Ryan developed an interest in guns. Even at the age of 12, he used to fire a .177 air gun at the cows in the fields behind the house, a neighbour recalled. Later, he went out at nights shooting rabbits. One night he met a man who was much bigger than him. They got into an argument before Michael pulled a gun out of his pocket and pointed it at the man. The man turned on his heels and ran.

'That just goes to prove the power of the gun,' Ryan boasted.

He collected ceremonial swords, military badges and medals, and military magazines. School friends say he preferred guns to girls. When he left school, one of the first things he did was get a small-arms licence.

During his last year at school, Ryan hardly ever turned up for classes. He left with no qualifications and drifted through a number of labouring jobs. Now, after his murderous rampage through his home town, Michael Ryan was back at school and – as ever – alone. The Chief Constable of the Thames Valley police, Colin Smith, claimed that prompt action by armed police officers prevented Ryan from killing more people than he did. But it was not until 5 p.m. that the police confirmed that Ryan was in the school. They surrounded it.

The local police admitted that they did know Ryan, but only in the way that most of the inhabitants of a quiet, friendly market town know each other. He had no criminal record. A local constable had visited Ryan's home in South View in June, just two months before the massacre, when Ryan had applied to have his licence extended to cover the 7.62 calibre automatic rifle. Ryan already had a firearms licence and, when he registered his new Kalashnikov, the police had checked on the house to make sure that the gun was stored securely. The officer they sent was Police Constable Trevor Wainwright. Wainwright said of Ryan: 'From local knowledge I knew he was not a yob or mixed with yobs. He was not a villain and I knew he did not have a criminal record. He was a loner but you could not hold that against him. The checks were very thorough.'

The young police officer had checked that the cabinet where Ryan kept the weapons was secure, then approved the extension of his licence and forwarded it to the headquarters of Thames Valley Police. In doing so, he had sealed the fate of his own parents, who were later shot by Ryan while they were on their way to visit their son.

While Michael Ryan was holed up in his old school, the children of his first victim, James and Hannah Godfrey, had been found. Apparently, despite witnessing the horrific murder of their mother, they had been tired and had had a little nap. When they awoke, they had gone to look for help.

They met Mrs Myra Rose, herself a grandmother, who was taking a stroll in the forest. She saw the two children coming down a hill towards her. The little boy was wearing a Thomas-the-Tank-Engine T-shirt and his sister had her hair tied back with a pink headband. Two-year-old James grabbed Mrs Rose's hand and refused to let go. Hannah, who was four, acted as spokesperson.

'A man in black shot my mummy,' she said. 'He has taken the car keys. James and me cannot drive a car and we are going home. We are tired.'

Seventy-five-year-old Mrs Rose lived in Bournemouth and was visiting friends in nearby Marlborough when she decided to go for a walk alone in the Savernake Forest. She found what the children were telling her hard to believe.

'It was such a horrific story for a little girl to tell,' Mrs Rose said, 'I did not know whether to believe it. The children were not crying.'

She was confused about what to do, but then she bumped into another family in the forest and told them what the children had said. One of them went to call the police and Mrs Rose sat down with the children to tell them stories.

'I don't think the youngsters really understood what had happened to their mother,' she told the newspapers later. 'James would not leave my side and I wanted to stay with the children.'

When the police came, they quickly found the bullet-riddled body of Susan Godfrey. Soon they were mounting a huge search of the 4,500-acre forest with teams of tracker dogs in case its glades contained the bodies of any further victims of Michael Ryan.

Talking to the police at John O'Gaunt School, Ryan appeared lucid and reasonable. He expressed no regret for killing Mrs Godfrey, nor any other of his victims. Only the murder of his mother seemed to trouble him.

Michael Ryan was thought of as a mummy's boy. Born when his mother Dorothy, a canteen lady, was 33, he was an only child and she lavished all her attention on him. A friend of the family described Ryan as a 'spoilt little wimp'. It was said: 'He got everything he wanted from his mother.' She would buy him a new car every year.

Ryan's father, Alfred, was a council building inspector and was also attentive. Michael was devoted to him. When he died in 1985, two years before his son made the name Ryan notorious, Michael seemed to go to pieces. 'He was his life, you see,' said Michael's uncle Leslie Ryan. 'When he went, Michael seemed to go.'

He became violent and unpredictable, and he focused more of his attention on his collection of guns. The family were relieved when they heard that Michael was about to get married. The date was set, then the wedding was called off.

He became violent and unpredictable

'He doesn't know whether he wants to be married or not,' his mother told relatives. 'First of all it's on and then it's off.'

Many doubt that there was a girl at all. He had certainly never been seen with one and was unnaturally close to his mother. Next-door neighbour Linda Lepetit said: 'It's unbelievable that he shot her. They got on so well. We could often hear them laughing and joking together. He had a natter to me and my children several times, but he was a bit of a loner.'

But others tell a different story. Dennis Morley, a friend of the family, claimed that Ryan used to beat his mother up.

'He used to hit his mother a lot,' said Morley. 'But he would not pick on a man.'

During his long conversations with the police from John O'Gaunt school, Ryan claimed to have been a member of the Parachute Regiment. He was not. But he was an avid reader of military and survivalist magazines, and he had fantasies about being a paratrooper.

Along with his usual attire of a brown jacket and slacks, he wore a pair of Dutch parachuting boots. He also wore sunglasses in all weather and was self-conscious about going prematurely bald. Even his only drinking buddy described Ryan as 'extremely quiet, he never gave anything away about himself'.

Apart from walking his labrador, Ryan's only recreation had been shooting. He belonged to two shooting clubs where he spent an hour twice a week. Andrew White, a partner in the Wiltshire Shooting Centre in Devizes, said: 'He'd come in for a chat, pick up his targets, go down to the range for an hour's shooting, come back, have another chat, and then go.'

But White did notice that, unlike some of the other riflemen at the 600-member club, Ryan would not use targets that showed a human figure or a soldier's head. He would insist on the standard circular accuracy targets.

During his negotiations with the police, Ryan confessed to the murders he had committed. Although he could shoot other people, he could not kill himself, he said. But at about 6.30 p.m. a muffled shot was heard from inside the school. Ryan did not answer any more. He had finally found the courage to kill himself.

The armed police still held back though. There were fears that Ryan had been holding hostages and they could not be sure what had happened inside the school. It was only at 8.10 p.m. that armed officers finally burst into the classroom to find Ryan shot with his own gun – and the Hungerford massacre was over.

Britain was so shocked by Michael Ryan's murderous outburst that the BBC quickly dropped several films they had scheduled which depicted gratuitous violence or gun play. The first casualty was an American film called *Black Christmas* which was due to go out on BBC 1 at 11.50 on the night of the massacre. It depicted a psychopath killing college girls and was replaced with the Dick Emery comedy *Oh You Are Awful!*.

The BBC's own film *Body Contact*, described as a 'stylish pastiche with echoes of *Bonnie and Clyde*', was also dropped. The ITV company Anglia dropped the western *Nevada Smith* and switched an episode of police drama *The Professionals* for a less violent one.

The day after the Hungerford massacre a fund was set up to provide support to the injured and the families of the dead. Local millionaire Peter de Savary gave £10,000. He had employed Ryan as a labourer when he was building his medieval theme park at nearby Littlecote House and about 80 per cent of the people who worked at his theme park lived in Hungerford. Another anonymous donor gave £10,000 and Newbury

District Council gave £5,000. Local radio stations GWR Radio and Radio 210 launched appeals. Soon smaller donations poured in and within a couple of days, the fund topped £50,000. Ryan's victims would also be eligible for compensation from the Criminal Injuries Compensation board. Murder victims' spouses and children under 18 would also be eligible for a bereavement award of £3,500 and a 'dependency' award.

Hardly a single person in Hungerford's small population was unaffected. In a community of that size everyone knew someone who had been killed. Quickly the Hungerford Family Unit was set up, giving 90-minute grief therapy sessions. It was staffed by social workers who had counselled victims' families from the Zeebrugge ferry disaster and the Bradford tragedy where football fans had been burnt to death in a football stand.

The local church also played a role, offering prayers for the victims and flying its flag at half-mast. They also offered prayers for the soul of Michael Ryan. However, the church soon found itself in an awkward position. While Michael Ryan's mother Dorothy had asked to be buried at Coine in Wiltshire, close to the village of Cherhill where she was born, Ryan himself was to be buried in Hungerford alongside his victims. Some residents of Hungerford muttered darkly that, if he was buried there, his body would be dug up and thrown out.

The Prime Minister at the time, Margaret Thatcher was on the streets of Hungerford two days after Michael Ryan. She visited the area where 14 people had been gunned down and the four houses that had been gutted when Ryan set his mother's house on fire. At the local vicarage she met some of the relatives of Ryan's victims and was soon close to tears. After visiting the wounded in the Princess Margaret Hospital in Swindon, Mrs Thatcher described the incident as 'not an accident in which we get a terrible tragedy, it is a crime, an evil crime'.

– Chapter 15 –

Lesbian Vampires and Satanic Cults

Tracey Wigginton, Kim Jervis, Lisa Ptaschinski, Tracey Waugh

NATIONALITY: AUSTRALIAN

NUMBER OF VICTIMS: 1

FAVOURED METHOD OF KILLING: STABBING

On the night of Friday 20 October 1989, four women met at the Club Lewmors, a lesbian dive, where they sipped champagne. Wigginton and Jervis were carrying knives – but Wigginton bragged that she would kill with her bare hands if she had to. Around 11.30 p.m., they left the club and began cruising the streets of Brisbane, Queensland, in Wigginton's green Holden sedan looking for a likely victim. On River Terrace, they spotted 47-year-old Edward Baldock, clinging drunkenly to a lamp-post. He had been out for a few beers and a game of darts with his friends in the Caledonia Club and was now slowly making his way home to his wife of 25 years. The women stopped and asked him if he wanted a lift home. He thought it was his lucky night, accepted and climbed in the back with Wigginton. They held hands. Wigginton instructed Ptaschinski to drive down to Orleigh Park, which was near Baldock's home. Ptaschinski parked under a fig tree near the deserted South Brisbane Sailing Club. Wigginton asked Baldock whether he wanted a good time. He was all for it. They got out of the car and walked down to the river bank, where they both undressed. A few minutes later Wigginton returned to the car, complaining that Baldock was too strong. Ptaschinski said she would help and Jervis handed her her knife. The two lesbian lovers walked back down to the river where Baldock sat, naked except for his socks. Wigginton urged Ptaschinski to creep up on him and stab him, but she did not have the nerve. She could not kill a poor old drunk. Instead, she collapsed in the sand in front of him and began to gabble. Wigginton had no such qualms. She stabbed Baldock repeatedly in the neck and throat until his head was nearly severed, then she drank his blood. She returned to the car satisfied and the elated women drove back to Jervis's flat, convinced that they had committed the perfect murder. It was only when they arrived at the macabre apartment that Wigginton realised that she had lost her bank card. She had dropped it while she was undressing. Panicked, the women drove back to Orleigh Park and scoured the area, but they could not find the card. They decided that Wigginton must have lost it elsewhere. On the way back to Jervis's flat, they were stopped for a routine check by a patrol car and Ptaschinski was breathalysed. The breath test was negative, but she had come out without her driving licence and the police took down the details of the car. The next morning, Baldock's naked body was discovered by two women out on an early morning walk. They called the police. Within minutes of their arrival, detectives found Wigginton's bank card in Baldock's shoe. They quickly discovered that the green Holden that had been stopped by a patrol car in the area was also registered to a Tracey Wigginton and put two and two together. At this point, they assumed that Wigginton was Baldock's mistress and she had murdered him in an argument over money. In the morning, the loss of Wigginton's bank card began to worry the four women more and more. If the card was found and any of them were questioned, they decided to say that they had been out fooling about in that area earlier the day before and that that's when Wigginton must have lost the card. However, the story had one major flaw. It did not take into account that they had been stopped in that same area by a patrol car that night. Acting on the theory that Wigginton was Baldock's aggrieved mistress, the police picked her up. But under questioning, she began to change her story from the one that they had agreed upon. She began to elaborate on it, mentioning that they had seen a suspicious-looking couple in the park. Later, she said that she had gone to the park in the evening and had fallen over a dead body in the dark, but had been too frightened to report it. Ptaschinski's nerve had gone the night before. With Wigginton in custody, it went again. She could not stand the waiting. She left the flat and began walking about in a confused state. As she wandered about aimlessly, the guilt gradually ate into her. She turned herself in at a nearby police station. Jervis and Waugh were arrested the next day. Under relentless questioning, Tracey

She beat Tracey mercilessly and poisoned her mind against men

Wigginton admitted that she was a 'vampire'. She was sent for detailed psychological examination. The doctors discovered that Tracey had been abandoned by her father and mother when she was a baby and was brought up by her grandparents George and Avril Wigginton. George was a profligate womaniser and Avril took out her hatred of her unfaithful husband on the children in her care. She beat Tracey mercilessly and poisoned her mind against men. Tracey turned to her genial grandfather for affection, but claimed that he had demanded sex with her after she had turned eight. At Catholic school, she became a lesbian and was known for her strange and evil behaviour. When she left school in 1982, she began calling herself Bobby and she went round to beat her grandmother up. She had a sado-masochistic relationship with a woman called Jamie who beat her with a strap and demanded total submission. She later underwent a lesbian 'wedding' performed by a member of the Hare Krishna sect and became a bouncer at a gay night club. After the 'marriage' broke up, she asked the club's owner, a man named John O'Hara, to help her have a baby. They had sex in front of six close friends. Tracey fell pregnant, but later miscarried. She began a stormy relationship with a woman named Donna Staib and although they lived together, they were both enormously promiscuous with other women. Around that time, Tracey dyed her hair 'midnight blue' and had her body tattooed with mystical signs. She and Staib shared a taste for horror videos. The night before Baldock's murder, they had watched a sequence of a man being shot in the forehead and his skull exploding over and over again in slow motion. The police feared that Wigginton's warped upbringing might be used in an insanity plea. But 24-year-old Wigginton took responsibility for her acts and was aware of their consequences. She pleaded guilty and was sentenced to life imprisonment. The other three women pleaded not guilty. They claimed that they had not thought that Wigginton was serious when she talked of killing and drinking people's blood and that they had been forced to go along with her because of her overbearing personality. Under cross-examination though, Ptaschinski admitted that she had been fascinated by the 'thrilling and chilling plan to murder a man to drink his blood'. In court, the three women claimed that Wigginton had occult powers. They said that she claimed to be the Devil's wife and practised mind control. They also insisted that the cross around Kim Jervis's neck had been broken by Wigginton's diabolical power, and she could disappear leaving only the eyes of a cat. Ptaschinski, 24, was found guilty of murder and sentenced to life. Jervis, 23, got 18 years for manslaughter. Only Waugh, 23, walked free from the court. Although she was the brightest of the four women and stayed in the background, the jury decided that she was completely under the evil sway of Tracey Wigginton.

Rodney Dale

NUMBER OF VICTIMS: 1 KILLED, 7 INJURED

FAVOURED METHOD OF KILLING: SHOOTING

NICKNAME: SATAN'S LAUGHING HITMAN

Rodney Dale, a 26-year-old Australian carved the satanic number '666' on the palms of his hands before he went on his rampage. On the afternoon of 17 April 1990, he shot eight people – one of whom died – in just thirty minutes in the Burleigh Heads district of Australia's Gold Coast. The '666' in the palm of his hands earned him the sobriquet 'Satan's laughing hitman' in the Australian press. With no warning at all, Dale went out on the balcony of his flat overlooking Tweed Street which was packed with Saturday afternoon shoppers at around 4 p.m. He was wearing a balaclava and carrying a rifle and a pump-action shotgun, and he started shooting. By the time the first police car arrived, one woman was lying badly wounded on the nearby Gold Coast Highway and the gunman was out on the road shooting randomly at anything that moved. A bridal party happened to be driving through the area at the time. A bridesmaid was hit in the leg and the driver of the bride's car was hit in the right hand, left arm and shoulder. But he managed to drive his passenger out of the area before he was rushed to hospital. The wedding went ahead, but the shooting, it is said, did put something of a damper on the proceedings. Seven more police cars and five ambulances rushed to the area. But another six women were wounded before 38-year-old Sergeant Bob Baker from Burleigh Police Station took decisive action. He pulled his Magnum pistol and walked straight across the road at the crazed gunman. 'Police! Put your gun down,' he shouted. In response, Dale turned his gun on the courageous policeman and started firing. What followed was something out of a western. The gunman loosed off bullet after bullet, but none found their mark. Sergeant Baker stood his ground and responded in kind. His fourth shot hit the gunman in the arm. He dropped his gun and surrendered. In Dale's flat was a note for his girlfriend saying he was 'going out hunting'. Neighbours described him as friendly, nice and happy. There were rumours that he was involved with a satanic cult. He never explained why '666' – the number of the Beast – was carved in his palms.

– Chapter 16 –

Jeffrey Dahmer

Jeffrey Dahmer

NATIONALITY: AMERICAN

NUMBER OF VICTIMS: 17 KILLED

MOTIVE: NECROPHILIA AND CANNIBALISM

FAVOURED METHOD OF KILLING: DRUGGING, STRANGULATION

REIGN OF TERROR: 1978–91

SENTENCE: 957 YEARS

Like Dennis Nilsen, Milwaukee mass murderer Jeffrey Dahmer kept the corpses of his victims around his home. But he wanted to possess them even more completely. So he ate their flesh because that way they would be a part of him and stay with him forever.

Dahmer began his murderous career in Ohio in 1978 at the age of 18. At that time, his parents were going through an acrimonious divorce. Dahmer's father had already left and his mother was away on a vacation. Dahmer was alone in the house and feeling very neglected. So he went out looking for company. He picked up a hitch-hiker, a 19-year-old white youth named Stephen Hicks who had spent the day at a rock concert. They got on well and Dahmer took Hicks back to his parents' house. They had a few beers and talked about their lives. Then Hicks said that he had to go. Dahmer begged him to stay, but Hicks was insistent. So Dahmer made him stay. He picked up a heavy dumbbell, beat him around the head and strangled him.

Dahmer dragged Hicks' body into the crawlspace under the house and dismembered it with a hunting knife. He had had plenty of practice – his childhood hobby had been dissecting animals. He wrapped Hicks' body parts in plastic bags and stashed them there. But the stench of rotting flesh soon permeated the house. That night, Dahmer took the remains and buried them in a nearby wood. But soon he became afraid that local children would discover the grave, so he dug up the body parts, stripped the flesh and pulverised the bones with a sledgehammer. Then he scattered the pieces around his garden and the neighbouring property. It was ten years before Dahmer killed again.

In 1986, Dahmer, then aged 26, was sentenced to a year's probation for exposing himself and masturbating publicly in front of two 12-year-old boys. He claimed he was urinating and promised the judge that it would not happen again.

Before his probation ended Dahmer moved to Milwaukee to live with his grandmother. He was a loner and would hang out in gay bars. If he did strike up a conversation with another customer, he would slip drugs into their drink. Often they would end up in a coma. Dahmer made no attempt to rape them or kill them, he was simply experimenting. But when the owner of the Club Bar ended up unconscious in hospital, Dahmer was barred.

Six days after the end of his probation, he picked up 24-year-old Stephen Tuomi in a gay club. They went to the Ambassador Hotel to have sex. When Dahmer awoke, he found Tuomi dead with blood around his mouth and bruising around his neck.

Dahmer had been drunk the night before and realised that he must have strangled Tuomi. Now he was alone in a hotel room with a corpse and any minute the porter would be checking whether the room had been vacated. He rushed out and bought a large suitcase. He stuffed Tuomi's body into it and took a taxi back to his grandmother's house. The taxi-driver even helped him drag the heavy case inside. Dahmer then cut up the body and put the bits into plastic bags which he put out for the rubbish collectors. He performed this task so well that he left no traces at all. When the police called around to ask him about the disappearance of Tuomi, there was no sign of a body and Dahmer found that he had got away with his second murder.

Sex, companionship and death were now inextricably linked in Dahmer's mind. Four months later, he picked up a young male prostitute. They went back to Dahmer's grandmother's house to have sex in the basement. Dahmer gave the boy a drink laced with a powerful sedative. When the young man was unconscious, he strangled him. He dismembered the corpse, stripped off the flesh, pulverised the bones and scattered the pieces.

Two months later, Dahmer met a 22-year-old homosexual who was broke. Dahmer offered him money to perform in a video. He had oral sex with Dahmer, in his grandmother's basement. When it was over, Dahmer offered him a drink, drugged him, strangled him and disposed of the corpse.

Dahmer's grandmother began to complain of the smell that persisted even after the rubbish had been collected. She then found a patch of blood in the garage. Dahmer said that he had been skinning animals out there. She accepted this excuse, but made it clear that she wanted him to move out.

Dahmer found himself a small apartment in a run-down, predominantly black area. On his first night there, he lured Keison Sinthasomphone, a 13-year-old Laotian boy back to the flat and drugged him. The boy somehow managed to escape. Dahmer was arrested and charged with sexual assault and enticing a minor for immoral purposes. He spent a week in jail, then was released on bail.

But Dahmer could not contain his compulsion to kill. While out on bail, he picked up handsome 26-year-old black bisexual Anthony Sears. Fearing that the police were watching his apartment, he took Sears back to his grandmother's basement. They had sex, then Dahmer drugged him and dismembered his body. He disposed of Sears' corpse in the rubbish, but kept the skull as a souvenir.

Back in court, the District Attorney pushed for five years' imprisonment for his assault on Keison Sinthasomphone. Dahmer's attorney argued that the attack was a one-off offence. His client was a homosexual and a heavy drinker, and needed psychiatric help, not punishment. Dahmer got five years on probation and a year on a correction programme.

It did not help. Dahmer was now set in his murderous ways. He picked up a young black stranger in a club and offered him money to pose for nude photographs. Back in Dahmer's flat, the youth accepted a drink. It was drugged. Once he was unconsciousness, Dahmer strangled him, stripped him and performed oral sex with the corpse. Then he dismembered the corpse, again keeping the skull, which he painted grey.

He craved more than the usual sex, murder and grisly dismemberment

He picked up another homosexual known as 'the Sheikh' and did the same to him – only this time he had oral sex before he drugged and strangled his victim.

The next victim, a 15-year-old Hispanic, was luckier. Dahmer offered him $200 to pose nude. He undressed but Dahmer neglected to drug him before attacking him with a rubber mallet. Dahmer tried to strangle him, but he fought back. Eventually Dahmer calmed down. The boy promised not to inform the police and Dahmer let him go, even calling a taxi for him.

Next day, when he went to hospital for treatment, the boy broke his promise and spoke to the police. But he begged them not to let his foster parents find out that he was a homosexual and the police dropped the matter altogether.

The next time Dahmer picked up a victim, a few weeks later, he craved more than the usual sex, murder and grisly dismemberment. He decided to keep the skeleton and bleach it with acid. He dissolved most of the flesh in the acid, but kept the biceps intact in the fridge.

When neighbours began to complain of the smell of putrefying flesh coming from Dahmer's flat, Dahmer apologised. He said that the fridge was broken and he was waiting to get it fixed.

Dahmer's next victim, 23-year-old David Thomas, was not gay. He had a girlfriend and a three-year-old daughter, but accepted Dahmer's offer to come back to his apartment for money. After drugging him, Dahmer realised that he did not really fancy his latest pick-up anyway. But fearing that Thomas might make trouble when he woke up, he killed him. This time he took more pleasure in the dismemberment, photographing it step by step.

He also photographed the dismemberments of Curtis Straughter and Errol Lindsey, holding onto their skulls as trophies.

Thirty-one-year old deaf mute, Tony Hughes, accepted $50 to pose nude. But by this time, Dahmer had become so blasé about the whole procedure that he kept Hughes' body in his bedroom for several days before he cut it up.

Dahmer's next victim was Keison Sinthasomphone's older brother, 14-year-old Konerak. Again things went badly wrong. Dahmer drugged the boy, stripped him and raped him but then, instead of strangling him, Dahmer went out to buy some beer. On his way back to the apartment, Dahmer saw Konerak out on the street. He was naked, bleeding and talking to two black girls. When Dahmer grabbed him, the girls hung on to him. One of them had called the police and two patrol cars arrived.

The police wanted to know what all the trouble was about. Dahmer said that he and Konerak had had a lover's tiff. He managed to convince them that 14-year-old Konerak was really 19 and, back at his apartment, he showed them Polaroids of Konerak in his underwear which seemed to back up his story that they were lovers. The police did not realise that the pictures had been taken earlier that day, while Konerak was drugged.

Throughout all this Konerak sat passively on the sofa, thinking his ordeal was over. In fact, it had only just begun. The police accepted Dahmer's story and left. Konerak was strangled immediately and then dismembered.

When Dahmer picked up 23-year-old Jeremiah Weinberger in a gay club, Weinberger asked his former roommate whether he should go with Dahmer. The roommate said: 'Sure, he looks OK.' Dahmer seems to have liked Weinberger. They spent the whole of the next day together having sex. Then Weinberger looked at the clock and said it was time to go – and Dahmer said he should stay for just one more drink. His head ended up in the freezer, next to Matt Turner's, an aspiring model Dahmer had picked up on Gay Pride Day in Chicago.

When Dahmer lost his job, he knew only one thing would make him feel better. He picked up a 24-year-old black man called Oliver Lacy, took him back to his apartment, strangled him and sodomised his dead body.

Four days later, 25-year-old Joseph Bradeholt – who was married with two children – accepted Dahmer's offer of money for nude photographs and, according to Dahmer, willingly joined in oral sex with him. His dismembered torso was left to soak in a dustbin filled with acid.

By the time Dahmer had killed 17 men, all in much the same way, he was getting so casual that it was inevitable that he would get caught. On 22 June 1991, he met Tracy Edwards, a young black man who had just arrived from Mississippi. He was with a number of friends. Dahmer invited them all back to his apartment for a party. He and Edwards would go ahead in a taxi and organise some beers. The others would follow later. Edwards went along with this plan. What he did not know was the Dahmer was giving his friends the wrong address.

Edwards did not like Dahmer's apartment. It smelt funny. There was a fish tank, where Dahmer kept some Siamese fighting fish. Dahmer told lurid tales about the fish fighting to the death and Edwards glanced nervously at the clock as he sipped his cold beer.

When the beer was finished, Dahmer gave Edwards a rum and coke. It was drugged. Edwards became drowsy. Dahmer put his arms around him and whispered about going to bed. Instantly, Edwards was wide awake. It was all a mistake. He had to be going, he said.

Before he knew it, his hands were handcuffed and Dahmer was poking a butcher's knife in his chest, ordering him to get undressed. Edwards realised the seriousness of his situation. He knew he had to humour the man and make him relax. Slowly, he unbuttoned his shirt.

Dahmer suggested that they go through into the bedroom and escorted Edwards there at knifepoint. The room was decorated with Polaroid pictures of young men posing naked. There were other pictures of dismembered bodies and chunks of meat. The smell in the room was sickening. The putrid aroma seemed to be coming from a plastic dustbin under the window. Edwards could guess the rest.

Dahmer wanted to watch a video with his captive friend. They sat on the bed and watched *The Exorcist*. The gruesome film made Dahmer relax as Edwards desperately thought of ways to escape.

The film over, Dahmer said, if Edwards did not comply with his requests, he would cut out his heart and eat it. Then he told Edwards to strip so that he could photograph him nude. As Dahmer reached for the camera, Edwards seized his opportunity. He punched him in the side of the head. As Dahmer went down, Edwards kicked him in the stomach and ran for the door.

Dahmer caught up with him and offered to unlock the handcuffs, but Edwards ignored him. He wrenched open the door and ran for his life.

Halfway down Twenty-fifth Street, Edwards spotted a police car. He ran over to it yelling for help. In the car he explained to the officer that a maniac had tried to kill him and he directed them back to Dahmer's apartment.

The door was answered by a well-groomed, good looking white man who seemed calm and composed. The police began to have second thoughts about the story Edwards had told them – until they noticed the strange smell.

Dahmer admitted that he had threatened Edwards. He looked contrite and explained that he had just lost his job and had been drinking. But when the police asked for the key to the handcuffs, he refused to hand it over and grew violent. The policemen pushed him into the flat and, in moments, had him face down

There were three human heads in the freezer

on the floor. They read him his rights. Then they began looking around the flat. One of them opened the fridge door.

'Oh my God,' he said, 'there's a goddamn head in here.'

Dahmer began to scream like an animal. The police rushed out to get some shackles. Then they began their search of the apartment in earnest.

The refrigerator contained meat, including a human heart, in plastic bags. There were three human heads in the freezer. A filing cabinet contained grotesque photographs, three human skulls and a collection of bones. Two more skulls were found in a pot on the stove. Another pot contained male genital organs and severed hands and there were the remains of three male torsos in the dustbin in the bedroom.

In the precinct, Dahmer seemed almost relieved that his murder spree was over. He made a detailed confession and admitted that he had now reached the stage where he was cooking and eating his victims' bodies.

Dahmer's cannibalism and his necrophilia were the cornerstones of his insanity plea. But the District Attorney pointed out to the jury that if Dahmer were found insane and sent to a mental hospital, his case would be reviewed in two years and, if he was then found to be sane, he could be out on the streets again. In June 1992 the jury found Jeffrey Dahmer guilty of the 15 murders he was charged with and he was given 15 life sentences, or 957 years in prison. The state of Wisconsin had no death penalty, but he still faced execution. He still had to be tried for the murders that took place in his parents' home in Ohio, which did have the death penalty. However, after serving two years in the state penitentiary, he was murdered by another inmate.

– Chapter 17 –

The House of Horrors

Fred West

ACCOMPLICE: ROSEMARY WEST

NATIONALITY: ENGLISH

NUMBER OF VICTIMS: FRED WAS CHARGED WITH 12 MURDERS, ROSEMARY WITH 10

FAVOURED METHOD OF KILLING: STRANGULATION

REIGN OF TERROR: 1967–94

MOTIVE: SEXUAL PERVERSION

On **24 February 1994**, the police turned up at 25 Cromwell Street, an ordinary three-storey house in central Gloucester in the south-west of England, with a warrant to dig up the back garden. The door was answered by Stephen West, the 20-year-old son of the householders Fred and Rosemary West. The police told him that they were looking for the body of his sister Heather, who had disappeared in May 1987 at the age of 16. Stephen's parents had told him that she had left home to go and work in a holiday camp in Devon and he believed that she was now living in the Midlands.

'I wanted to know the reasons why they thought Heather was buried there but they wouldn't tell me,' said Stephen, disingenuously. Among the surviving West children there was a running joke that Heather was buried under the patio.

'I told one of the detectives that they were going to end up making fools of themselves,' said Stephen. 'He just replied "That's up to us".'

As the police went about their business, Stephen and his mother Rosemary tried to contact his father Fred, who was working on a building site about 20 minutes' drive from Gloucester. Eventually they got through to him on the mobile phone in his van.

'You'd better get back home,' Rosemary told Fred. 'They're going to dig up the garden, looking for Heather.'

That was at 1.50 p.m. 56-year old Fred did not turn up at home until 5.40 p.m. It has never been explained what he was doing during the intervening four hours. Fred said that he had been painting and that he had taken ill as a result of the fumes while he was driving home. He had had to pull over and passed out at the roadside. Others suspect that he was disposing of evidence.

When Rosemary, 44, was interviewed, she told the police that Heather had been both lazy and disagreeable, and they were well rid of her. Fred said that she was a lesbian who had got involved in drugs and, like his wife, seemed unconcerned with her disappearance.

'Lots of girls disappear, take a different name and go into prostitution,' he said, seemingly more concerned about the mess the police were making raising the paving stones of his patio.

That night the middle-aged Fred and Rosemary West stayed up all night, talking. Geoffrey Wansel, author of *Evil Love* based on 150 hours of taped interviews with Fred West, says that they cooked up a deal. Rosemary was to keep silent, while Fred said that 'he would 'sort it out' with the police the following day, and that she had nothing to worry about as he would take all the blame'.

The next morning, Fred stepped into a police car outside and told Detective Constable Hazel Savage, who had instigated the search: 'I killed her.'

At Gloucester police station, Fred told detectives how he had murdered his daughter, cut her body into three pieces and buried them, adding: 'The thing I'd like to stress is that Rose knew nothing at all.'

When Rose was told of Fred's confession, she claimed that Fred had sent her out of the house the day Heather disappeared. She had no knowledge of Heather's death.

But 20 minutes, after he had confessed, Fred West retracted everything he had said.

'Heather's alive and well, right,' he insisted. 'She's possibly at the moment in Bahrain working for a drug cartel. She has a Mercedes, a chauffeur and a new birth certificate.'

West was adamant that the police could dig as much as they liked, but they would not find Heather. However, later that day, the excavation team unearthed human remains. When confronted with this, West again confessed to murdering his daughter. Heather, he said, was headstrong. During an argument he had slapped her for insolence, but she had laughed in his face. So he grabbed her by the throat to stop her. But he gripped too hard. She stopped breathing and turned blue. When he realised what he had done, he tried to resuscitate her, but he did not have any medical training. In desperation, he dragged her over to the bathtub and dowsed her with cold water.

It was then his story struck a disturbing note. To run cold water over her, he said, he found it necessary to take her clothes off. When the cold water treatment did not work he lifted her naked body out of the tub and dried her off. He tried to put the corpse in the large rubbish bin, but she would not fit. He realised that he would have to dismember her, but first he would have to make sure that she was dead, so he strangled her with her tights.

'I didn't want to touch her while she was alive,' said West. 'I mean, if I'd have started cutting her leg or her throat and she'd have suddenly come alive...'

According to his own account, West was squeamish. Before he began his gruesome task, he closed Heather's eyes.

'If somebody's sat there looking at you, you're not going to use a knife on that person are you?' he told the police.

First he cut off her head. This made a 'horrible noise... like scrunching'. It was very unpleasant. Then he began cutting her legs off. Twisting one of her feet, he heard 'one almighty crack and the leg come loose'.

With the head and legs removed, Heather's dismembered corpse fitted neatly into the rubbish bin. That night when the rest of the family was asleep, he said, he buried Heather in the garden, where she had lain undiscovered for seven years. Now the police had found her. But hers was the only body in the garden, he told them, so they could call off the excavation.

However, Professor Bernard Knight, the pathologist the police had called in, soon realised that among the remains the excavation team had unearthed, there were three leg bones. Clearly, there was more than one body buried in the garden at 25 Cromwell Street.

Again, Fred West was forced to make a confession, though again he tried to limit the damage. He agreed to accompany the police back to the garden and show them where he had buried the two other girls – 17-year-old Alison Chambers and 18-year-old Shirley Robinson, who had both disappeared in the late 1970s. However, he did not tell them about the six other bodies he had buried underneath the floor of the cellar and bathroom of the house. West did not want to be labelled a serial killer. He was also house-proud and did not want the police tearing apart his home.

West did not want to be labelled a serial killer

Born in 1941 in the village of Much Marcle, some 14 miles north-west of Gloucester, Fred West was the last of a long line of Herefordshire farm labourers. His parents, Walter and Daisy West, had six children over a ten-year period who they brought up in rural poverty.

A beautiful baby with blond hair and piercing blue eyes, Fred was his mother's favourite. A doting son, he did everything she asked. He also enjoyed a good relationship with his father, who he took as a role model. However, as he grew, he lost his good looks. His blond hair turned dark brown and curly. He had inherited some of his mother's less attractive features – narrow eyes and a big mouth with a large gap between his front teeth. Some put this down to gypsy blood. Crueller commentators called him simian.

Scruffy and unkempt, West did not do well at school. He was a troublesome pupil and was thrashed regularly. His mother, now seriously overweight and always badly dressed, would turn up at his school to remonstrate with the teachers. This led to him being teased as a 'mummy's boy'. He left at 15, practically illiterate and went to work, like his father before him, as a farmhand.

By the time he was 16, West had begun to take an interest in girls. He tidied himself up a bit and aggressively pursued any woman that took his fancy. This included his next of kin: West claimed to have made his sister pregnant and that his father had committed incest with his daughters.

'I made you so I'm entitled to have you,' West claimed his father said. But then, West was a practised liar.

At 17, West was involved in a serious motorcycle accident. One leg was broken and was left permanently shorter than the other. He also suffered a fractured skull that left him in a coma for a week. A metal plate had to be put into his head. Dr Keith Ashcroft of the Centre for Forensic Psychophysiology in Manchester believes that damage to his frontal lobes left West with an insatiable need for sex. After the accident he was prone to sudden fits of rage and seems to have lost control over his emotions.

It was then that he met a pretty 16-year-old girl named Catherine Bernadette Costello, nicknamed Rena. She had been a petty thief since childhood and was constantly in trouble with the police. The two misfits quickly became lovers, but the relationship was halted when Rena returned home to Scotland a few months later.

Eager for more sex, Fred became offensively forward. One night while standing on a fire escape outside a local youth club, he stuck his hand up a young woman's skirt. She reacted furiously, knocking him over the balustrade. In the fall, he banged his head again and lost consciousness. This may well have aggravated the frontal lobe damage caused by the motorcycle accident.

Fred West then embarked on a career in petty theft. In 1961, he and a friend stole cigarette cases and a watchstrap from a local jewellers. They were caught red-handed with the stolen goods on them and were fined. A few months later, he was accused of getting a 13-year-old girl, a friend of the family, pregnant. Fred was unrepentant. He did not see anything wrong in molesting underage girls.

"Doesn't everyone do it?" he said.

He was convicted but his general practitioner's claim that he suffered from epileptic fits saved him from serving a jail sentence. However, he showed no sign of changing his ways. His family threw him out and he went to work on buildings sites where, again, he was caught stealing. There were more allegations that he was having sex with underage girls.

West's parents eventually relented and let him return to the family home in Much Marcle. Then in the summer of 1962, Rena Costello returned from Scotland and took up with Fred again. By this time Rena had added burglary and prostitution to her rap sheet, which hardly recommended her to his parents.

Fred and Rena married secretly that November and they moved to Scotland. Rena was pregnant and Fred's parents believed that the baby she was carrying was his. In fact, the child's father was an Asian bus driver. When Rena's daughter Charmaine was born in March 1963, Fred got Rena to write to his mother, explaining that their baby had died and they had adopted a mixed-race child.

West's voracious sexual appetite was also causing problems, though his interest in straightforward vaginal sex was minimal; he preferred bondage, sodomy and oral sex. Although she had been a prostitute, Rena was not always willing to comply with Fred's urges. However, at the time, West was driving an ice-cream truck, which gave him easy access to other young women and he was unfaithful on a daily basis. Their marriage went through a rocky patch with frequent separations. But in 1964, Rena gave birth to West's child, Anne-Marie.

West was involved in an accident in the ice-cream truck that had resulted in the death of a young boy. The accident had not been his fault, but he was concerned that he might lose his job. Fred and Rena had also met a young Scottish woman named Anne McFall whose boyfriend had been killed in an accident. Together, the three of them, plus Rena's two children, moved to Gloucester, where West got a job in a slaughterhouse. It was while working there that West developed a morbid obsession with corpses, blood and dismemberment.

West's marriage became increasingly unstable. Rena fled back to Scotland but Fred refused to let her take the two children with her. Missing her daughters, Rena returned to Gloucester in July 1966 to find Fred and Anne McFall living together in a caravan. Around the time there had been eight sexual assaults in the area committed by a man who matched West's description. Increasingly worried about the safety of her children, Rena went to the police and told them that her husband was a sexual pervert and totally unfit to raise her daughters. This was when Constable Hazel Savage first became involved in the case.

By the beginning of 1967, McFall was pregnant with West's child. She put pressure on him to divorce Rena and marry her. In July, West responded by killing McFall and burying her in Letterbox Field in Much Marcle, near the caravan site. She was eight months pregnant. West not only murdered his lover and their unborn child, he painstakingly dismembered the corpse, removing the foetus, which he buried alongside McFall's body parts – though some were missing. When the corpse was unearthed in 1994, the fingers and toes could not be found. This was to be his hallmark in future crimes.

After Anne McFall's disappearance, West was noticeably nervous. But when Rena moved into the caravan with him in 1967, West became his old self again. With West's encouragement, Rena went to work as a prostitute again. Meanwhile, he began to openly molest four-year-old Charmaine.

On 5 January 1968, pretty 15-year-old Mary Bastholm was abducted from a bus stop in Gloucester. She had been on the way to see her boyfriend and had been carrying a Monopoly game. The pieces were found strewn around the bus stop. West always denied abducting Mary Bastholm, but he knew her. He was a customer at the Pop-In Café, where Mary worked. Mary often served him tea when he had been employed to do some building work behind the café. Mary had also been seen with a woman answering the description of Anne McFall and one witness claimed to have seen Mary in West's car. Most people who have studied the case are convinced that Mary Bastholm was another of Fred West's victims.

A month after Mary Bastholm went missing, West's mother died after a routine gallbladder operation and West became seriously unstable. He changed jobs several times and launched into a series of petty thefts. Then his life changed. On 29 November 1968, while working as a delivery driver for a local baker, he met the 15-year-old girl who would become his second wife and partner in crime.

Rosemary Letts was born in November 1953 in Devon. Her background was disturbed. Her father, Bill Letts, was a schizophrenic. He demanded total obedience from his wife and children, and used violence to get his way.

'If he felt we were in bed too late,' said Rose's brother Andrew, 'he would throw a bucket of cold water over us. He would order us to dig the garden, and that meant the whole garden. Then he would inspect it like an army officer, and if he was not satisfied, we would have to do it all over again.'

A martinet, he enjoyed disciplining his children and was always on the lookout for reasons to beat them.

'We were not allowed to speak and play like normal children,' said Andrew. 'If we were noisy, he would go for us with a belt or chunk of wood.'

His wife Daisy also suffered in the violent outbursts.

'He would beat you black and blue until Mum got in between us,' Andrew said. 'Then she would get a good hiding.'

His savage attitudes and his mental instability did little to recommend him to employers and he drifted through a series of low-paid, unskilled jobs. Short of housekeeping money and in the thrall of a violent husband, Daisy Letts suffered from severe depression. She had already given birth to three daughters and a son when she was hospitalised in 1953 and given electroshock therapy. At the time she was pregnant with Rosemary and it is thought that these shocks could have had an effect on the child as she developed in her mother's womb.

Rosemary was noticeably different from the other Letts' children. In her cot she developed the habit of rocking violently and sometimes she rocked so vigorously that she could move her pram across the room, even when the brake was on.

As she grew older, she rocked only her head – but for hours on end as if she was in a trance. The family soon realised that she was a bit slow. They called her 'Dozy Rosie'. However, with big brown eyes and a clear complexion, she was a pretty child. This appealed to her father and, by doing everything he asked without question, she became the apple of his eye and escaped the beatings he meted out to the other children although there were rumours that she had an incestuous relationship with her father and that he molested young girls.

Things did not go well for Rosemary when she went to school though. With no appreciable intellectual gifts, she did not do well academically. As she grew older, she developed a tendency towards chubbinesss and was teased relentlessly. In response, she lashed out.

As an adolescent, Rose became precocious sexually. After taking a bath, she would walk around the house naked, then climb into bed with her younger brother and fondle him. Her father forbade her to go out with boys her own age. Not that many were interested. Both her reputation as an ill-tempered, sullen, aggressive loner and her chubbiness put the local boys off. Instead she concentrated on the older men in the village.

After 15-year-old Mary Bastholm disappeared from a bus stop in Gloucester in January 1968, girls in the area were on their guard. But Rosemary's growing interest in sex meant that she would not stay home and, on one occasion, one of the older men she was seeing raped her.

At the beginning of 1969, Daisy Letts could stand life with her violent husband no longer. She left and moved in temporarily with her older daughter Glenys and her husband, Jim Tyler. Free from her father's strictures, the 15-year-old Rose spent all her time going out. Her brother-in-law said that Rose carried on with a numer of older men and that she had even tried to seduce him. After a few months, to everyone's surprise, Daisy moved back to Bill, bringing Rose with her. It was then that Rose met 28-year-old Fred West.

Whatever Bill Letts's shortcomings as a parent, he tried to keep his underage daughter away from West. When Bill discovered that Rose was having sex with West, he reported him to the Social Services. This proved ineffective, so Bill turned up at West's caravan and threatened him. The relationship was halted briefly when West went to prison for theft and failure to pay fines. But Rose was already pregnant with West's child. At 16, she left her father's house and moved into West's caravan to take care of Rena's two daughters.

In 1970, Rose gave birth to the ill-fated Heather. With Fred in jail, no money and three children to take care

Her temper flared constantly

of, the teenage Rose found it hard to cope. Her temper flared constantly. She particularly resented having to take care of another woman's children and treated Charmaine and Anne-Marie abominably.

In the summer of 1971, eight-year-old Charmaine went missing. Rose told Anne-Marie that their mother Rena had come to get her. There is no doubt that Rose killed her. Colin Wilson, author of *The Corpse Garden*, believes that she was not responsible for her actions. He thinks that Rose 'simply lost her temper, and went further than usual in beating or throttling her. She was, as Anne-Marie said, a woman entirely without self-control; when she lost her temper, she became a kind of maniac.'

West could not have killed Charmaine as he was in jail at the time. However, he was complicit in concealing her body under the kitchen floor of 25 Midland Road, a house in Gloucester they had recently moved into. When the body was found, the fingers and toes were missing, just like Anna McFall's. Fred and Rose were now bound together by their crime. Later, when Rose's father came to take her away from West, West said: 'Come on, Rosie, you know what we've got between us.'

This upset Rose, Bill Letts noted. Afterwards Rose told her parents why she could not leave

'You don't know him!' she said. 'You don't know him! There's nothing he wouldn't do – even murder!'

In the 1960s, a large number of West Indian immigrants had come to Gloucester. They were largely single men and Rose invited many of them over to the house for sex – both for fun and to earn a little extra money. Fred encouraged this. He was a voyeur and enjoyed watching her have sex through a peephole. Although over-sexed, Fred would only join in if the sex involved bondage, sadism, lesbianism or vibrators. He also took suggestive pictures of Rose, using them in advertisements in magazines for 'swingers' and other publications where he advertised her services as a prostitute.

Eventually Rena came to look for her daughter Charmaine. Unable to get any sense out of Fred or Rose, Rena visited Fred's father, Walter, in August 1971, hoping he could shed some light on what happened to Charmaine. As a result, Fred decided to kill Rena. It seems that he got her back to the house in Midland Road, got her drunk and strangled her. He dismembered her body, put the bits in bags and buried her in Fingerpost Field near Much Marcle in the same general area as he buried Anna McFall. Again the fingers and toes were missing.

Fred and Rose began employing their neighbour, Elizabeth Agius, as a babysitter. On more than one occasion, when the Wests returned home, Elizabeth asked them where they had been. They said they had been cruising around looking for young girls, preferably virgins. Fred explained that he had taken Rose along, so then they would not be afraid to get into the car with him. Elizabeth thought they were joking, but later Fred propositioned her. The Wests later drugged and raped her. They were deadly serious.

In January 1972, Fred and Rose married at Gloucester Registry Office. And in June, they had another daughter who they named Mae. They decided they needed a bigger house to raise their growing family and accommodate Rose's prostitution business and they moved into 25 Cromwell Street. It had a garage and a spacious cellar. Frank as ever, Fred told Elizabeth Agius that he planned to convert the cellar into a room where Rose could entertain her clients. Or he would soundproof it and turn it into his 'torture chamber'. This, in fact, was what he did.

Its first inmate was his own eight-year-old daughter, Anne-Marie. He told her that he and Rose were such caring parents that they were going to teach her how to satisfy her husband when she got married. They stripped her and gagged her. Her hands were tied behind her back and Rose held her down while Fred raped her. This hurt her so much that

Anne-Marie could not go to school for several days. She was warned not to tell anyone, otherwise she would be beaten. The rapes continued. On one occasion she was strapped down so her father could rape her quickly during his lunch hour.

Fred and Rose continued cruising the vicinity, looking for young girls. At the end of 1972, they picked up 17-year-old Caroline Owens, who they hired as a live-in nanny, promising her family that they would take care of her. Caroline was very attractive, and Fred and Rose both tried to seduce her. She found them repellent, but when she said she was leaving, they stripped her and raped her. Fred threatened that if she told anyone about it: 'I'll keep you in the cellar and let my black friends have you. And when we're finished we'll kill you and bury you under the paving stones of Gloucester.'

Caroline believed him. Terrified, she kept silent. But she could not hide her bruises from her mother, who wrung the truth from her and called the police.

The matter came to court in January 1973, but West was able to convince the magistrate that Caroline had consented to sex. Despite West's long criminal record, the magistrate did not believe that the Wests were capable of violence and they got off with a small fine. By this time Fred was 31. Rose was 19 and pregnant for the third time.

The Wests still needed a nanny and seamstress Lynda Gough moved into 25 Cromwell Street to take care of the children. Soon after, they murdered her. Then Fred buried her dismembered body under the floor of the garage. Again he removed her fingers and toes, although this time her kneecaps were missing too. When Lynda's family asked what had happened to her, they were told she had moved on. The police were not called and there were no repercussions. Soon after, in August 1973, the West's first son, Stephen, was born.

Having got away with so much, the Wests began killing just for the fun of it. In November 1973, they abducted 15-year-old schoolgirl Carol Ann Cooper and took her back to Cromwell Street where they amused themselves with her sexually. After about a week, they got tired of her and killed her, either suffocating or strangling her. Then her body was dismembered and buried under the house.

The following month, 21-year-old university student Lucy Partington went home to Gotherington near Cheltenham for the Christmas holidays. She was the cousin of novelist Martin Amis. On 27 December, she went to visit a disabled friend. She left to catch a bus home shortly after 10 p.m. and was waiting at a bus stop on the outskirts of Cheltenham when the Wests offered her a lift. It is almost certain that she would not have got into the car if Rose had not been there. The Wests took her back to Cromwell Street where they raped and tortured her for about a week, then murdered her, dismembered her body and buried it under the house.

Fred cut himself while dismembering Lucy's corpse and went to the hospital to have the wound stitched on 3 January 1974. By then Lucy – like Carol Ann Cooper – had been reported missing, but there was nothing to connect either of the girls to the Wests. Their bodies were concealed in Fred's home improvement scheme. This involved enlarging the cellar and turning the garage into an extension to the main house. The only thing remotely suspicious about this was that Fred's home improvements were done at strange hours of the night. However, West did attract police attention. To pay for his home improvements – and the concrete he covered the corpses with – he committed a series of thefts and fenced stolen goods.

Three more young women – 15-year-old schoolgirl Shirley Hubbard, 19-year-old Juanita Mott from Newent in Gloucestershire and 21-year-old Swiss hitch-hiker Therese Siegenthaler – ended up under the cellar floor at 25 Gloucester Street. They had been tortured and dismembered. The Wests had subjected them to extreme bondage, using plastic covered washing lines and ropes to suspend them from one of the beams in the cellar, and gagging them with tights, nylon socks and a brassiere. In 1976, the Wests enticed a young woman from a home for wayward girls back to Cromwell Street where she was taken to a room where two naked girls were being held prisoner. She was forced to watch while the two girls were tortured. Then she was raped by Fred and sexually assaulted by Rose. Later during the court case, she gave evidence as 'Miss A'.

It is likely that one of the girls was Anne-Marie, Fred's daughter who was the regular target of the couple's sexual sadism. But Fred not only raped and tortured his own daughter, he brought home other men to have sex with her.

By 1977, Fred had extensively remodelled the house. Upstairs he had constructed extra bedrooms so they could take in lodgers. One of them was 18-year-old Shirley Robinson. A former prostitute with bisexual inclinations, she had sex with both Rose and Fred.

Rose fell pregnant by one of her West Indian clients and gave birth to Tara in December 1977. At the time Shirley was also pregnant, carrying Fred's child. Rose was unhappy about this. She feared that Shirley would displace her in Fred's affections. So she had to go. In July 1977, Shirley Robinson was murdered. By this time, the cellar was full, so Shirley and her unborn child were buried in the back garden at 25 Cromwell Street.

In November 1978, Rose gave birth to another daughter. She was Fred's child and they named her Louise. There were now six children in the household and, from an early age, they were aware of what was going on. They knew that Rose was a prostitute and that Anne-Marie was being sexually abused by her father. Anne-Marie eventually fell pregnant by Fred, but it was an ectopic pregnancy which took place in the fallopian tube rather than the womb itself and the foetus had to be aborted. She then moved out to live with her boyfriend, so Fred turned his sexual attentions on Heather and Mae. Heather tried to resist and was beaten.

Not even the loss of Rose's father, who died of a lung ailment in May 1979, put the Wests out of their stride. Several months later, they abducted a troubled 17-year-old from Swansea named Alison Chambers, raped and tortured her, then murdered her and buried her in the back garden.

In June 1980, Rose gave birth to Fred's second son, Barry. In April 1982, Rose had Rosemary Junior, who was not Fred's child. Then in July 1983, Rose had yet another daughter, Lucyanna. Like Tara and Rosemary

Junior, she was mixed race. It is thought that the Wests kept on carrying out sexual abductions throughout this period. But as they did not bury any of the victims at 25 Cromwell Street and refused to confess to any murders during the early 1980s, we cannot be sure.

However, having eight children in the household took its toll on Rose's temper. She became increasingly irrational and beat them without provocation. This began to loosen the children's bond of loyalty. Their continued silence was the Wests' only protection. In May 1987, 16-year-old Heather told a girlfriend about her father's sexual abuse and the beatings, and her mother's profession. The girl told her parents, who were friends of the Wests. When Fred and Rose heard of this, they murdered Heather and told the other children that she left home. However, Fred asked his 13-year-old son Stephen to help him dig a hole in the back garden where he later buried Heather's dismembered body.

Fred and Rose set out to expand the prostitution business by advertising in specialist magazines. They were on the lookout for young women to pimp, who might also be willing to join in their sadistic perversions. A prostitute named Katherine Halliday joined the household. But when she was introduced to the Wests' collection of whips and chains, the black bondage suits and masks, she took fright and left.

The Wests' campaign of rape and murder had been going on for 25 years, but only now did they begin to run out of luck. One of the very young girls that they had abducted and raped told her girlfriend what happened. The girl went to the police and the case was assigned to Hazel Savage, now a detective constable. She knew of Fred from 1966 when Rena had told her about his sexual perversions.

On 6 August 1992, the police arrived at 25 Cromwell Street with a search warrant. They were looking for evidence of child abuse, found a mountain of distasteful pornography and arrested both Fred and Rose. Fred was charged with the rape and sodomy of a minor and Rose was charged with assisting him.

DC Savage set about interviewing the Wests' friends and family members. Anne-Marie talked openly about the abuse she had suffered at Fred's hands. She also expressed her suspicions about the fate of

Charmaine, who Savage had known from her investigations in 1966. Rena, it seemed, had also gone missing. Savage checked tax and national insurance records which showed that Heather had not been employed, drawn benefits or visited a doctor in five years. Either she had moved abroad or she was dead.

The younger children were taken into care. Unable to cope without Fred, Rose tried to kill herself by taking an overdose of pills. But her son Stephen found her in time and saved her life. In jail Fred became self-pitying and depressed. But still his luck held. The case against him collapsed when two key witnesses decided not to testify against them and he was released.

However, DC Savage now launched an inquiry into the whereabouts of Heather. The West children joked that she was under the patio. They said Fred had threatened them that if they did not keep their mouths shut about the goings-on in 25 Cromwell Street they would end up under the patio like Heather.

Digging up a 900-square-foot garden was a huge undertaking and was bound to attract media attention, especially since the extension to the house had been built over part of the garden. But Detective Superintendent John Bennett eventually got a warrant.

Fred West knew that it was only a matter of time before the evidence of his long murder spree would be unearthed. He told his son that he had done something really bad and would be going away for a while.

'He looked at me so evil and so cold,' said Stephen. 'That look went right through me.'

After the discovery of the bones in the garden, Fred was charged with the murder of Heather, Shirley Robinson and Alison Chambers. To protect Rose, Fred took full responsibility for the murders.

The police now broadened the investigation to look into the disappearance of Rena and Charmaine. Fred was assigned an 'appropriate adult' named Janet Leach. She was usually assigned to befriend and assist juveniles or the mentally subnormal when they were taken into custody. Fred West was thought to fall into this second category. Leach asked Fred whether there were any more bodies. West admitted that there were and sketched a map of the cellar and bathroom, showing where six more bodies lay. He admitted to murdering the girls he had buried there, but not to raping them. The girls, he insisted, wanted to have sex with him. However, he did not even know the names of some of his victims. One he called simply 'Scar Hand' because of a burn on her hand. Therese Siegenthaler he referred to as 'Tulip' under the mistaken impression that she was Dutch, though she was, in fact, Swiss. This made it difficult for the police to identify the bodies. With large numbers of people being reported missing each year, it was a mammoth task to match a set of remains to a missing person's report.

Of course, Fred West did know the names of some of his victims. He admitted to murdering his first wife Rena and his lover Anne McFall and burying their bodies in the fields near Much Marcle. He also admitted to the murder of Charmaine, Rena's eldest daughter. With his help the bodies of Rena, Anne McFall and Charmaine were found. However, he refused to cooperate with the Mary Bastholm case and her body has never been located.

From the start the police were convinced that Rose West was involved in the murders, even though she feigned shock at her husband's confessions and denied everything. She played the naive and innocent victim of a murderous and manipulative man. Along with Stephen and her eldest daughter Mae, she was moved to a police safe house in Cheltenham. The house was bugged by police but she never said anything which implicated herself. However, on 18 April 1994 she was charged with a sex offence and taken into custody. The murder charges would come later.

By this time the world's media had turned up in Gloucester. TV crews from America and Japan filmed interviews in the street and journalists quickly dubbed 25 Cromwell Street the 'House of Horrors'.

The fact that a serial killer had been operating in Gloucester for over 25 years came as a shock to its citizens. They had got away with it because, with the exception of Lucy Partington, the Wests had deliberately targeted people who drifted in and out of society and whose disappearance would not be noticed. Nevertheless the international attention the Wests had brought the city came as a terrible blow to Gloucester's civic pride.

On 13 December 1994, Fred West was charged with 12 murders. He and Rose appeared together in court. In the dock, Fred tried to comfort Rose, but she pulled back from him, telling the police that he made her sick. Fred found the rejection devastating. He wrote to her, saying: 'We will always be in love… You will always be Mrs West, all over the world. That is important to me and to you.' She did not respond.

Just before noon on New Year's Day at Winson Green Prison in Birmingham, 54-year-old Fred West hanged himself with strips of bedsheet. He had picked his moment well. The guards were at lunch and he had clearly planned his suicide so that he would not be discovered and resuscitated.

This left Rose alone to face ten counts of murder. Clearly she could not have been involved in the murder of Rena and Anne McFall as they had been killed before she knew Fred. Her trial opened on 3 October 1995. However, there was little direct evidence to link her to the murders. Instead the prosecution, led by Brian Leveson QC, aimed to construct a tight web of circumstantial evidence to prove Rose's guilt.

A number of key witnesses – including Caroline Owens, Miss A and Anne-Marie – testified to Rose's sadistic assaults on young women. The most damning evidence came from Anne-Marie, who fixed her stepmother with a withering stare as she described how she and Fred had embarked on a campaign of sexual abuse when she was eight.

Another witness, Caroline Raine, a former beauty queen, told the court of the night in 1972 when Fred and Rose abducted her when she was hitchhiking across Gloucestershire and sexually assaulted her. The prosecution suggested that this was a blueprint for how the Wests picked up their victims. In this case, Caroline Raine escaped with her life and the Wests were prosecuted and fined over the incident at the time. From then on, it was clear that Fred and Rose had made up their minds that future victims would not be allowed to live to tell the tale.

Fred's confidante Janet Leach also gave crucial evidence. She testified that Fred had told her privately that Rose was involved in the murders

– and that Rose had murdered Charmaine and Shirley Robinson by herself. However, he said that he made a deal with Rose to take all the blame himself. At the time, this confession, given in confidence, had put her under so much stress that she suffered a stroke. It was only after Fred's suicide that she felt the bond of confidentiality had been lifted and she told the police what he had said to her. Giving testimony put her under enormous stress. She collapsed and had to be taken to the hospital, and the trial was adjourned for several days.

The defence, led by Richard Ferguson QC, maintained that evidence of sexual assault was not the same thing as evidence of murder. He made the case that Rose did not know that Fred was murdering the girls they had abused and burying them around the house.

Ferguson made the mistake of putting Rose on the witness stand. She did not impress the jury. The prosecution rattled her by making her angry. She appeared obstructive and defiant. The prosecution also managed to force her to confess how badly she had treated the children and she gave the general impression of being unscrupulous and dishonest.

The defence played taped interviews with Fred West, where he said that he had murdered his victims when Rose was out of the house. But it was not difficult for the prosecution to show that Fred was an inveterate liar, so everything he said was open to doubt.

In his closing speech, Leveson maintained Rose was the dominant force in the Wests' murderous partnership. She was, he told the jury, the 'strategist'.

'The evidence that Rosemary West knew nothing is not worthy of belief,' he said.

Ferguson, closing for the defence, maintained that the evidence for murder only pointed to Fred. There was no proof that Rose had known anything, let alone participated. The jury did not believe him. It quickly came to the unanimous verdict that Rosemary West was guilty of the murders of Charmaine West, Heather West, Shirley Robinson and the other girls buried at the house. The judge sentenced her to life imprisonment on each of the ten counts of murder. In 1996, her request to appeal was turned down.

David Blunkett, the Home Secretary during this period, later told Rosemary West that she would never be allowed out.

In October 1996, Gloucester City Council demolished 25 Cromwell Street. There were calls to create a memorial garden on the site, but there were fears that it would be turned into a ghoulish shrine, so it was left as a landscaped footpath leading to the city centre.

Four years after Rose West was sentenced her son Stephen revealed to the police that he was convinced that his father had killed 15-year-old Mary Bastholm. He said that, while visiting his father in prison shortly before he died, West had boasted that Bastholm's body would never be found. He also talked of a number of other victims and crowed: 'They are not going to find them all, you know, never.'

When Stephen asked specifically asked him about Mary Bastholm, West replied: 'I will never tell anyone where she is.'

However, to the police, West had continued strenuously denying that he had killed Bastholm, although she had been seen in his car. Mary Bastholm's brother Peter said he was relieved by the news, though his parents had both died without learning the fate of their only daughter.

Later in 1998, Fred West's cousin William Hill was jailed for four years after being convicted of one count of rape and three charges of indecent assaults. Like West, Hill preyed on young women and one of his convictions was for a series of indecent assault on a 15-year-old girl over an extended period in the early 1980s. He tried to kill himself in jail but failed. Fred West's brother John succeeded in hanging himself in jail while awaiting the verdict after being tried for raping Anne-Marie.

Anne-Marie tried to kill herself by throwing herself from a bridge near Gloucester, but was rescued. She had previously tried to kill herself during the trial by taking an overdose, but was rushed to hospital and had her stomach pumped. Stephen West tried to hang himself at his home in Bussage, near Stroud, after his girlfriend left him. He survived when the rope snapped.

In December 1998, Gordon Burn, the author of *Happy Like Murderers*, another book about the Wests, claimed that the bones removed from the victims' bodies – usually fingers, toes, but in some cases kneecaps and entire shoulder blades – had been buried near Pittville Park in Cheltenham, close to the bus stop where Fred first met Rose in 1970. Burn said that the location held an 'almost spiritual' significance for the Wests.

He was interviewed by Chief Constable of Gloucestershire, Tony Butler, and Detective Chief Inspector Terry Moore who had taken over the case after Detective Superintendent John Bennett had retired.

'Out of all the books it's probably the best written and the most interesting,' said Moore. 'He has got some things right and some things wrong."

As to the bones, Moore said: 'There are various theories but nothing has come to light. The secret has gone to the grave with Fred and Rose is not saying anything.'

In 2000, Rosemary West secured legal aid to launch a new appeal. Her lawyer, Leo Goatley, said that West may 'unearth new photographic evidence, which would prove that her husband, Fred West, was the sole killer'. The hope was that she would 'be cleared by anatomical photographs of women which were taken by Fred West and seized by police during an earlier investigation in 1992'. The photographs, he asserted, were time stamped and would help his client prove she was not present at the time. The originals, he said, had been destroyed, but Goatley was confident that 'copies would have been made or details of the photographs chronicled by police'. He also said that excessive publicity and chequebook journalism prevented her getting a fair trial, and an application was made to the Criminal Cases Review Commission on 20 October 2000.

But the application was doomed to failure when a TV documentary aired an interview with Janet Leach who revealed that Fred West had confessed to killing many more than the 12 victims he had been charged with murdering.

'Fred said that there were two other bodies in shallow graves in the woods but there was no way they would ever be found,' she told the interviewer. 'He said there were twenty other bodies, not in one place but spread around and he would give police one a year. He told me the truth about the girls in the cellar and what happened to them so I don't see why he would lie about other bodies.'

She also said that West had confessed to the murder of Mary Bastholm. She was one of two young woman 'in shallow graves in the woods, but there was no way they would ever be found'.

'No one has even scratched the surface of this case,' said the documentary's producer. 'Social services had three hundred missing-people files and one hundred missing girls. There were two girls from Jordansbrook children's home who were making a living as prostitutes from twenty-five Cromwell Street.'

The programme also described how West had told his solicitor that he believed 'the spirits of his victims were coming up through the floor from the cellar where they were entombed'.

'When they come up into you it's beautiful,' West is alleged to have said. 'It's when they go away you are trying to hold them, you feel them flying away from you and you try to stop them. You can't send them back to where they were.'

Soon after this Rosemary West abandoned her appeal and told the press that she had resigned herself to spending the rest of her life in Durham's high-security prison. She also apologised to her step-daughter Anne-Marie for 'the abuse she suffered' and expressed a desire to be reconciled to her.

Then, on 22 January 2003, the BBC reported that 'the wedding between jailed serial killer Rose West and session musician Dave Glover has been called off – just days after it was announced. The pair have been writing to each other for a year, but Mr Glover is reported to have pulled out because of the publicity.' Bass player Glover, 36, had been working regularly with the band Slade for 18 months, but his contract was then terminated.

A spokesman for the band said: 'It has all come as an incredible shock. At no point had Dave Glover discussed this. It's like marrying Hitler.'

West and Glover had announced their intention to marry on 19 January. Rose West explained that she wanted to give 'this young man his life back'.

– Chapter 18 –

Doctor Death

Dr Harold Shipman

 **NATIONALITY:** ENGLISH

NUMBER OF VICTIMS: 215+

FAVOURED METHOD OF KILLING: INJECTING PETHIDINE/MORPHINE

BORN: 1946

PROFESSION: GP

MARRIED: YES

REIGN OF TERROR: EARLY 1970s–98

Dr Harold Shipman is thought to be the most prolific serial killer ever. He is said to have killed at least 215 people and perhaps as many as 400 over a career of murder that lasted nearly 30 years. Yet he was an ordinary GP working in the English Midlands.

Born into a working-class family in Nottingham on 14 June 1946, Harold Frederick Shipman was known as Fred or Freddy. Although the family lived in a red-brick terraced council house like any other, under the influence of his mother, Vera, they set themselves apart from others.

'Vera was friendly enough,' said a neighbour. 'But she really did see her family as superior to the rest of us. Not only that, you could tell Freddy was her favourite, the one she saw as the most promising of her three children.'

Shipman's sister Pauline was seven years his senior, his brother Clive, four years younger than him. But he was the apple of his mother's eye and she decided that it was Harold that was going make a success out of life. She also decided who Harold could play with and, to set him apart from the other boys, she insisted that he wore a tie while the others dressed more casually.

A confident and clever child, Shipman did well at junior school and was accepted by High Pavement Grammar school. There he failed to shine in the classroom, but made his way by dogged hard work.

Where he did shine was on the running track and the football field. But he did not involve himself in the camaraderie of sport. His unshakeable belief in his innate superiority alienated those who would otherwise have been his friends. An isolated adolescent, he had to cope as his beloved mother wasted away with terminal lung cancer. He would race home after school to make her a cup of tea and chat with her. It was clear that she found great solace in his company. It is thought that Shipman learned his engaging bedside manner then. He would also play out his mother's deathbed scene over and over with the elderly women that would become the majority of his victims.

Towards the end of her life, Vera was in great pain. Shipman watched in fascination as the family doctor injected her with morphine. It took away the pain, but it did not stop Vera growing thinner and frailer. Then on 21 June 1963, at the age of 43, his mother died. Shipman himself was just 17. The loss seems to have left him with no regard for human life or feelings towards others.

Two years after his mother died, Shipman was admitted to Leeds University Medical School, after re-sitting the entrance examinations. At university he was a loner and most of the teachers and his fellow students at Leeds could barely remember him. Those who did, claim that he looked down on them, seemingly bemused by the way his fellow students behaved.

'It was as if he tolerated us,' said one. 'If someone told a joke he would smile patiently, but Fred never wanted to join in. It seems funny, because

I later heard he'd been a good athlete, so you'd have thought he'd be more of a team player.'

However, on the soccer pitch he revealed another, darker side. His intense need to win made him extremely aggressive both on and off the ball.

At school, Shipman had never shown much interest in girls.

'I don't think he ever had a girlfriend,' said one teacher. 'In fact, he took his older sister to school dances. They made a strange couple. But then, he was a bit strange, a pretentious lad.'

However, at university he quickly acquired a girlfriend. She was daughter of his landlord, a 16-year-old window-dresser name Primrose, three years his junior. She also came from a strict background with a mother who controlled her acquaintanceships. No calendar girl, Primrose was delighted to have found a boyfriend. They married in November 1966 when she was 17 and five months pregnant.

he revealed another, darker side

Shipman's sense of superiority was not dented even when he had to re-sit a number of exams at medical school. But he eventually got the grades to graduate and moved on to a mandatory period of hospital training, becoming a junior house doctor at Pontefract General Infirmary. It is thought that he began his career of killing there – murdering at least ten patients, including a four-year-old girl.

In 1974 he joined a medical practice in Todmorden in Calderdale, West Yorkshire. By this time he had two children. In this small Yorkshire town, Shipman blossomed. No longer the withdrawn loner, he was suddenly outgoing and became respected by both his patients and his fellow practitioners, who welcomed the up-to-date information they got from a young doctor, fresh from medical school. But the staff under him at the practice saw a different side of Shipman. He was often rude and liked to belittle his juniors, frequently berating them as 'stupid'. He also had a way of manipulating the other doctors and the general opinion was that he was a control freak – though he was also seen as hard-working, enthusiastic and sociable.

But soon problems surfaced. He began having blackouts. He told the other partners he suffered from epilepsy. However, the true reason for the blackouts was soon revealed. The practice's receptionist Marjorie Walker discovered some discrepancies in the local chemists' narcotics ledgers. The records showed that Shipman had been prescribing large amounts of pethidine – a morphine-like analgesic whose addictive properties are still in dispute – in the names of several patients and on behalf of the practice itself. These discrepancies were investigated by partner Dr John Dacre.

The matter came to a head at a staff meeting. Partner Dr Michael Grieve recalled the scene: 'We were sat round with Fred sitting on one side and up comes John on the opposite and says, "Now young Fred, can you explain this?"'

Dacre then laid before Shipman all the evidence that he has been collecting. It clearly showed that Shipman had been prescribing pethidine to patients who never received it.

'In fact, the pethidine had found its way into Fred's very own veins,' said Grieve.

Realising his career was on the line, Shipman begged for a second chance. When this was refused, Shipman hurled his medical bag to the ground. His colleagues were shocked by this petulant outburst. Soon after, Shipman's wife Primrose stormed into the room, screaming that her husband would never resign.

'You'll have to force him out!' she shrieked.

Indeed, that is what they did. Shipman left Todmorden and checked into a drug treatment centre in York. He was found guilty of forgery and prescription fraud, and was fined £600, but he was not struck off by the General Medical Council.

'If Fred hadn't, at that point, gone straight into hospital,' said Grieve, 'perhaps his sentence would have been more than just a fine. I think it's perhaps the fact that he put his hand up and said "I need treatment" and went into hospital, and then the sick-doctor routine takes over.'

This was probably also the reason he was not struck off the medical register.

There is now some doubt that Shipman had been using all the pethidine himself and there are those who believe that Shipman had been using it to kill patients in Todmorden.

Two years later, Shipmen got a post at the Donnybrook Medical Centre in Hyde, Greater Manchester, with surprising ease.

'His approach was "I have had this problem, this conviction for abuse of pethidine",' said Dr Jeffery Moysey of the Donnybrook Centre. '"I have undergone treatment. I am now clean. All I can ask you to do is to trust me on that issue and to watch me".'

But they did not watch him closely enough. Again, he appeared to be a dedicated, hard-working doctor, who earned his colleagues' respect and his patients' trust. And, again, he was seen as bullying and abusive by those under him – though he was skilled at masking this in front of his peers. But this time there were no blackouts, and no suspicion of drug abuse. This left him free to kill.

He stayed at the Donnybrook clinic for 16 years. Then in 1993, after falling out with the partners, he set up on his own as a GP with Primrose as his part-time receptionist. Such was his reputation in Hyde that he attracted a large number of patients. It is not known how many of them he killed.

The first person to suspect that something was wrong was local undertaker Alan Massey. He noted that Shipman's patients seemed to be dying at an unusually high rate. But there was also a curious pattern to their deaths and a strange similarity to the corpses when he called to collect them.

'Dr Shipman's always seem to be the same, or very similar,' said Massey. 'They could be sat in a chair, could be laid on the settee, but I would say ninety per cent were fully clothed. There was never anything in the house that I saw that indicated the person had been ill. It just seems the person, where they were, had died. There was something that didn't quite fit.'

The undertaker was so troubled that he questioned Shipman about it.

'I asked him if there was any cause for concern,' said Massey. 'He just said: "No, there isn't."'

Shipman showed Massey the book in which he recorded the details of death certificates he had issued. In it, he entered the cause of death and noted any causes for concern. He assured Massey that all the deaths were straightforward. There was nothing to worry about. Anybody who wanted to inspect the book had free access. As Shipman showed no unease when questioned, Massey was placated and took no further action. But his daughter, Debbie Brambroffe, who was also in the business, was not so easily mollified. She enlisted the support of Dr Susan Booth, who came from a nearby practice.

By law a doctor from an unrelated practice must countersign cremation documents. The fee paid for this service is known cynically as 'cash for ash'. So when Dr Booth turned up at the funeral parlour to countersign some of Shipman's cremation forms, Brambroffe told her of her misgivings.

'She was concerned about the number of deaths of Dr Shipman's patients that they'd attended recently,' said Dr Booth. 'She was also puzzled by the way in which the patients were found. They were mostly female, living on their own, found dead sitting in a chair fully dressed – not in their night-clothes lying ill in bed.'

Booth confided in her colleagues and one of them, Dr Linda Reynolds, contacted the coroner John Pollard. He, in turn, contracted the police. Shipman's medical records were examined surreptitiously, but nothing untoward was found as the causes of death and treatments matched perfectly. What the police did not then know was that Shipman re-wrote his patients' notes after he had killed them.

Recently this preliminary investigation has been widely criticised as the police did not check to see whether Shipman had a criminal record. Nor did they consult the General Medical Council. Had they discovered Shipman's history of drug abuse and forgery, they might have dug a little deeper and put an end to Shipman's killing spree there and then.

Shipman was eventually stopped by the dogged determination of Angela Woodruff, the daughter of Kathleen Grundy who died suddenly on 24 June 1998. A former mayor, Mrs Grundy was a tireless worker for local charities and a wealthy woman. Even though she was 81, she had boundless energy and her death came as a shock to the many people who knew her.

When she failed to show at an Age Concern club where she helped serve meals to elderly pensioners, someone was sent to her home to find out if anything was wrong. They found her lying on a sofa, fully dressed. She was already dead, so they called her GP, Dr Shipman.

It transpired that he had visited Mrs Grundy a few hours earlier, and was the last person to see her alive. The purpose of his visit, he said, had been to take blood samples for a study on ageing. Shipman then pronounced her dead and her daughter, Angela Woodruff, was contacted. Shipman assured Mrs Woodruff that a post-mortem was unnecessary as he had seen her mother shortly before her death.

After Mrs Grundy was buried, Mrs Woodruff got a phone call from a firm of solicitors who claimed to have a copy of Mrs Grundy's will. Woodruff was a solicitor herself and her firm had always handled her mother's affairs. They held a will that Mrs Grundy had lodged with them in 1996.

The moment Woodruff saw the new document, she knew it was a fake. It was a form that you can obtain from a post office or newsagents. And it was filled in sloppily, poorly worded and was badly typed.

'My mother was a meticulously tidy person,' she said. 'The thought of her signing a document which is so badly typed didn't make any sense. The signature looked strange, it looked too big.'

It also asked for the body to be cremated, which Woodruff knew was not her mother's wish. And, tellingly, it left £386,000 to Dr Shipman.

'It wasn't a case of "Look, she's not left me anything in her will,"' Woodruff said. 'But the concept of Mum signing a document leaving everything to her doctor was unbelievable.'

The obvious conclusion was that Dr Shipman had murdered her mother for profit. Mrs Woodruff went to the Warwickshire police, who passed the investigation on to the Greater Manchester force where it ended up in the hands of Detective Superintendent Bernard Postles. Once he saw the new will, he agreed with Angela Woodruff's conclusions.

'You only have to look at it once and you start thinking it's like something off a John Bull printing press,' he said. 'You don't have to have twenty years as a detective to know it's a fake.'

A post-mortem was required to get conclusive proof that Kathleen Grundy had been murdered, so the police applied to the coroner for an exhumation order. Such orders are rare. The Greater Manchester Police is one of the largest police forces in the country. It was formed in 1974 and since then there had not been a single disinterment.

'We did not have one officer who had ever taken part in an exhumation,' said Detective Superintendent Postles. 'We had to ask the National Crime Squad for advice.'

By the end of the investigation of the Shipman case, Greater Manchester Police would be all too familiar with exhumation.

Mrs Grundy's body was disinterred one August night amid gusting wind and driving rain just five weeks after she had been buried in Hyde. The mud-streaked coffin was opened and hair and tissue samples were taken for analysis. At the same time, Shipman's office and home were raided, so he had no chance to conceal or destroy any evidence. Shipman showed no surprise at this turn of events. Rather, he registered bemused contempt as the warrant was read.

There were some odd things about Shipman's home. The police found mysterious pieces of jewellery, presumable stolen from his victims, and the house was littered with newspapers and filthy old clothes. For a doctor's home, it was little short of insanitary.

One of the first things the police found was the typewriter Shipman had used to type the fraudulent will. Shipman said that Mrs Grundy sometimes borrowed it. However, Shipman's fingerprints were found on the document, but there were none of Mrs Grundy's fingerprints on it – and none belonging to those people who were purported to have witnessed it.

When the toxicology reports came back from the lab, Detective Superintendent Postles realised that he had an open-and-shut case. The cause of death was an overdose of morphine. What's more, death would have occurred within three hours of receiving the lethal injection.

Postles was astounded. As a doctor, Shipman would have known morphine is one of the few poisons that remains easily identifiable in body tissue for centuries. There were plenty of other drugs that would have been lost against the background. For example, had Shipman used insulin, which the body produces naturally, to kill Mrs Grundy the case would have been impossible to prove. As it was, Shipman's only defence was to claim that the respectable old lady was a junkie. Psychologists speculate that he wanted to be caught. Why type the forged will on his own typewriter? And why use a drug so easily traced? Others think he saw himself as invincible. As a doctor, he believed, his word would never be questioned.

The publicity surrounding the Grundy case brought a torrent of phone calls from other relatives of Shipman's patients who had died in similar circumstances. The police immediately broadened the scope of the investigation. A pattern quickly emerged. The cause of death recorded by Dr Shipman often bore no relation to the symptoms the patient had suffered prior to their demise and Shipman was usually present at the death or had visited the patient immediately before. He also urged families to cremate their dead. But clearly the police could only proceed with cases where the relatives had ignored this advice and had buried the body.

In each case, Shipman also insisted that no further investigation into the cause of death was necessary. People trust their doctors. Even if they questioned him, Shipman could show that their loved one had died of a condition consistent with their medical history. His story would be backed by the computerised medical records he kept. Shipman would hurry to his office to rewrite immediately after he had killed one of his patients. Kathleen Grundy's medical notes, for example, clearly showed that she was a morphine addict. This was clearly ludicrous. From the moment he asserted this, his credibility crumbled.

Convinced of his superiority, Shipman claimed he was a computer expert, but he did not know was that his hard drive recorded every alteration he made to the patient's record, along with the time it was made. The police called in their own experts to demonstrate that he had fabricated his patients' medical histories after their deaths to cover his tracks.

One of the earlier cases the police pursued was that of Winnifred Mellor, a healthy 73-year-old who played football with her grandchildren and was planning a trip to the Palestine when she died mysteriously at three in the afternoon on 11 May 1998 after a visit from Shipman.

The police confronted Shipman with the fact that, soon after she was dead, he added to her notes that she had suffered 'chest pains' on 1 October 1997 – ten months earlier. Shipman claimed he had no recollection of making that alteration, but the police were able to point out that the addition had been made using his user name and his password.

'It doesn't alter the fact I can't remember doing it' was Shipman's feeble reply.

'You attended the house at three o'clock,' said the officer interviewing him. 'That's when you murdered this lady. You went back to the surgery and immediately started altering this lady's medical records. You tell me why you needed to do that.'

'There's no answer,' said Shipman.

In a further interview, Shipman was accused of killing Winnifred Mellor with a morphine overdose, then altering her records to show a history of angina.

'The levels were such that this woman actually died from toxicity of morphine, not as you wrongly diagnosed,' Shipman was told. 'In plain speaking you murdered her. One feature of these statements from the family was they couldn't believe their own mother had chest pains, angina and hadn't been informed.'

'By... by whom?' asked Shipman.

'By her,' said the officer.

'By her, thank you,' said Shipman, sarcastically.

'They also found it hard to believe because she didn't have a history of chest complaints and heart disease and angina, did she, Doctor?' the officer asked.

'If it's written on the records then she had the history and therefore...'

'The simple truth is you've fabricated a history to cover what you've done,' said the officer. 'You'd murdered her and you make up a history of angina and chest pains so you could issue a death certificate and placate this poor woman's family, didn't you?'

'No,' said Shipman.

'We've got a statement from a Detective Sergeant John Ashley, who works in the field of computers,' the officer said. 'He has made a thorough examination of your computer, doctor, and the medical records contained on it. What he's found is that there are a number of **arrogant and supercilious** entries that have been incorrectly placed on this record to falsely mislead and to indicate this woman had a history of angina and chest pains. What have you got to say about that, doctor?

'Nothing,' said Shipman.

It was clear that he was not going to co-operate in any way with the police, who found him arrogant and supercilious throughout the investigation. Nevertheless, the evidence against him accumulated. He was charged with 15 counts of murder and one of forgery – over the will – and went to trial in Preston on 5 October 1999.

Shipman's defence counsel Nicola Davies, a 46-year-old medical lawyer, began the proceedings with an application to have the case thrown out as Shipman could not receive a fair trial because of 'inaccurate, misleading' reporting of the case. Taking nearly two days, she reviewed the media coverage of some 150 patients' cases, the investigation of Shipman himself and intense interest in the exhumations. Richard Henriques, for the crown, countered with the fact that the reports had alerted other families to the possible fate of their relatives.

Ms Davies then asked for the court to hold three separate trials. She argued that the case of Kathleen Grundy should be prosecuted separately as it alone had any alleged motive – that of greed. A second trial should cover only patients who had been buried as only in these cases was there physical evidence of cause of morphine poisoning.

A third trial, she said, should cover those who had been cremated, where no physical evidence existed.

Henriques argued that the cases were inter-related and trying them together would present a comprehensive picture.

Ms Davies petitioned for evidence showing how Shipman had accumulated stocks of morphine to be disallowed. In 28 cases, he had continued prescribing for patients after they had died, and kept the drugs for his murderous purposes. He also prescribed morphine to living patients who did not require strong painkillers.

The judge, Mr Justice Forbes, denied all three petitions. The trial would continue with the original 16 charges on the indictment.

On 11 October 1999, the jury was sworn in and the case for the prosecution was made by Richard Henriques. He was one of the top Britain's barristers and had handled the 1993 Jamie Bulger trial, where two ten-year old boys were found guilty of kidnapping, torturing and murdering the two-year-old on Merseyside.

Henriques' opening statement in the Shipman case pulled no punches.

'None of those buried – nor indeed cremated were prescribed morphine or diamorphine,' he said. 'All of them died most unexpectedly. All of them had seen Dr Shipman on the day of their death.'

He ruled out the possibility of euthanasia or mercy killing as a motive, as none of those who had died was suffering from a terminal illness. Henriques simply concluded that Shipman killed the 15 patients whose names were on the indictment simply because he enjoyed doing so.

'He was exercising the ultimate power of controlling life and death,' Henriques said, 'and repeated the act so often he must have found the drama of taking life to his taste.'

His first witness was Angela Woodruff, who explained that she had spoken to Dr Shipman after the Hyde Police had phoned to tell her that her mother was dead.

'Exactly what he said was difficult to remember,' she said. 'It's very hazy because I was very, very upset. Dr Shipman said he had seen my mother on the morning of her death. He said he had seen her at home.'

She was then questioned about the fake will that left everything to Shipman. She dismissed it as a fake, citing her mother's meticulous attention to detail. This was supported by her mother's diary, where every event was scrupulously recorded in pristine penmanship.

She also testified to the health of her 81-year-old mother. 'She was just amazing,' she said. 'We would walk five miles and come in and she would say: "Where's the ironing?" We used to joke she was fitter than we were.'

In the ensuing cross-examination, Ms Davies attempted to show that Mrs Woodruff's relationship with her mother had been less than harmonious. This impression was totally disproven by the diary and other witnesses.

Government pathologist Dr John Rutherford took the jury through the gruesome details of the post-mortem procedure, explaining how body tissue was collected and analysed. He demonstrated that victims cited in the indictment had not died from old age or disease and that, typically, morphine poisoning was the cause of death.

A fingerprint expert then demonstrated that Mrs Grundy had not handled the 'will', though Dr Shipman had. Calligraphy analyst Michael Allen then took the stand and dismissed the signatures on the document as 'crude forgeries'.

Computer analyst Detective Sergeant John Ashley then testified that Shipman falsified his patients' medical histories. The recorded interviews showing Shipman's reaction to being confronted with this was then entered into the record.

In the second week of the trial, district nurse Marion Gilchrist was called. She recalled Shipman's reaction when he realised he was about to be arrested for the murder of Mrs Grundy. He broke down and said: 'I read thrillers and, on the evidence they have, I would have me guilty...'

Then he said: 'The only thing I did wrong was not having her cremated. If I had had her cremated I wouldn't be having all this trouble.'

At the time, the nurse put this down to black humour.

Another witness testified that Shipman had said: 'If I could bring her back, I would; look at all the trouble it's caused.' As to the will, he had said: 'I was going to say I didn't want the money but, because of all this trouble, I will have it.'

Shipman had then claimed he was going to use most of the money for philanthropic purposes.

Dr John Grenville, who had reviewed Shipman's notes, expressed shock at how quickly Shipman had pronounced Mrs Grundy dead.

'I would examine the body carefully to ensure death had occurred,' he said. 'If I found no pulse at the neck, I would look for a more central point.'

Grenville also pointed out that Shipman made no attempt to revive the patient, which would have been standard medical practice.

As the details of each case were presented, other patterns emerged. Shipman told bystanders that he had called 999, but when he checked and found the patient dead, he would pick up the phone and pretend to cancel the ambulance – though none was on its way.

This occurred in the case of Lizzie Adams who was murdered on 28 February 1997. Although she was 77 year old, she still loved dancing. Her dance partner William Catlow dropped in at Mrs Adams' Coronation Street home the day she died to find Shipman inspecting her magnificent collection of crystal and porcelains. In the next room, Lizzie lay dying.

'I just burst past him,' Catlow told the court. 'She felt warm. I said: "I can feel her pulse."'

According to Catlow, Shipman said: 'No, that's yours. I will cancel the ambulance.'

But telephone records showed that Shipman had not phoned for an ambulance that day. He later persuaded the family to have her body cremated.

Shipman also claimed to have called an ambulance when he killed 64-year-old Norah Nuttall on 26 January 1998. Her son Anthony said he had left his mother alone for just 20 minutes, returning to find Dr Shipman leaving the house.

'I asked him what was wrong,' said Anthony. 'He said: "I have rung an ambulance for her." I ran in and she looked like she was asleep in the chair. I took her by the hands and shook her, saying, "Mum, Mum."'

Then Shipman touched her neck and told the son: 'I'm sorry, she has gone.'

Naturally, the family did not find this at all satisfactory and Norah Nuttall's sister went to Shipman's office to examine the dead woman's records because she wanted more details of her sister's death. Annoyed, Shipman told his staff: 'I knew it would happen, I told you it would happen.'

He quickly made up a story of how Norah had phoned his office to say she was ill. Later he claimed he had been paged and, as he happened to be nearby, he made a house call. The telephone records proved that both of these stories were fabrications.

Shipman was caught in another lie. He had said that his reason for visiting Kathleen Grundy was to collect blood samples for a study on ageing. When he was asked what had happened to them, he said they had been sent for analysis. But the prosecution demonstrated that Shipman was not involved in any study on ageing. When confronted, Shipman then remembered that he had left the samples under a heap of notes and, once they were no longer useful, he thrown them away. This did little to bolster his credibility.

The court was also struck by Shipman's lack of compassion toward the bereaved. Lorry driver Albert Lilley broke down as he told of the way Shipman announced the death of his wife, 58-year-old Jean Lilley, after he had killed her on 25 April 1997.

'He said: "I have been with your wife for quite a while now, trying to persuade her to go to the hospital, but she won't go. I was going to come and have a word with you and your wife, and I was too late,"' Lilley testified. 'I said: "What do you mean too late?" He said: "You are not listening to me carefully."'

It seemed Shipman actually took pleasure in forcing Lilley to guess his wife had died. Shipman played a similar guessing game with Winnifred Mellor's daughter Kathleen.

'He said: "Did you realise that your mother has been suffering from chest pains?" and I said: "No",' Kathleen told the court. 'He said: "She called this morning and I came to see her and she refused treatment." So

I said well I'll be up as soon as I can. He said: "No, no there's no need for that. So I said has she gone to hospital?" And he said: "There's no point in sending her to hospital." And I just went silent then, and he didn't say anything neither. And then I just realised what he was not saying. And I said do you mean my mother's dead? He said: "I see you understand."'

Winnifred Mellor's neighbour Gloria Ellis played a key role in securing his conviction. She had witnessed Shipman's visit to Winnie Mellor just hours before her death. When he returned later, he knocked on Gloria Ellis's door. He said he had come to see Winifred Mellor. He could see her sat in a chair and thought she was dead. So the two of them went to Winifred Mellor's house and found her dead in a chair.

Then, when Gloria asked: "You were here before, weren't you?" Shipman did not answer.

"Has Gloria had a stroke?" she asked.

Shipman then grew hostile. He called her a 'stupid girl'. Far from being stupid, she recorded to the minute the times of Shipman's visits.

Shipman was similarly heartless in the case of 63-year-old Ivy Lomas, the only one of the 15 to have died in his surgery. Detective Constable Philip Reade had gone to the doctor's office hoping Shipman would help him locate Ivy's next of kin.

'He was laughing,' said Reade. 'He said he considered her such a nuisance that he was having part of the seating area permanently reserved for Ivy with a plaque to the effect "Seat permanently reserved for Ivy Lomas".'

Shipman also told Reade that as he left the room Ivy 'could have taken her last breath'. Once again, he had made no effort to resuscitate the woman. Instead, he left her alone while he attended other patients.

'This was a medical emergency,' said Dr Grenville. 'I would have given my entire attention to this particular patient.'

But Shipman knew Ivy was beyond resuscitation. She was dying from an overdose of morphine.

Henriques pointed out that 'the poisoner fears pathology, ambulances and hospitals'. And Shipman went to great lengths to avoid any sort of investigation. When 68-year-old Pamela Hillier died in mysterious circumstances on 9 February 1998, a paramedic from the ambulance service suggested they call the police. Shipman said simply: 'I don't think there is any need to do that.'

Mrs Hillier's family was also far from happy with Shipman's cavalier attitude to the diagnosis. When entering the cause of death on the death certificate, he said: 'Let's put it down to a stroke.' This made no sense to the relatives. Pamela Hillier had been both strong and active before Shipman paid a visit. Her son Keith wanted a post-mortem, but Shipman advised against it, saying that it was 'an unpleasant thing... to put my mum through'.

Shipman also went to great lengths to persuade families to have their loved ones cremated. In the case of Kathleen Grundy, he had even ticked the cremation box on the relevant form. But fortunately Angela Woodruff knew that her mother wanted to be buried.

Shipman's defence tried, against all odds, to paint a picture of him as an old-fashioned family doctor – one prepared to go the extra mile for his patients – as well as a family man with a loving wife and well-adjusted children (Shipman and his wife had four children in all, but all were grown up before his addiction to murder was uncovered).

Naturally his previous convictions of drug abuse and forgery went unmentioned. But still they had to overturn the forensic evidence.

Davies questioned whether it was possible to tell whether the morphine found in the bodies came from a single overdose – as the prosecution contended – or from multiple doses.

'I can't say,' the forensic analyst replied.

Plainly, the defence hoped that if they could convince the jury that the morphine in the victims' bodies came from long-term use, they could contend that they had not been murdered by Dr Shipman, but that they were drug addicts who had been killed by their own habit. They were clutching at straws.

The prosecution then put American forensic expert Dr Karch Steven on the stand. He described the technique he had used. It was new and details of the procedure had only been published in *The Lancet* the year before. This technique proved conclusively that none of the victims had been a long-term morphine user. In each case, the narcotic in the tissue came from a single, massive overdose.

Shipman maintained he never carried morphine, so he could not have killed any of his patients. This assertion was overturned by the family of 69-year-old Mary Dudley, who had died on 30 December 1990 – though Shipman had not been charged with her death. Mary's daughter-in-law Joyce Dudley had received a phone call from Shipman telling her: 'I'm afraid your mother-in-law has only got about half an hour left to live.'

By the time, Joyce and her husband Jeffery arrived at Mary's house in Werneth Road, his mother was dead. Shipman told them she had died from a heart attack.

'And this is when he said to me and Jeff that he "gave her a shot of morphine" for the pain,' Joyce Dudley recalled.

The records also detailed his over-prescribing of morphine. He said he had prescribed 2,000 milligrams of morphine to Frank Crompton, who was suffering from prostate cancer. Although Mr Crompton was not in pain, Shipman said he wanted to have the morphine on hand in case pain developed later. Crompton, Shipman maintained, was afraid of becoming a drug addict and threw away the ampoules. Later, Shipman said that he talked to Crompton again and persuaded him that it was best if he kept some morphine in the house and ordered another batch. Crompton had since died, but it seems likely that Shipman purloined both consignments.

Shipman's staff found it difficult to keep track of his drug usage. When a batch of morphine went missing, he said that he had given it to a colleague who had loaned him some in an earlier emergency. He also said he had a supply of diamorphine – that is, heroin – that he had found lying on the office doormat one morning when he arrived at work. It must have been dropped through the letter box, he maintained. Henriques pressed Shipman relentlessly on his 'magic mat' where restricted drugs simply materialised overnight. Otherwise Shipman took unused supplies from patients who had died.

'What he tended to do is over-prescribe to individuals who legitimately required diamorphine, certainly in the days just prior to them dying,' said Detective Superintendent Bernard Postles. 'What he would do then is go along to the home, offer to dispose of any excess that was left at the house, and he would take that away.'

In one case, Shipman obtained enough diamorphine to kill 360 people.

Jim King had a narrow escape in 1996 when Shipman incorrectly diagnosed cancer. He treated him with massive doses of morphine, saying 'You can take as much morphine as you wish' because 'of course it didn't really matter, I was dying anyway'.

King then came down with pneumonia and Shipman made a house call. Again he said he had to give King an injection. But King's wife was wary, perhaps because both King's father and aunt had died after one of Shipman's visits. At her insistence, King refused the injection.

'I kept telling him no, no, I don't want it,' said King. 'He was a bit arrogant about it, a kind of snotty attitude towards me, a little bit.'

This probably saved King's life and kept more morphine out of Shipman's hands. Later, the Kings learned that Shipman had indeed killed their relatives.

In his summing up, Mr Justice Forbes urged caution. After all, no one had actually seen Shipman kill any of his patients.

'The allegations could not be more serious – a doctor accused of murdering fifteen patients,' he said. 'You will have heard evidence which may have aroused feelings of anger, strong disapproval, disgust, profound dismay or deep sympathy.'

However, he said, common sense must prevail.

At 4:43 p.m. on 31 January 2000, the jury returned a unanimous verdict. Shipman was guilty on all 15 counts of murder and one of forgery.

Shipman betrayed no sign of emotion as the verdict was read. His wife Primrose, wearing black and flanked by her two sons, remained impassive. When his previous convictions – including one for forgery – were read, there was a gasp in the courtroom. Sentence was to be passed immediately.

'You have finally been brought to justice by the verdict of this jury,' said the judge. 'I have no doubt whatsoever that these are true verdicts.

The time has now come for me to pass sentence upon you for these wicked, wicked crimes.

'Each of your victims was your patient. You murdered each and every one of your victims by a calculated and cold-blooded perversion of your medical skills, for your own evil and wicked purposes.

calculated and cold-blooded perversion of your medical skills

'You took advantage of, and grossly abused their trust. You were, after all, each victim's doctor. I have little doubt that each of your victims smiled and thanked you as she submitted to your deadly ministrations.'

He handed down a life sentence for each of the murders and a four-year sentence for forgery. Normally a judge writes to the Home Secretary to recommend the length a prisoner sentenced to life should serve. Mr Justice Forbes broke with the tradition and announced his recommendations there and then.

'In the ordinary way, I would not do this in open court,' he said. 'But in your case I am satisfied justice demands that I make my views known at the conclusion of this trial. My recommendation will be that you spend the remainder of your days in prison.'

At the end of the 57-day trial, only 15 murders had been dealt with. There were no immediately plans to try Shipman for any more murders. As he was already serving 15 concurrent life sentences, what was the point?

However, the police were convinced that those 15 were only the tip of the iceberg. The first murder that Shipman had been convicted of happened in 1996, but the police were convinced that Shipman's killing spree started long before that. An audit conducted by Professor Richard Baker of the University of Leicester estimates that he murdered at least 236 patients over a 24-year period. Professor Baker examined the number and pattern of deaths among Shipman's patients, and compared them with those of other practitioners' patients. There was a noticeably higher rate of death among elderly patients. Deaths were often clustered at certain times of the day and they usually occurred when Shipman was present. And his records did not match with the patients' known symptoms.

Detective Chief Superintendent Bernard Postles, who headed the original investigation, noted the death toll estimated in Baker's audit was 'broadly in keeping with the number of deaths investigated by Greater Manchester Police during the course of the investigation'. However, John Pollard once said 'we might be looking at a thousand'. No one will ever know. Shipman was eventually prosecuted for just 15. Professor Baker's study made for distressing reading for the friends and relatives of patients who died while in the Shipman's care and the police started a special helpline for those concerned.

An official inquiry was set up under high court judge Dame Janet Smith. It scrutinised the records of nearly 500 of Shipman's patients who had died between 1978 and 1998. The inquiry's report concluded that Shipman had murdered at least 215 of his patients – 171 women and 44 men, between the ages of 41 and 93. However, Janet Smith said, 'The full toll may be higher', and cited a real suspicion that Shipman had killed 45 more people, though there was not enough information to be certain. And in another 38 cases, there was too little evidence to form any clear opinion on the cause of death.

Dame Janet found Shipman's 'non-violent' killing almost incredible.

'The way in which Shipman could kill, face the relatives and walk away unsuspected would be dismissed as fanciful if described in a work of fiction,' she said.

Even more incredible was that he could murder so many people without arousing suspicion for decades.

Later Dame Janet upped the estimate of how many people Shipman killed by 15 – bringing his total murder toll to an estimated 230 – after investigating his activities during the three years he was a junior house doctor at the Pontefract General Infirmary in the 1970s. She said that Shipman had certainly unlawfully killed three men there and that his death toll at the hospital was 'between ten and fifteen patients'. Dame Janet had decided to investigate Shipman's activities in Pontefract when

Sandra Whitehead, a student nurse who had worked with him for three years, recalled the high death rate in the hospital and contacted police.

'In many cases I have been unable to reach a definite conclusion,' she said. However, of the 137 deaths she investigated at Pontefract – 133 of which Shipman had signed a death certificate or cremation order – she was suspicious about 14 which were 'probably natural but there is one or more feature of the evidence that gives rise to some suspicion or unease'.

The commission found that Shipman had been present in at least one third of the cases he had certified, compared to an average of 1.6 per cent for other doctors. It was also found that an unusually high percentage of the deaths had occurred between 6 p.m. and midnight.

It now seems that Shipman's first victim was probably 67-year-old Margaret Thompson, who had been recovering from a stroke. She died in March 1971, and records indicated that Shipman had been alone with her at the time.

Dame Janet said Shipman had murdered 54-year-old Thomas Cullumbine, 84-year-old John Brewster and 71-year-old James Rhodes in April and May 1972. She also had 'quite serious suspicions' about the deaths of 74-year-old Elizabeth Thwaites, 72-year-old Louis Bastow, 70-year-old John Auty Harrison and four-year-old Susan Garfitt. She was possibly his youngest victim and a break from his normal pattern, as all his other victims were elderly.

A sufferer from cerebral palsy, Susan Garfitt had been admitted to Pontefract General Infirmary on 11 October 1972 with pneumonia. Her mother, Ann Garfitt, recalled Dr Shipman telling her in a soothing voice that the child was going to die and that further medication would only prolong her suffering. After asking him to be kind to the child, Mrs Garfitt went for a cup of tea. When she returned, a nurse told her that Susan had died. Looking back, she wondered whether Shipman had taken her request for kindness as tacit consent to performing euthanasia on her child. In the circumstances, the inquiry decided that Shipman had probably given the child a lethal injection. Other serial killers who have worked in health care often warn that a patient is going to die before killing them.

In three cases – 86-year-old Butterfield Hammill, 57-year-old Cissie MacFarlane and 49-year-old Edith Swift – Shipman had administered inappropriate treatment injecting 'dangerously large doses of a sedative drug'.

'There is some evidence that he liked to test the boundaries of certain forms of treatment,' said Dame Janet. 'It is quite likely that some of the deaths Shipman caused resulted from experimentation with drugs.'

In her opinion many of these patients would have died anyway, perhaps within a few hours, but Shipman's drug experiments hastened their deaths. These deaths usually occurred during the evening shift when there were fewer medical personnel around to see him at work. Then he made unusual entries in their medical records, including strange comments on their deaths. There were also notations that were similar to those seen on the notes of patients he was convicted of killing. Shipman mocked his patients, dismissing them with the abreviations FTPBI (Failed To Put Brain In) and WOW (Whining Old Woman).

In all, Dame Janet positively identified 218 victims, though 45 cases might merit further investigation, making a total that could exceed 260. However, the final report has discounted the claim of former prisoner Jonathan Harkin that Shipman confessed to 508 murders while he was held in prison in Preston.

The report also criticised the Greater Manchester Police, saying that 'three of Harold Shipman's victims could have been saved if police had investigated properly'. An internal inquiry was also found to be 'quite inadequate'. The police later apologised to the families of Shipman's last three victims.

Dame Janet also criticised the coroners, saying that, in future, they 'would be backed by a team of expert investigators to ensure that a homicidal doctor such as Shipman would not be able to exploit the system again'.

The enquiry also found that the post-mortem examination of 47-year-old Renate Overton, who lingered in a coma for over a year after

Shipman gave her a lethal injection in 1994, was inadequate and there should have been an inquest. Dame Jane said: 'Had the circumstances of her admission to hospital been fully investigated at that time, there is a real possibility that it would have been appreciated that Shipman had deliberately administered a lethal dose of morphine – it was a missed opportunity.'

Shipman claimed over a hundred more victims after Mrs Overton died on 21 April 1995.

Shipman maintained his innocence to the end, though he enjoyed being the star turn at his trial. At 6 a.m. on 13 January 2004, he was found hanging in his cell at Wakefield jail. An inquiry found that he had committed suicide using bed sheets tied to the bars of his cell window. He was not on suicide watch, though he had been at Durham jail beforehand. He had been moved to Wakefield the previous June to make it easier for his wife to visit him.

It was said that Shipman was 'obnoxious and arrogant to the prison staff. Just before Christmas his enhanced status was reduced to basic. He was deprived of the television set in his cell and had to wear prison uniform rather than his own clothes'. However, some privileges had been restored shortly before he died.

'He was showing no signs whatsoever of pre-suicidal behaviour at all,' said a spokesman.

Shipman's wife and four children never accepted that he was guilty. They even believed that he had been murdered in his cell.

With Shipman dead, the reason he killed will never be known. The murders seemed to provide no sexual thrill. There were no signs of violence, no hint of sadistic excitement. And, except in the case of Kathleen Grundy, there was no apparent motive. Serial killers often like to toy with their terrified victims, to glory in their power over them. But Shipman's victims did not know what was happening to them. They all seem to have died peacefully, often in their own homes in surroundings where they felt safe.

Some psychiatrists speculate that he hated older women, often saying that the elderly were a drain on the National Health Service. Others feel he had a deep masochistic need to re-create the scenario of his mother's death – though an unshakeable belief in their own superiority is not usually a trait found in masochists.

Dr Richard Badcock, a psychiatrist at Rampton High Security Hospital, spoke at length with Shipman after the conviction. He believed that 'Shipman's choice of career might have been influenced by his developing tendencies towards necrophilia, perhaps originally triggered by the death of his mother from cancer when he was 17'. Having complete control over life and death 'can give a sense of power and omnipotent invulnerability in itself', Dr Badcock theorised.

The fact that he left so many clues have led some to believe that Shipman wanted to be found out and stopped, as if he was fighting a compulsion he could not control. On the other hand, his sense of superiority may have led him to believe that he could do whatever he wanted without fear of discovery. But there is a contradiction inherent in that too. He must have known that he was not as clever as he made out as he had already been caught forging prescriptions and stockpiling drugs.

South Manchester coroner John Pollard speculated that Shipman 'simply enjoyed viewing the process of dying and enjoyed feeling the control over life and death', while the official report simply stated that he was 'addicted to killing' in the way he was addicted to painkillers around the time the murders started.

– Chapter 19 –

Columbine

Eric Harris and
Dylan Klebold

NATIONALITY: AMERICAN

AGE: 19 AND 17

REIGN OF TERROR: 20 APRIL 1999

NUMBER OF VICTIMS: 13 KILLED, 23 INJURED

FAVOURED METHOD OF KILLING: SHOOTING

FINAL NOTE: 'GOOD WOMBS HATH BORNE BAD SONS'

At 11.10 a.m. on 20 April 1999, 19-year-old Eric Harris drove into the student car park at Columbine High School in Littleton, a suburb of Denver, Colorado and parked his 1986 grey Honda Civic in a space assigned to another student. Harris, who avowedly hated Jews, gays and blacks, together with his co-conspirator 17-year-old Dylan Klebold, had chosen that day deliberately because 20 April was Hitler's birthday.

Soon after, Klebold arrived in his 1982 black BMW and parked in a space assigned to another student in the south-west senior car park. Their two cars flanked the lower level of the school cafeteria. This was their target.

Harris got out of his car and spoke to a fellow student, telling him to flee the school because he liked him. The student took his advice. He was the only person they would willingly spare that day.

A few minutes later Harris and Klebold walked into the school cafeteria, carrying two large duffel bags containing enough explosives to kill most of the students who would be arriving for lunch. They put the bags on the floor beside two lunch tables where they did not look out of place among the hundreds of other backpacks and bags scattered around the cafeteria. Each of the duffel bags contained a 20lb propane bomb timed to explode at 11.17 a.m. At that time there would be 488 students in the cafeteria.

The two would-be assassins then returned to their cars to watch the explosion. According to their home-made videotapes, they planned to shoot down anyone who escaped the blast. Their cars were also fitted with bombs and timers set to explode when, afterwards, the two had gone back into the school on a further killing spree.

Around the same time, there was a small explosion in a field on the east side of Wadsworth Boulevard three miles from the school. Harris and Klebold had left two backpacks there, filled with pipe bombs, aerosol canisters and small propane tanks. These were diversionary devices, aimed to keep the police and the fire department from tending the devastation at the school. However, only the pipe bombs and one of the aerosol canisters exploded, but this had set the grass on fire. The couple, it seems were inexpert bomb-makers and, fortunately, the devices in the cafeteria failed to go off. But that did not mean that those at Columbine High School would get off scot-free.

At 11.19 a.m. Harris and Klebold were seen standing together at the top of the west steps, the highest point on the campus. Both were wearing black trench coats, which hid 9mm semi-automatics, and were carrying a duffel bag and a backpack. A witness heard one of them say: 'Go! Go!'

Then they pulled shotguns out of their bags and began shooting at the other students around them. The first shots killed Rachel Scott and injured Richard Castaldo who were eating their lunch on the grass outside the school library. Lance Kirklin, Sean Graves and Daniel Rohrbough were hit by gunfire as they came out of the side door of the cafeteria. Five other students, who had been sitting on the grass to the west of the stairs, tried to run and were shot at. They made for the outdoor athletic storage shed. Michael Johnson suffered gunshots wounds, but managed to take cover there with the others. Mark Taylor was gunned down.

Klebold then descended the stairs to the cafeteria and shot Daniel Rohrbough again at close range, killing him instantly. He also shot Lance Kirklin a second time, again at close range, but Kirklin miraculously survived.

After entering the cafeteria briefly, perhaps to ascertain why the bombs had not gone off, Klebold rejoined Harris at the top of the stairs. Meanwhile Harris shot at Anne Marie Hochhalter, hitting her numerous times as she sought cover in the cafeteria. Then the two gunmen were seen lighting explosive devices and throwing them into the car park, onto the school's roof and onto the grassy slope outside.

Witnesses then heard one of the gunmen shout: 'This is what we always wanted to do. This is awesome!'

By then, the police had begun to get calls. The cafeteria supervisor called Jefferson County Sheriff's Deputy Neil Gardner – the community resource officer at Columbine High School – on the school's radio, saying he was needed in the rear car park of the school. And a student called 911, reporting that a girl was injured in the lower south car park of the high school.

'I think she's paralysed,' the caller said.

This message was conveyed to Deputy Paul Magor, who was on his way to the grass fire on Wadsworth. Deputy Gardner was pulling onto Pierce Street and heading south to the student car park when he heard the call 'Female down in the south lot of Columbine High School' and switched on his siren. Motorcycle patrolman, Deputy Paul Smoker also heard the call and radioed in that he was on his way.

At 11.24 teacher William 'Dave' Sanders and staff members Jon Curtis and Jay Gallatine went into the cafeteria and told the students to get down under the lunch tables. Meanwhile teacher Patricia 'Patti' Nielson saw two male students outside the west entrance of the school carrying what she thought were toy guns. She assumed that they were being filmed as part of a school video production. As it was, they were causing a bit of a commotion and she was on her way to tell them to knock it off when

Harris fired into the doorway. Nielson was showered with shards of glass and metal fragments, cutting her knee, forearm and shoulder. Student Brian Anderson was also injured by flying glass when he was caught between the inner and outer doors and Harris fired at the doors in front of him. Although injured, Nielson and Anderson managed to flee into the school library. At the time Harris and Klebold were distracted by the arrival of Deputy Gardner, who pulled up in the lower south car parks with his lights flashing and siren wailing.

As Gardner stepped out of his patrol car, Harris fired about ten shots at him before his rifle jammed. Gardner returned fire. For a moment, Gardner thought he had hit Harris. But seconds later Harris was firing again, spraying bullets around the car park, before he retreated into the school through the west doors.

In the cafeteria, the students were painfully aware that they were involved in something much more serious than a school prank. They fled up the stairs to the second level with Sanders directing them to safety down the hallway to the eastern exits. Hiding under the counter in the library, Nielson made a 911 call to report that shots were being fired. Smoke began wafting in through the doorway and she yelled at students to take cover under the tables.

At 11.25 Jefferson County Sheriff's Office put out a general alert: 'Attention, south units. Possible shots fired at Columbine High School, 6201 South Pierce, possibly in the south lower lot towards the east end. One female is down.'

Gardner also called for back up.

'Shots in the building,' he radioed. 'I need someone in the south lot with me.'

Then he sent a 'Code 33'. This means 'officer needs emergency assistance.'

Jefferson County Deputies Scott Taborsky and Paul Smoker soon arrived at the west side of the school and began to attend to two wounded students lying on the ground near the sports fields. Then Smoker saw Gardner down the hill to his right, brandishing his service revolver. A gunman carrying a semi-automatic rifle appeared inside of the double doors and Smoker yelled a warning to Gardner. Harris then leant out of a broken window and began shooting. Smoker returned fire and Harris disappeared, but Smoker could still hear gunfire from inside the building.

By this time, Harris and Klebold were in the main north hallway and began firing at students there. They were laughing.

Student Stephanie Munson and another student walked out of a classroom into the hallway. A teacher yelled at them: 'Run! Get out of the building!' They fled towards the eastern exit. Stephanie was hit in the ankle, but both managed to escape, finding safety across the street in Leawood Park.

Klebold chased some other students down the hallway, stopping near the phone booth in the main lobby. A student on the phone with her mother looked to see the sleeve of a black trench coat and a 9mm pistol shooting towards the main entrance. She dropped the phone and hid in a nearby restroom. Klebold then ran back towards the library. When she could hear no more commotion from the hallway, the girl went back the phone. She whispered to her mother, telling her to come pick her up, then escaped through the east doorway.

Dave Sanders was on the second level outside the library when he saw a gunman coming down the hallway. He had turned to run away when he was shot. However, he managed to crawl to the science block where fellow teacher Richard Long helped him into classroom SCI-3. There, two Eagle Scouts, Kevin Starkey and Aaron Hancey, gave him first aid. Despite their efforts, Sanders died.

Outside Deputy Magor set up a road-block on Pierce Street where a teacher and students told him that someone was patrolling the school with a gun. Then he received a report that hand-grenades had gone off at the school. These were, in fact, pipe bombs which Harris and Klebold had set off in the hallway. They threw two more down the stairwell into the cafeteria and fired into the hallway outside the library.

Students were now running from the school, seeking safety behind Taborsky's patrol car on the west side. They told the police that gunmen were inside the school randomly shooting at people with UZIs or shotguns and throwing hand-grenades. The younger of the two gunmen was of high school age. The other was 'taller, a little older'. Both were wearing black trench coats.

By this time, deputies were ringing the school and more reports of injuries were coming in. Deputy Gardner was requesting emergency medical help to the west side when he came under fire from a large calibre weapon.

Harris and Klebold then walked into the school library and told the students to get up. When Harris shot up the front counter, one student, who was hiding behind the photocopier, was injured by flying splinters of wood. Another student was killed before Harris and Klebold began a gunfight out of the windows with the police. Then they turned their attention back on the students in the west section of the library, killing four and injuring four more. They shot out the display cabinet near the front door before firing their guns into the east section of the library, injuring five and killing three. Reloading, they went into the centre section where they killed two more students and injured another two. One gunman yelled: 'Yahoo.'

In the seven-and-a-half minutes the gunmen were in the library they killed ten people and wounded 12 more. Those who survived did so only because they hid until they were evacuated later by a S.W.A.T. team: Patti Nielson managed to hide in a cupboard; another teacher hid in the periodicals rooms; and two of the library staff sought refuge in the library's TV studio. At 11.30 Jefferson County Patrol Deputy Rick Searle began evacuating the students, some of them wounded, who had taken cover behind Taborsky's patrol car. He moved them to a safe location at Caley Avenue and Yukon Street south-west of the school where a triage point was set up. At the south end of the student car park Deputy Kevin Walker provided cover for the students fleeing from the cafeteria. Through the windows on the upper level, he saw one of the gunmen wearing a 'white T-shirt with some kind of holster vest' leading to speculation that there were three gunmen. They didn't know that by this time, Harris had discarded his black trench coat.

Fearing the situation was escalating, Deputy Magor radioed the Sheriff's Office that more help was needed. However, the Denver Police Department was already on its way as one of its officers had a son who a student at Columbine and had called his father.

Minutes later, the Jefferson County S.W.A.T. team, led by Lieutenant Terry Manwaring, was on the way to the high school, and they quickly established a command post at the corner of Pierce Street and Littlewood. Jefferson County Sheriff's Office also requested assistance from other agencies. Soon after the Colorado State Patrol turned up and took up positions on the north-east side of the school by the tennis courts. Firefighters from Littleton's fire department also arrived on the scene.

At 11.35, the gunmen shot their last victim. Then they made their way down the hallway to the science block. On the way, they peered in through the windows of the classrooms, making eye contact with some of the students. But they made no attempt enter the classrooms or harm anyone. However, several students saw Harris and Klebold shooting into empty rooms. Then they taped an explosive device to the door of a storage room. But they did not appear to be particularly eager to get into any of the locked classrooms. They could easily have shot the locks off. But, by this point, the gunmen seemed to have run out of steam. Their killing spree was over. Now their behaviour appeared directionless.

They rained down more pipe bombs into the cafeteria from the library hallway above – but everyone who had been there had already either been killed, escaped or taken cover.

As explosions that blew out windows of the cafeteria, several students run out and took cover behind cars, while Deputy Walker covered them with his gun. He radioed in that he had students with him, but he did not have any safe route to get them out of the car park. Meanwhile a 911 call was received from 17 students hiding in the kitchen who feared that the gunmen were closing in on them.

Around 30 students who had been in the library made their escape out of the west doors and took cover behind patrol cars. Deputy Taborsky, who was with them, reported that he had been told the gunmen were wearing bullet-proof armour and that one of them was probably 'Ned

Harris'. His informant had more than likely said 'Reb', which was Harris' nickname.

Harris and Klebold went down into the cafeteria. On the stairs, Harris knelt down with his rifle resting on the banister and loosed off several shots into one of the large 20lb propane bombs hidden in a duffel bag in an attempt to set it off. He failed. Klebold then walked over to the bomb and fiddled with it.

The two of them took swigs from the water bottles on the school lunch tables. A witness then heard one of the gunmen say: 'Today the world's going to come to an end. Today's the day we die.'

Today the world's going to come to an end

Klebold threw something at the propane bomb. The cylinder failed to detonate, but there was a small explosion. This started a fire which set the sprinklers off.

Denver Metro S.W.A.T. arrived and Jefferson County Undersheriff John Dunaway authorised the S.W.A.T. teams to enter the school. A live bomb was found nearby at Wadsworth and Chatfield, and at 11.55 the command post received a description of one of the suspects. He was, informants said, 'Eric Harris, five foot ten inches, thin build, shaved blond hair, black pants and white T-shirt, light blue gym backpack.'

Ambulances turned up to evacuate the wounded. Meanwhile Harris and Klebold wandered around the cafeteria, inspecting the damage they had done. They looked in the kitchen, then went back upstairs to the library.

The media had already picked up on the story and the command post asked Channel Seven's news helicopter to pick up a deputy so he could make an aerial survey of the school. Meanwhile Fire Department paramedics attempted to rescue Lance Kirklin, Sean Graves and Anne Marie Hochhalter who were lying wounded outside the cafeteria, but the gunmen fired on them from a second-storey library window. Deputy Walker spotted the muzzle flashes and returned fire, and Deputy Gardner joined in the firefight. Then, with the Denver police officers providing cover fire, the paramedics managed to retrieve the three wounded teenagers from in front of the cafeteria. The gunfire from the library window then stopped and Deputy Gardner seized the opportunity to evacuate the 15 students who were taking cover behind his patrol car. More students made their escape through the side door of the cafeteria.

At 12.06, the first S.W.A.T. team arrived at the east main entrance to the school. Manwaring then ordered Deputy Allen Simmons to take his Jefferson County S.W.A.T. team into the school through the south-east doors. Using the fire truck as a shield, Manwaring led the second team around to the west side where students had reported gunfire. However, by this time, Harris and Klebold were already dead. They shot themselves shortly after that last gunshot was fired from the library window.

The triage point at Caley and Yukon began dispatching the wounded to hospital by ambulance and helicopter. Bomb squads from Jefferson County, Denver and Arapahoe County were soon supplemented by bomb experts from Littleton Fire Department, the Bureau of Alcohol, Tobacco and Firearms (ATF) and the Federal Bureau of Investigation (FBI). They began examining the diversionary device found at Wadsworth and Chatfield, while others were sent to the homes of the suspects.

At the command post on Pierce, there was a report that a gunman and hostages were at the front door of the school. Moments later a lone student came out of the main door and ran to the fire truck. The teenager was quickly checked for weapons. It was soon ascertained that he was not one of the gunmen.

On board Channel Seven's news helicopter Sergeant Phil Domenico conducted a survey of the school's roof. Meanwhile extra staff were called into Jefferson County Sheriff's office which was now inundated with calls from the world's media. Parents and students were gathered at Columbine Public Library and Leawood Elementary School, where counselling was provided.

An officer from the Salvation Army called in a mobile kitchen, which was set up near the command post. Then the Red Cross moved into Clement Park to provide food and water for the media, students and their families.

At 12.17, a young man wearing a white shirt and black pants and carrying a .22 rifle and a knife was see walking along the west side of the school. He was arrested at gunpoint. The rifle was found not to be loaded. The young man said he had heard of the shooting on the TV and came to 'help the police'.

At 12.20, a student being interviewed on TV said that the gunmen shot one of his friends. He said that there were two or three gunmen and they were armed with automatic weapons, sawn-off shotguns and pipe bombs. He did not know their names but said they were part of Columbine's 'Trench Coat Mafia'.

The Trench Coat Mafia was a loose association of disaffected youths who complained that they were harassed by the school's athletes – the 'jocks'. There were some 21 members. Some worked at Blackjack Pizza with Harris and Klebold. Others knew them from school. They identified themselves by wearing black trench coats or dusters. In the senior class photograph of 1999 several members – including Harris and Klebold – posed as if pointing weapons at the camera. Some had actually seen the pipe bombs and CO_2 cartridge devices Harris and Klebold had made, but none of them knew that they were planning the Columbine killings.

By 12.35 Manwaring's S.W.A.T. team was at the back entrance of the school on west side's upper level. Their first objective was to rescue two students lying in front of the west doors. The fire truck inched up to the west doors and two Denver S.W.A.T. members grabbed Richard Castaldo. They laid him on the bumper of the fire truck, then Deputy Taborsky transferred him to his patrol car and rushed off to seek medical assistance. Next the S.W.A.T. team tried to retrieve the bodies of Rachel Scott and Daniel Rohrbough. The situation remained chaotic as, at this point, no one knew the gunmen were dead. Students inside the school continued calling 911, their parents and the media with reports of hostage taking, explosions and as many as eight roaming gunmen as well as the sound of gunshots coming from the auditorium, the gymnasium, the music rooms, the science block, the business wing and the school's offices. The firing they heard probably came from the S.W.A.T. team during their rescue of Richard Castaldo at the school's upper west entrance. Meanwhile other schools in the area were 'locked down' with no one being allowed to enter or leave.

Manwaring's S.W.A.T. team then asked for a floor plan of the school. Soon after another ten-man S.W.A.T. team from Jefferson County, under the command of Sergeant Barry Williams, arrived at the command post on Pierce Street.

Deputy Simmons, leader of the first S.W.A.T. team that entered the school on the east side, called for back up. The school covered 250,000-square-foot and had numerous rooms and hallways that had to be searched. It was full of students hiding, some injured and in need of assistance.

Two S.W.A.T. marksmen positioned themselves on the rooftops of houses on West Polk Avenue, the first street south of the school. From there, they had a clear view over the south car park, the cafeteria and the library windows.

Williams' S.W.A.T. team moved into position at the north-west corner of the school, directly opposite the point where Simmons' team had entered the building. They planned to make their way to the cafeteria and the library. But a bomb blocked the outside west doors to the upper level and the library and instead they had to enter by breaking the window of the teachers' lounge, situated next to the cafeteria.

Inside they were met with the deafening noise of fire alarms and the flash of strobe lights from the burglar-alarm system. Tiles were hanging from the ceiling and water was pouring under the door to the cafeteria. Along with the noise of the sprinklers, there was a hissing sound, which Williams feared might be coming from a broken gas pipe. Quickly his team cleared the kitchen and back storage areas, evacuating the staff and students hiding there through the teacher's lounge window. They evacuated another 60 students from the school's music area on the second floor, and continued to work from west to east on the lower level while Simmons' S.W.A.T. team worked from east to west on the upper.

Simmons' S.W.A.T. team evacuated 30 students and faculty from south-facing classrooms on the upper level before meeting up with

Williams' team who had, by then, cleared the stairs to that level. The teams continued to receive warnings from the squads inspecting the diversionary bombs placed on Wadsworth that there could be similar devices planted throughout the school, and also received messages from the S.W.A.T. marksmen that there were more injured students on the upper levels, including one **'1 bleeding to death'** student who had hung a banner out of the window with '1 bleeding to death' scrawled across it. A little later three males dressed in black clothing and matching the general description of the gunmen were arrested in a field north of the high school. They were not Columbine students and identified themselves as the 'Splatter Punks'. They insisted they had shown up at Columbine High School out of curiosity. Cleared of any involvement in the shooting, they were released.

At 2.30, President Clinton was scheduled to make an announcement about the American economy. Instead he talked about Columbine.

'Ladies and gentlemen, we all know there has been a terrible shooting at a high school in Littleton, Colorado,' he said. 'Because the situation, as I left to come out here, apparently is ongoing, I think it would be inappropriate for me to say anything other than I hope the American people will be praying for the students, the parents and the teachers and we'll wait for events to unfold and there will be more to say.'

In the library, Patrick Ireland, who had been shot, slipped in and out of consciousness. Nevertheless, he slowly made his way to the west window. Sergeant Domenico in the news helicopter spotted him trying to climb out of a broken window on the second floor. Below him was a concrete sidewalk. Deputies sent in an armoured vehicle with members of the Lakewood S.W.A.T. team, who caught the young man as he fell.

Williams' S.W.A.T. team eventually reached the library where there were numerous bombs among the survivors. Among the 12 dead they found there were two males who had self-inflicted gunshot wounds to the head. They matched the description of the gunmen.

By 4.45, the S.W.A.T. teams had finished their search of Columbine High School. The building had been cleared and the two suspects were dead. The massacre at Columbine was over. Between them Harris and Klebold had killed 12 of their schoolmates and one teacher, and injured 23 others. More fatalities followed. Greg Barnes, a 17-year-old school basketball star who saw his best friend killed in the shootings hanged himself the following year and Carla Hochhalter, the 48-year-old mother of a girl injured in the shootings, shot herself.

But Columbine, it seemed, had got off lightly. According to their video-taped testimony, Harris and Klebold had planned to blow up a sizeable part of the school with hundreds of students in it. As it was it took several days for the authorities to find and defuse all the bombs they had left behind them. The bomb-making factory in Harris's garage had turned out over thirty pipe bombs as well as the two larger propane devices. Examining their diaries and websites, the police learned that the two had originally conceived a larger plan to reduce the school to rubble, then blow up a plane over New York City. They wanted a film made of their story and discussed who should direct, Steven Spielberg or Quentin Tarantino.

The couple left videotapes to assist with the production. In one, Harris appeared with a sawn-off shotgun he called Arlene, after his favourite character in the video game *Doom*.

'It's going to be like f***ing *Doom*,' he said. 'Tick, tick, tick… Ha! That f***ing shotgun is straight out of *Doom*.'

They also idolised Hitler. But the motivation for the killings was not clear. One survivor recalled that Harris and Klebold ordered all the jocks who had harassed them to stand up.

'We're going to kill every one of you,' they said.

But in the end the killings were blindly indiscriminate.

'They shot at everybody,' said one survivor, 'including the preps, the jocks and the people who wore Abercrombie and Fitch clothes. But it would be hard to say they singled them out, because everybody here looks like that. I mean, we're in white suburbia. Our school's wealthy.

Go into the parking lot and see the cars. These kids have money. But I never thought they'd do this.'

In another tape Harris and Klebold also thanked Mark Manes and Phillip Duran for supplying them with the weapons they needed.

Manes was later charged, under a Colorado state law forbidding the sale of handguns to a juvenile, with selling a Intrac TEC-9, 9mm pistol to Klebold for $500. He was also charged with possession of a dangerous or illegal weapon as he had gone shooting with Harris and Klebold in March 1999 and had fired one of their sawn-off shotguns. He supplied one hundred rounds of 9mm bullets to Harris on the night of 19 April. Pleading guilty, he was sentenced to six years in a state penitentiary.

Phillip Duran, who worked with Harris and Klebold at Blackjack Pizza, was charged with brokering the deal with Manes and handling a sawn-off shotgun during target practice. He was sentenced to four-and-a-half years in jail. Both Duran and Manes denied any knowledge of Harris and Klebold's plans.

Eighteen-year-old Robyn Anderson, a friend of Harris and Klebold, also admitted accompanying Harris and Klebold to a gun show in late 1998 and buying two shotguns and one rifle which were later used in the killings. But as the purchase had been made from a private individual rather than a licensed gun dealer, no law had been broken.

Some attempt was made to blame their parents, but both the Harrises and Klebolds seem to have provided an exemplary family life. Both boys felt remorse for their parents.

'It f***ing sucks to do this to them,' said Harris on one of the tapes they left behind. 'They're going to be put through hell once we do this.' Speaking directly to them, he added: 'There's nothing you guys could've done to prevent this.'

Klebold told his mother and father that they had been 'great parents' who had taught him 'self-awareness, self-reliance... I always appreciated that.' He added: 'I am sorry I have so much rage.'

In an attempt to explain what they were about to do, Harris quoted Shakespeare's *The Tempest*, saying: 'Good wombs hath borne bad sons.'

On the morning of the shootings, just before they set off for Columbine High School, Harris and Klebold made one final videotape, saying goodbye to their parents. Klebold said: 'It's a half hour before Judgement Day… I didn't like life very much… I just know I'm going to a better place than here.'

Harris concluded: 'I know my mom and dad will be in shock and disbelief… I can't help it… That's it. Sorry. Goodbye.'

Other titles from Summersdale

EXECUTION
A GUIDE TO THE ULTIMATE PENALTY

'Essential reading for all gore junkies' *Sunday Express*

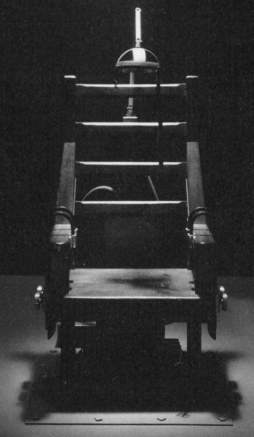

GEOFFREY ABBOTT

Execution
A Guide to the Ultimate Penalty

Geoffrey Abbott

£9.99 Pb

Execution is a gruesomely fascinating account of methods of judicial execution from around the world and through the ages, and includes such hair-raising categories as death by cannibalism, being sewn into an animal's belly and a thousand cuts.

In his own darkly humorous style, Geoffrey Abbott describes the instruments used and their effectiveness, and reveals the macabre origins of familiar phrases such as 'gone west' or 'drawn a blank', as well as the jargon of the underworld.

From the preparation of the victim to the disposal of the body, *Execution* answers all the questions you are ever likely to ask, and some you would never want to imagine.

A former Beefeater at the Tower of London, writer and TV personality Geoffrey Abbott has his own collection of vintage torture instruments and is the author of nineteen books including *The Executioner Always Chops Twice* and *Lipstick on the Noose*.

HOW IT FEELS

TO BE ATTACKED BY A SHARK

edited by MICHELLE HAMER

also

SHOT IN THE HEAD

ABDUCTED BY ALIENS

CRUSHED BY AN AVALANCHE

AND OTHER TRUE STORIES

How It Feels to be Attacked by a Shark

Michelle Hamer

£6.99 Pb

'When I felt his teeth hit my bone I thought he was going to break me.'

How does it feel to be attacked by a shark or crushed in an ice crevasse? Do you wonder what it's like to be brainwashed by a cult – or to weigh 36 stone? Can you imagine what it's like to be shot in the head?

If you think it could never happen to you, read on. These compulsively readable true-life stories tell of unexpected experiences with the extreme, the horrifying and the simply bizarre.

In gripping detail, ordinary people recall how they survived the unthinkable and what they discovered in life-defining moments, revealing the strength of the human spirit to rise to the challenge of extraordinary circumstances.

Michelle Hamer is a journalist based in Australia. She is married with four children – all born by Caesarian section, and she'll happily tell anyone who'll listen just how that feels.

[REVISED AND UPDATED]

conspiracy
theories

kate tuckett

Conspiracy Theories

Kate Tuckett

£5.99 Pb

Just because you're paranoid doesn't mean they're not after you…

Worried that the world is run by a sinister cabal operating at the very highest level of government? You could just be right. Bringing together startling evidence on topics ranging from JFK to Bush, Roswell to Harry Potter, Chernobyl to the curse of the Kursk submarine and Bruce Lee's death to Space Shuttle Columbia, *Conspiracy Theories* has a cover-up for every occasion.

GEOFF THOMPSON

WATCH MY BACK

'I train for the first shot
– it's all I need.'

'LENNIE MCLEAN HAD THE BRAWN, DAVE COURTNEY HAD THE
CHARM, BUT GEOFF THOMPSON IS IN A CLASS OF HIS OWN.' FHM

Watch My Back

Geoff Thompson

£7.99 Pb

Watch My Back is the story of one man's search for courage.

Depressed, intimidated by life and indoctrinated to believe that this was his lot, Geoff Thompson, on the verge of a breakdown, decided to fight back. In a bid to confront his fears, he took a job as a bouncer in one of Britain's roughest nightclubs.

His life was never to be the same again.

Over the next ten years, and after being involved in hundreds of brutal and bloody fights that left two of his friends murdered and many more in prison, the bullied 11-stone youth turned himself into a fearsome fighting machine with an unparalleled reputation as a knockout specialist. Seduced by beautiful women, attacked by maniacs with knives, guns (and a pair of garden shears), chased and locked up by the police and sought after by top establishments to 'clean up' their clubs, Geoff reached the top of his trade and became addicted to violence.

Then it all changed.

After being nearly killed in a gang attack, and almost killing one of his attackers in a savage car park match-fight, he was forced to reassess his relationship with violence.

This is the story of an ordinary man who faced his fears and took himself from bedsit to bestseller but very nearly got killed on the way.

Geoff Thompson is one of the UK's most respected martial artists and a prolific writer. His film *Brown Paper Bag* won Best Short Film at the 2004 BAFTAs.

www.summersdale.com